The Arab Ba'th Socialist Party

History, Ideology, and Organization

The Arab Ba'th Socialist Party

History, Ideology, and Organization

Kamel S. Abu Jaber

Foreword by Philip K. Hitti

New Preface by Tariq Tell

HESPERUS

The Arab Ba'th Socialist Party
History, Ideology and Organization
By © Dr. Kamel S. Abu Jaber 1932–2020

Published by Hesperus Press Limited
167-169 Great Portland Street, 5th Floor, London, England, W1W 5PF
www.hesperus.press

The Arab Ba'th Socialist Party first edition published in 1966 by Syracuse University Press, Syracuse, New York Library of Congress Catalog Card: 66-25181

Designed and typeset by Roland Codd
Printed in the United Kingdom

ISBN (paperback): 978-1-84391-991-9
ISBN (electronic book): 978-1-84391-992-6

For Loretta, Linda, and Nyla

Note on the spelling of *Ba'th*

Ba'th, Arabic for resurrection, is transcribed in various ways, also like Ba'ath, Baath or Baas. In this study Ba'th is used. It is the most widely used spelling in academic literature, and is also the transcription closest to the original Arabic بَعْث.

Contents

Foreword

Of the numerous political parties that have mushroomed in the contemporary Arab world, the Ba'th is one of the very few that by its ideology, organization, and effectiveness qualifies to be so called. The majority of the others revolve on personalities and stand ready to bargain and compromise.

As a school of thought the Ba'th draws upon Western Socialist-humanist sources. But its leaders and spokesmen, though mostly European educated, disclaim any such indebtedness.

They emphasize, rather overemphasize, the rootedness of their doctrines in Arabism and Islamism. Meanwhile they consider Moslem Brotherhood reactionary, hold little rapport with other Socialist parties in the area, and look upon Communists as rivals rather than allies. Nevertheless they have lately developed within their ranks a leftist wing.

The increasing importance of this party in recent years may be indicated by the fact that its advocates seized power in Iraq for seven months in 1963 and in Syria they have retained it since 1963. In February of 1966 the leftists among them gained control in Syria.

This book by Dr. Abu Jaber is a descriptive and analytical study of the Ba'th party in its genesis, ideology, structural organization, and historical development. It is the only one of its kind in English known to me. It represents years of research by an Arab-born, American-educated author who, thanks to a

Ford Foundation fellowship, had a year of graduate work and research at Princeton University and another year of travel in the area concerned. The result is a worthy contribution not only to our knowledge of a leading political party but to Arab politics in general.

PHILIP K. HITTI
Princeton, N.J.
May 11, 1966

Preface

The activities and ideology of the Ba'th party have been of special interest to me for many years. That the Ba'th party today, in power in Syria, is of great interest to many of us concerned with the contemporary problems of the Arab world is only natural, for it is the first "ideological" party to achieve power there.

This book outlines the genesis, development, and character of the Ba'th Socialist party in the Arab world, with particular emphasis on Syria, where it has thrived. It explores the ideas of early Arab Socialists and outlines the history of the Ba'th party's activities, ideology, and organization. (It does not purport to be a general discussion of Arab politics.)

Research for this study was done primarily in Arabic sources, for two reasons: (1) Material in Western languages on the subject of Arab socialism in general and on the Ba'th in particular is scarce. (2) It will benefit the reader, in my opinion, to see the ideas of Arab socialism as translated from their original text. (Unless otherwise indicated, translations in the text and appendixes are by the present author.) However, many books and articles in English were of great value in suggesting areas of research and in providing insight sometimes fresh but often stereotyped – about the emergence of ideology in a developing region of the world.

Transliteration from Arabic to English has been kept simple. The most familiar English form has been used wherever possible and diacritical marks have been kept to a minimum.

It would be impossible to list individually the countless people and organizations that helped me in the preparation of this study. I would like to thank my friend Professor Frank Munger of Syracuse University, whose insights and suggestions added much to this book. My thanks also go to the Ford Foundation and the Foreign Area Training Program, whose financial assistance made it possible for me to research and write this book both at Princeton University and in the Arab world. Special gratitude goes to Philip K. Hitti of Princeton University, who has written the Foreword.

I wish also to acknowledge the assistance of many individuals – both members and nonmembers of the Ba'th party in Syria, Jordan, and Lebanon – who wish to have their names withheld. Special thanks go to Dr. Bashir al-Dauk, owner of the Tali'ah Publishing House in Beirut, who placed his private collection of newspapers and books at my disposal.

The views expressed in this book are solely those of the author and in no way reflect on the Ford Foundation, the Foreign Area Training Program, or any of the individuals who helped in its preparation.

KAMEL S. ABU JABER
Knoxville, Tennessee
February 1966

Author's Introduction

On the chill morning of February 23, 1966, tanks again rumbled ominously into the streets of Damascus, seizing control of strategic points in the city and surrounding the residence of President Muhammad Amin al-Hafiz: another *coup d'état* was being staged. Once more the entire world was made aware of the struggle for power in Syria. This time, however, it was a struggle within the Ba'th party, with civilian and military elements the protagonists. Unlike some of the previous Syrian "revolutions," this one was bloody; the dead and injured numbered some four hundred persons. The injured included President Hafiz and his son and two daughters. Most of those top leaders of the Ba'th opposed to the *coup* were apprehended, and their fate is still undetermined.

This latest coup was perpetrated by a group of left-wing Ba'thist army officers who claim to have staged it "to purify the revolution of March, 1963." It was aimed against the right-wing Ba'thists who, according to the leftists, were deviating from the proper revolutionary path.

If anything, this latest palace revolt emphasizes the division within the Ba'th party – an omnipresent division which has manifested itself in several major splits within the party over the years. This internal split underscores the failure of Arab Socialists in general to create and sustain a united front against the conservative elements in Arab society.

The new split within the Ba'th did not come as a complete surprise to anyone familiar with the inner conflict of the party. This *coup* of February, 1966, was in fact the second one at tempted by the same group of leftist army officers within two months. Following the unsuccessful *coup* of December, 1965, the left wing of the party was ousted.[1] Premier Yusuf Zayen, a civilian physician who was leader of the extremists, was asked to resign by the National Command of the party and replaced by the moderate Bitar. The new government formed by Bitar included "moderate Syrian friends of President Gamal Abdel Nasser" and was to emphasize "moderation [in its Socialist program] and some liberalization of the economy with mild encouragement to small business."[2] The Bitar government, bearing in mind Syria's isolation in the sphere of Arab politics and the stagnant economic situation, sought a rapprochement with Nasser and a moderate application of the Ba'th Socialist program.[3]

Clearly displeased with the turn of events, the extreme leftists within the Ba'th, led by Zayen and Major General Salah Jadid, former chief of staff, awaited the right moment to stage a counter *coup*. The leadership now in control of Syria does not represent the gamut of the Ba'th party. It is composed mainly of extreme leftists vesting almost exclusive authority in the military wing of the party who were unhappy with Bitar's attempt "to get the army out of politics."[4]

The reasons behind the latest split within the party are varied and complex. Foremost among them was the apparent split between the civilians and the military.[5] Backed by Hafiz and the right wing of the party, Bitar attempted to assert civilian authority over the military. In September, 1965, Jadid, the strong man behind the new junta, was dismissed as the army's chief of staff and a number of other army officers were later transferred to less sensitive posts.[6] Bitar claims the new *coup* to be a reflection of the selfish desire of certain army officers to impose their views on the party.[7]

Behind the civilian-military split lay personal rivalries and jealousies among the top leadership of the party, both civilian and military. This personal rivalry took on the appearance of an ideological struggle with the left wing, composed mainly of officers who support Jadid, outbidding their rivals in their zealous approach to socialism. These extreme leftists were also unhappy about the attempted rapprochement with Nasser. They looked to the left – to Moscow, even Peking. In fact, the new government formed after the new group took over was immediately criticized by Nasser.[8] On the other hand, the Soviet Union was extremely sympathetic.[9] The new regime cooperated closely with the local Communist party. Khalid Bakdash, secretary general of the Syrian Communist party, was allowed to return to Syria, and Samih Atiyyah, a member of the Communist party, was made minister of communications by the new regime.[10] Zayen, the new premier, visited Moscow in April, 1966, with a group of economic specialists and secured a generous commitment from the Soviet Union to finance a dam on the upper Euphrates in Syria.[11]

In or out of power, the Ba'th – as this book will reveal-has not learned to live in peace with itself; inner struggles continue to rock the party from time to time.

June 1966

Preface to the Second Edition

Jordanians pursuing graduate studies in the US were relatively rare in the early 1960s. Even fewer were those like Kamel Abu Jaber who had worked their way through an American college rather than being sent abroad on state scholarships. Thus on returning to Amman for his PhD fieldwork on the Ba'th Party in 1963, it was only natural that Abu Jaber had to constantly field questions about the topic of his research. The most memorable of these interrogations occurred during an encounter with Falah al-Madadha, a 'family friend' and famously reactionary Undersecretary of the Ministry of the Interior. In the late 1950s, Madadha had played a leading role in King Hussein's suppression of the 'Jordanian National Movement' (JNM), a left leaning coalition of radical nationalists among whom Ba'thists held a pivotal place. He now wanted to know why a promising young scholar in a Western university would waste his time on 'an insignificant and anti-Jordanian movement,' advising Abu Jaber to 'study something more worthwhile.'[1]

In berating the Ba'th Party, Madadha used the Jordanian idiom, '*Hizb Hamil*,' perhaps best translated as a 'feckless party of troublemakers.'[2] As a member of one of Jordan's long-established landholding families, with a father proud of his Bedouin heritage and still rooted in the bucolic rhythms of the family estate in al-Yadudah,[3] Abu Jaber would have understood perfectly this choice of words. '*Hamil*' was the term East Bank farmers used for stray livestock brought into the family flock by careless shepherds. Among Jordan's *fellahin*, the word was used for recalcitrant members of the village household: young, unmarried men who shirked their communal work and had to be coerced into fulfilling their allotted tasks. The implication was that the Ba'th was an alien, disruptive element in Hashemite Jordan. Whether their interests were academic or political, loyal members of the Jordanian elite should give Ba'thism a wide berth.

The Pan-Arab radicalism of the Ba'th and its sometime ally, the charismatic Gamal Abdel Nasser, was indeed at odds with a conservative, pro-Western Hashemite monarchy wrapped in the mantle of the British sponsored Great Arab Revolt. Yet as Abu Jaber was well aware, most members of his generation had invested in a different version of Arabism. For these young, educated *effendiyya*, the 'Arab Socialism' and non-aligned, Third World nationalism shared by Nasser and the Ba'th's were seen as the surest path to Arab unity. For the Ba'th, this would lead in turn to socio-political modernization and the material prowess needed to liberate Palestine and put right the injustices of the 1948 *Nakba.* Abu Jaber's own research revealed an extensive network of Ba'thist activists in Syria, Iraq, Lebanon and Jordan that supported their party's revolutionary vision of Arab 'renaissance.' Most stayed loyal to its ideals after the breakup of the United Arab Republic, the short-lived (1958–1961) Egyptian-Syrian union headed by Nasser but formed through Ba'thist prompting. They remained wedded to the Ba'th slogan of 'Unity Liberty and Socialism' even after the party's break with Nasser and the failure of the Tripartite Unity Agreement between Syria, Iraq and Egypt in 1963.

In the hothouse atmosphere of Arab politics during the 1960s, it is of little wonder that Abu Jaber persisted with his study of the Ba'th, completing his PhD in Syracuse on the topic in 1965, having earlier spent a year (1962–1963) on doctoral research at Princeton with Ford Foundation funding. It was there that he came under the influence of the Lebanese American scholar Philip Hitti, then very much the doyen of Middle East Studies in the US. Hitti recognized the singular contribution of Abu Jaber's work on the Ba'th Party and his influence may well have been key to Abu Jaber obtaining a visiting professorship at the American University of Beirut, his *alma mater*. In Beirut, Abu Jaber filled in for the Palestinian historian Hanna Batatu, using his office while the latter was on research leave, no doubt working on his own book on the social origins of the revolutionary forces in Iraq.[4] These forces included the Iraqi Ba'th whose members temporarily seized power – we now know with US encouragement – in the course of the bloody overthrow of the regime of Abd al-Karim Qasim in 1963.

While in Beirut, Abu Jaber got to know such AUB luminaries as 'Eli Salem, Yusuf Ibish,... Kamal Salibi' and through them 'was introduced not only to the intellectual community of Beirut but also to some of the most influential political opinion leaders and politicians of Syria and Lebanon.' He completed the work needed to transform his dissertation into the present book, amplifying his doctoral research with material from the AUB's vast trove of Arab newspapers and magazines. He also gained full access to a unique collection belonging to Bashir al-Dauk, the owner of the radical publishing house, al-Tali'ah This private library included the only complete archive of the Ba'th Party's official newspaper, *al-Ba'th*. Beirut's status as the preferred destination of Arab politicians in exile, and its proximity to Damascus where the Ba'th had regained power over Syria in 1963, allowed Abu Jaber to enrich his work with interviews with the key protagonists of the 'Arab

Cold War.'[5] This included 'many Iraqi Ba'th Party leaders then in exile in Damascus or Beirut, and most of the Ba'th leaders in Jordan.'[6] He also interviewed the party's founders, Michel Aflaq (for Abu Jaber, the Ba'th party's 'philosopher'), Salah al-Din al-Bitar (its 'tactician') as well as Munif al-Razzaz, the Jordanian who became head of its National Command in 1965.[7]

Such contacts, along with the publication of the first edition of the *Arab Ba'th Socialist Party* by Syracuse University Press in 1966, would have been duly noted by Jordan's ubiquitous security services. On returning to Jordan in the wake of the June 1967 War, and despite having given up a post at an Ivy League college in the US, Abu Jaber still needed recourse to the proverbial *wasta* (mediation) to obtain an academic job. He only secured an appointment to a teaching position at the University of Jordan after the intervention of the reformist Prime Minister Wasfi al-Tall, who maintained close relations with a number of leading Ba'thists. These included his old AUB classmate Razzaz, Kamal al-Sha'ir[8] and former Free Officers affiliated to the Ba'th such as Mahmud al-Ma'ayta and Shahir Abu Shahut. This appointment would shift Abu Jaber's career onto a different path, including a reconciliation with the Jordanian authorities and two terms of ministerial office at the request of King Hussein.

While he published many other books in the course of a long academic career capped by a sixteen-year spell at the University of Jordan (1969–1985), Abu Jaber does not seem to have returned to the topic of his doctoral research. Nor did he update the *Arab Ba'th Socialist Party* by drawing on the steady flow of publications on the brutal consolidation of Ba'thist rule in Syria and Iraq under Hafez al-Asad (1970–2000) and Saddam Hussein (1979-2003).[9] Indeed, his introduction to the 1966 edition of the *Arab Ba'th Party* hints at a premonition of the violence that was to envelop Ba'thist politics in the coming decades. Its opening paragraph registers his dismay at the bloodshed that accompanied the overthrow of Amin al-Hafiz by the military wing of the Ba'th in February of the same year. Abu Jaber's fear was that with Salah Jadid's coup, the ever-present schism between the Ba'th Party's radical and moderate wings would be resolved by means of a bloody, military led lurch to the left. Aflaq's original vision of a gradualist, genuinely Arab socialism would lose out to a doctrinaire Soviet inspired import that threatened to plunge the region into social revolution.

In any event, such fears proved unfounded, although the rise of the Ba'th's military wing in Syria under Salah Jadid and Hafez al-Asad drove the historic leadership of the party into what would prove permanent exile. Aflaq and his comrades resurfaced in a purely decorative role, as the toothless 'National Command' (*Qiyadat Qawmiyya*) of a rival Baghdad based party after the Iraqi Ba'th returned to power – again through military coup – in 1968. By then, the Arab defeat in the Six Day War of June 1967 had set in train a deep-seated reconfiguration of radical Arab politics. Schemes for Arab unity were abandoned in favor of the consolidation of independent nation (in Arabist parlance '*qutri*') states still trapped within the borders set by colonial rule. Armed guerilla movements predicated on a local *wataniyya* (in effect *qutri* centered patriotism), notably a PLO dominated by Yasir Arafat's Fateh, replaced the Ba'th as the modular forces of Arab liberation. Nasser's death in September 1970 and the 1973 Arab Israeli War completed the eclipse of Pan-Arabism. The oil price revolution that followed precipitated a shift from *Thawra* to *Tharwa* 'revolution to wealth,' consolidating a new regional order lubricated by petrodollars that flowed through the once imperial structures that Nasser and his generation had sought to overthrow.

Under this new dispensation, schemes for socialism and Arab unity took a back seat, as the erstwhile revolutionaries invested in a market led *infitah* (market opening), in a bid to turn political power into economic wealth that they could pass on to their offspring. In both Syria and Iraq, the two wings of the Ba'th transformed from a revolutionary vanguard into an instrument of state patronage, both undergirding strangely parallel – and peculiarly savage – 'States of Barbary.'[10] A movement that once dreamt of radical renaissance, revolution and Pan Arab unity was now reduced to little more than a fig-leaf disguising narrow, tribal-sectarian autocracies. Personal rule and grossly inflated personality cults[11] replaced the old Ba'th's collective leadership and ended forever the party's tendency to 'swallow its rulers.'[12]

Faced with the dismal prospect offered by the regimes of the Asads and Saddam Hussein, it is tempting to conclude that Abu Jaber's book is hopelessly dated, or that it cannot offer much to the contemporary reader. However, we should resist this conclusion and the 50/50 hindsight it assumes, for Kamel Abu Jaber's *Arab Ba'th Party* is important precisely because its conception and outlook predates the rise of these 'Republics of Fear.'[13] Based on a deep engagement with the key Arabic sources, his analysis of the genealogy of the Ba'th's socialist ideas is lucid and remains compelling. A vast array of Arabic press material, enlivened by interviews with the major protagonists of the Ba'th, allows Abu Jaber to chart the party's rise to the brink of regional hegemony in the late 1950s. His dispassionate analysis of the divisions within the Ba'th – and the disagreements that turned Nasser from the party's ally into its nemesis in the mid-1960s – exposes the contradictions that ensured that its bid for Arab unity remained unfulfilled.

Despite its academic form, the *Arab Ba'th Party* breathes life into an optimistic moment in the modern history of the Arab East, when a different world seemed possible and Arabs could credibly dream of unity, national progress and the righting of historic wrongs. Therefore, students of the politics of the Middle East must be grateful that Kamel Abu Jaber chose to ignore the warnings muttered by the likes of Falah al-Madadha and persist with his chosen research topic. Two generations of scholars have already had cause to welcome his readiness to take the risk of publishing his findings in the first edition of this book. All of us must now commend Hesperus Press for re-issuing it for use by the new cohorts of global historians working on the anti-colonial movements that dominated the first decades of formal independence in the Arab World.

Tariq Tell
Beirut
2023

And the years shall pass,
And the Ba'th will remain
Beyond the years
A beautiful dream.

Kamal Nasser
Poet of the Ba'th Party

1 Beginnings of Arab Socialism

Only rarely does an idea receive the ready and widespread acceptance gained by the idea of *Ishtirakiyyah* (socialism) in the Arab world since the end of the Second World War. Indeed, as the Arabs gradually win their independence, they are turning increasingly to socialism. While some Arab nations, such as Jordan and Saudi Arabia, have not officially adopted it as a state policy, they have introduced certain aspects of the welfare state and the idea of "social justice" is gaining ground.

The present mushrooming of Socialist ideas cannot be explained simply in terms of the Arabs wish to improve their lot after independence. It is evident that Arab socialism had adherents as early as the late nineteenth century. At that time major Arabic magazines and newspapers were engaged in heated debates about socialism. Dr. Yakoub Sarrouf, owner and publisher of the influential magazine *al-Muqtataf* (Selections), was an ardent advocate of *laissez-faire* theories and the arch-enemy of socialism in Egypt. In 1889 *al-Muqtataf* jeered at the Socialist concept of equality. "Equalizing people," it claimed, is against nature and is "immoral." The author of this article then added, "Competition is an essential prerequisite to progress."[1] Another influential opponent of the Socialists was the magazine *al-Hilal* (The Crescent), which branded socialism "immoral" and claimed it would kill private initiative. It also questioned the government's ability to run nationalized enterprises.[2]

The fact that the two major Egyptian magazines of the time declared themselves anti-Socialist suggests that socialists had a number of powerful adherents. Indeed, socialism had gained the support of influential men, one of whom was Dr. Shibli Shumayyil, termed the first Arab Socialist.[3] Shumayyil was a Social Darwinist who believed socialism the inevitable result of progress. To stave off the charge that socialism teaches the distribution of wealth without justice, Shumayyil said, "It [socialism] does not [simply] teach the distribution of wealth… but justice in the distribution of profits between labor and capital."[4] He defined socialism as "the reform of society through the reform of each individual within it."[5]

Salamah Musa, another influential advocate of Socialist ideas, wrote in the early part of the twentieth century. Returning to Egypt from Britain, where he was educated, Musa began to support a moderate and democratic program of socialism. In 1910 he wrote an article eulogizing British socialism and outlining its history.[6] Influenced by the writings of George Bernard Shaw, during his stay in Britain he had joined the Fabian Society. Musa holds the distinction of having written the first book on socialism in Arabic, *al-Ishtirakiyyah* (Socialism) (Cairo: al-Matba'ah al-Ahliyyah, 1913).

Musa thought of socialism as an "economic order," not a comprehensive philosophy. While he recognized the existence of two classes and the fact that the "machine" made it possible for the few to be rich while the many remained poor, he neither envisioned nor advocated class struggle.[7]

To replace the existent "putrid system," he advocated a limited program of socialism based on nationalization to be carried out in stages, beginning with public utilities. No one would have the right of inheritance, and ownership would be restricted. His Socialist program included free education, social services, housing, limited hours of work, social security, and workmen's compensation.[8]

In his earlier writings Musa did not allude to nationalism and the desire for independence. Later on, however, with the formation and rise of the Wafd party in Egypt, he realized it was impossible to be a Socialist without being a nationalist.[9] Indeed, with the struggle for independence carried on by the Wafd party, Musa found himself suddenly in its ranks. "The Egyptian Socialist finds himself with the Wafd," he said, "for the Wafd is a call for independence. It is impossible for a Socialist to think in any Socialist program unless independence be achieved."[10] His words, were to prove prophetic not only in Egypt but in many other parts of the Arab world as well, where only after independence did Socialist ideas flourish.

Another major Arab intellectual of the Socialist school was Nicola Haddad. A politically active man, he defended socialism in magazines, newspapers, and books and even published his own magazine. Influenced by the writings of Eugene Debs, the American Socialist, he established an Arab Writers Association in New York in 1910 and there issued his magazine *al-Jami'ah* (The Universal). To keep the magazine in print, he enlisted the help of Amin al-Rihani and Anton Farah, both prominent writers.[11]

In 1920 he wrote a book defining his ideas on socialism, *al-Ishtirakiyyah* (Cairo: Dar al-Hilal). While this book is longer than Musa's, it is fundamentally quite similar to it. Like Musa, Haddad believed in democratic socialism and that economic democracy cannot be achieved without political democracy. He also believed that capitalism had failed and must be replaced. His book, though, has a more sophisticated critique of *laissez-faire* ideas than Musa's. Competition, it says, had brought about the reverse of its avowed purpose. Instead of alleviating the ills of society, it compounded them and caused the rise of two classes: the "exploiters" and the "exploited." Instead of competition there should be cooperation. "Since people must cooperate in making a living, and in production, why should they not share in its enjoyment each according to his efforts?" Like Musa, he advocated a drastic reduction in the amount of property to be owned, asserting that only personal belongings should be allowed. Abolition of private property would also eliminate inheritance: "Each individual will inherit from society [only] his right to work, earn a living, and his right to be protected against misery and poverty."[12]

Haddad's socialism was to be brought about by a program of nationalization with compensation. He also advocated Henry George's idea of progressive taxation "which would abolish the value of property." He clearly rejected the use of violence as too extreme and rejected the Bolshevik experiment for this reason. Socialism must be brought about freely through the formation of Socialist parties; it must use democratic means. In his treatment of freedom for the individual, he was somewhat vague. He stated that complete freedom characterizes the animals of the jungle. As society advances, it demands more and more cooperation. This necessitates new limits on freedom for the benefit of the individual. In a Socialist state, the limits on freedom must be in accordance with "justice" – a justice that applies to everyone in the society, thus obviating tyranny.[13] Like Musa, Haddad visualized his society as one in which everyone could get employment according to his ability. He called for social services, free education, public grounds, and parks.[14]

The first Arab Socialist writers were educated in the West and imbued with Western ideas. They brought Western Socialist ideas into the Arab world and saw no advantage in labeling them as "Arab", as later Arab intellectuals were to do. For this reason some later Arab writers looked upon those of pre-1920 vintage as mere "imitators".[15] The early Arab Socialists were not satisfied with spreading Socialist ideas through writing alone; they favored forming political parties. As early as 1908, upon his return to Egypt from studying in France, Dr. Muhammad Jamal al-Din organized the Blessed Socialist party *(al-Hizb al-Ishtiraki al-Mubarak)*, which emphasized agrarian reform but neglected nationalism.[16] Despite some support from urban areas, this movement soon disintegrated. In 1920 Musa and a few other intellectuals organized the second Socialist party in the Arab world: the Egyptian Socialist party (*al-Hizb al-Misri al-Ishtiraki*). This party continued its activities until 1930, when it too disintegrated.[17]

Another party, initially non-Socialist, began in Egypt in the 1920s. Young Egypt (*Misr al-Fatat*) finally regularized its efforts in 1933 under the leadership of Ahmad Hussein. It aimed at liberating Egypt from British control, demanded an end to feudalism and improvement of peasant conditions. In 1940 it changed its name to the National Islamic party and in 1946 to the Democratic Socialist party. It published a newspaper called *al-Ishtirakiyyah*, repeatedly banned and censored by the Farouq regime. During the Second World War, Hussein was jailed on the charge of being a Fascist sympathizer. He denied this charge in a pamphlet called *Egypt's War Effort*, which he published in 1947 in New York.[18] In 1950 Ibrahim Shukri, vice president of the party, won a seat in Parliament. Shortly afterward he was thrown in jail because of his vocal opposition to the government, and the party paper was shut down.

At first Egypt was the center of Arab Socialist ideas and movements, but they were taking root in other parts of the Arab world as well. In Iraq in 1931 a group of Western-educated liberals formed what was later to be know as the Ahali Group. Like its predecessors and contemporaries in Egypt, this group, or party, failed to gain mass support. And, while it was in doctrine a Socialist party, it referred to its ideology as *Sha'biyyah* (populism) rather than Ishtirakiyyah, for the latter word carried with it in Iraq – and indeed throughout the Arab world – a stigma of immorality that "shocked most of its followers."[19]

The young men who formed the Ahali Group were liberals who preached the welfare of the people, protection of human rights, state responsibility for health and education. They reorganized the institutions of family and religion and denied the existence of class struggle. Finally they demanded liberty and equality for the masses, thus combining economic and political democracy. Having no common background, the men in the group soon divided into factions.[20]

Certain features of the Socialist movement in the Arab world prior to the Second World War stand out. First, while there seems to have been a substantial amount of agitation on behalf of some intellectuals in favor of Socialist ideas, they appear to have made very little headway even among the intelligentsia. The lack of appeal for the illiterate masses can best be ascribed to the contention that socialism was "immoral," a charge very effectively exploited by the conservatives. As for the intelligentsia, they were too much preoccupied with independence and nationalism to become involved with socialism.[21] Thus, it was only after independence had been won that Socialist ideas flourished in the Arab world, whereas just a generation earlier prominent Arab Socialists lamented that socialism could not vaunt a single champion.[22]

Sporadic efforts toward socialism prior to the Second World War were successfully offset by the conservatives, by government suppression as in Egypt, or by factionalism and lack of organization.[23] Perhaps this accounts for the confusion and irresolution that have beset contemporary Arab Socialists.

Writing about contemporary politics in the Middle East, Manfred Halpern states, "Next to nationalism, no ideology in the Middle East is more popular than socialism."[24] This statement, while accurate, is surprising in light of the fact that until recent years adoption of Socialist ideology in the Middle East had been given no serious consideration. One theory put forth in explanation of this is that "socialism remained merely a wing of the nationalist movement, an embryo waiting for the national revolution to triumph before it [could] be born."[25] Such an explanation certainly applies to the Arab Ba'th Socialist party, the roots of which go back to 1943 but which did not come of age until Syria became independent in 1946.

Gebran Majdalany lists two main currents of Arab socialism today.[26] The first and more important is that of the Ba'th Socialist party, whose aim is to join the entire region of the Arab world, which it considers united by culture and aspiration. The second current is represented by certain parties which base their action (or in the case of certain Iraqi parties which have since gone out of existence, based their action) on the present political possibilities without regard or commitment to ideology. The Progressive Socialist party in Lebanon represents this tendency. Until 1963 it rejected Arab unity ideas and declared that Lebanon's "particular situation" gives it unique attributes and that its destiny should be decided by Lebanon alone.[27] In Iraq this tendency was represented by three political parties that came into legal existence in 1946: the National Democratic party (*al-Hizb al-Watani al-Demoqrati*), the National Unity party (*Hizb al-Wihdah al-Wataniyyah*), and the People's party (*Hizb al-Sha'b*). These three Socialist parties were very close and in fact agreed on most points in their programs; it was only because of personal rivalries that three parties, rather than one, came into being. These parties called for social services, public education, agrarian reform, equality regardless of race or religion, strengthening of the democratic regime, freedom for labor to unionize, and creation of cooperative societies. To achieve such a comprehensive program, they advocated high progressive taxes, inheritance taxes, a planned economy, close supervision of large domestic and foreign companies, and nationalization of public utilities.[28]

To the above two Socialist currents listed by Majdalany, a third, the Nasserite movement, should be added. Until February and March, 1963, when the Ba'th party took control of the governments of Iraq and Syria, it was only in the U.A.R. that socialism and Socialist ideas were put into practice – a fact which of itself distinguished the Nasserites from the other parties. In addition, Nasser's socialism essentially differs from other varieties in its denial of certain political liberties – a denial which the Ba'th and the others, at least in theory, do not condone. Nasser's brand of socialism is a way... to economic and political freedom" and "for this end it utilizes power."

Nasser's course is "*to act positively* with all the components of power."[29]

The principal concern of this book is to examine the scope and substance of that brand of Arab socialism advocated by the Ba'th party, relating it to the events that motivated the Arab world after the Second World War. It also points up the similarities between the varieties of Arab socialism. These similarities are great, the emphasis on the political rather than the social is striking. Arabs, it seems – whether Nasserites, Ba'thists, or otherwise – are concerned with the political first, the social second. In the Ba'th hierarchy of values, Arab socialism comes after Arab unity. This preoccupation with the political coupled with intense anti-Western sentiment is shared by all Arab Socialists.

Political instability, social change, and intense feelings of nationalism have been plaguing the Arab world in recent years. Rising to the challenge of an advancing Western culture, the developing areas of the world are groping for identity and for social and political institutions and ideologies that will help them withstand general pressure to conform to Western standards.

Although they use Western terminology and attack their problems from an ethical position developed in the West, Arab Socialists deny their Western heritage. Instead they insist that their socialism is indigenously Arab, as are their values and approaches. Like similar political thinkers in other developing areas of the world, the Ba'thists are seeking identity in an age of conformity – an age when Western culture has become almost universal.

The success or failure of the Ba'th party to achieve its programs is intimately linked with the prevailing political conditions of the world. Two power blocs, the disunity of the Arab world, rivalry among Arab leaders, and the internal economic and political difficulties of developing countries contribute to the present chaos in the Arab world – a chaos reflected in the Ba'th party.

The present study traces the evolution of Socialist ideas in the Arab world, then moves into a systematic study of the history, ideology, and organization of the Ba'th party. It points up the strength and influence of a minority dedicated to the idea of achieving change. Change, for the Ba'th party, must be not only political but social and economic as well. Indeed, the party demands a change in the Arab self that ultimately will be reflected in Arab society as a whole. Whether the Ba'th approach is utopian or whether such change can be effected only time will tell.

This study reveals the changes Western ideas undergo when adapted to the needs of the Arab world. In the Arab world Western socialism appears in a new guise and is called Arab socialism. For Western ideas cannot be transplanted whole to other parts of the world. Eventually they mix with certain local traditions and practices to form a new species.

While Arab leaders use Western words, they impart special meaning to them. When Michel Aflaq, the cofounder of the Ba'th party, speaks of individual liberty, he does not necessarily mean that practiced in the West. He means something new, uniquely Arab. This makes it difficult for Western political analysts, who at times take what they read at face value, to understand the writings of Middle Easterners. Also, many Westerners reading, say, Aflaq or Nasser cannot fathom the intense emotional content of their words. This is perhaps an indication that Western culture has attained such a high degree of stability that it has forgotten the spicy and fiery zeal of its own reformers. Today's Ba'thists are the Luthers, Rousseaus, Owens, and Marxes of the rising Arab world. They have a vision, a program, a dream.

In essence this book attempts to prove the strength of the nationalist desire for political as well as ideological independence. Because of this desire the Ba'th party, like other Socialist movements in the developing world, stresses its independence of capitalism and Western socialism alike.

As an ideological movement, the Ba'th party epitomizes the agonies and hopes of a large number of Arabs who are intent on achieving change and modernization. Ba'th history is characterized by the often frustrated hopes of modern Arabs to bring about unity, socialism, and liberty. The party reflects the situation of the Arab world as a whole, rife with division, personal jealousies, and ideological disputes. It seems amazing, in fact, that the party has been able to survive as many crises as it has. That it has is no doubt attributable, in part, to Aflaq's judicious leadership.

Even his enemies speak of Aflaq with deference. Followers hail him as a "new" man in the Arab world – a man who shuns political office, prestige, and wealth. Arabs see Aflaq as an ascetic philosopher – a lesser Gandhi. His popular image as a "clean" politician has helped bolster the image of the Ba'th as an ideological – as opposed to an opportunistic, office-seeking – movement. Aflaq's refusal to assume public office has helped him maintain his grip on the party and has enhanced his reputation. Further, not being in office has insulated him from criticism for any public action on the part of the Ba'th. His middle-of-the-road position also gives him flexibility in dealing with party crises. He can exert his influence in any direction and make it seem right. One problematic aspect of Aflaq, from the standpoint of the party, is the fact that he is a Greek Orthodox Christian. This has made him somewhat less than ideal to lead a political party whose program of socialism and unity touches potentially on the whole Arab world-a world dominated by Islam and sensitive to religious differences.

Michel Aflaq was born in 1910 to a middle-class Damascene family. His father, an ardent nationalist, was arrested by both the Ottomans and the French.[30] His mother, although advanced in years, is still very much interested in politics and a firm believer in Arab nationalism.[31] Thus Aflaq grew up in a home where politics was a favorite topic.

At the age of eighteen, like many ambitious young Syrians of his day, Michel went to Paris to study at the Sorbonne in the Faculty of Arts. Active in politics before his departure, he maintained his interest in Paris. There he founded an Arab Students' Union, and through meeting with students from other Arab countries his Syrian nationalism expanded to Arab nationalism. At the Sorbonne he read the works of Marx, which opened his eyes to the enormous importance of the social problems facing humanity. Though influenced by Marx, he never became a Communist; he was too much of a humanist for that.[32] Upon his return from France in 1932, Aflaq taught history in the government schools. From 1933 to 1936 he was attracted by the Communists, hoping for their support of Arab nationalism. His pro-Communist leanings colored his teaching and put him at odds with his superiors. During this period he even wrote for the Communist magazine *al-Tali'ah* (The Vanguard), an association which lasted until 1936. Of these years he recently said:

> During this period I admired the hardiness of the Communists struggle against the French. I used to admire the toughness of the young men in the Communist party. After 1936 and the assumption in France of the Léon Blum Front government, I became disenchanted and felt betrayed.[33]

Aflaq felt betrayed since the Blum government was not more sympathetic to the nationalist cause in Syria.

Another man important to the Ba'th party is Salah al-Din al-Bitar. His life and activities have been so closely interwoven with Aflaq's that he has frequently been overlooked and sometimes forgotten. Born to a middle-class Damascene family, Bitar early developed into an Arab nationalist bent on removing the French from Syria.

He received his high school education in Damascus and in 1928, with Aflaq, went to the Sorbonne, where he studied physics. When he returned from France in 1932, he took a teaching position in the government schools.

Like many young intellectuals of his time, Bitar could not stand aloof from the politics of his era and concentrate exclusively on his teaching. His friendship with Aflaq no doubt influenced him to become involved in politics. Like Aflaq, he harbored Marxist tendencies for a time, only to become disenchanted after the formation of the Blum government. Both he and Aflaq were certain that it was futile to hope for sympathy for their cause from France, regardless of who was in power there. This convinced them of the "imperialist nature" of Western European socialism.

Both men carried their nationalistic ideas to the classroom, which did not please their superiors. They constantly voiced objection to the educational programs, which they claimed were "slanted by the imperialists."[34] They objected to the outdated methods of instruction and examination and when after many warnings the Ministry of Education fined them a fifteen-day salary deduction they wrote a fiery letter of resignation in which they accused the minister of education of incompetence and of bowing to the imperialists.[35]

The years following their resignation were difficult for both of them. Since neither had an independent income, they were forced to depend on their families and private tutoring for livelihood. From 1940 to 1943 they toyed with the idea of establishing a political party based on their nationalistic ideas. During this time, at weekly meetings in their homes with students and friends, their political ideas took form.

Events in Iraq in 1941 when Rashid Ali carried out his *coup d'état* in an effort to offset the British attempt to bring Iraq into the Second World War led Aflaq and Bitar to form a Syrian

Committee to Aid Iraq. Events in Lebanon in 1943 finally brought their idea of creating a party to fruition.

From this point on Aflaq's life became totally enmeshed in politics. He became an unsuccessful candidate for the Syrian Parliament in 1943. At that time he and Bitar backed Shukri al-Quwatli, then president of Syria, in an effort "to combine the national effort" in the struggle for independence.[36] In 1947, after independence, and in 1949, Aflaq again ran for office without success. After these three defeats he decided never to enter parliamentary elections again. He claimed to have lost in 1949 because of the government's fraudulent practices against him.[37]

Aflaq has been a political prisoner several times. In 1939 the French arrested him; in 1948 the national government of Shukri al-Quwatli; in 1949 the leader of the first Syrian *coup d'état*, Husni al-Zaim; and in 1952 and 1954 Adib al-Shishakli. In 1952 he escaped from prison to Lebanon, but Shishakli pressed the Lebanese government to deport him and he had to take exile in Italy for four months.

In his entire political career, Aflaq has held only one official political appointment, that of minister of education in the Atasi Ministry of 1949. He held this position for only three months and only under pressure "since all political parties had to be represented and I was forced to take the job. I tried not to be the one representing our party but could not succeed." Aflaq claims to have an aversion to "political jobs"; he would "rather think."[38]

Aflaq wields strong influence over several thousand young Arabs. From 1943 to 1965 he was secretary general of the Ba'th party. In 1965 he was replaced by Dr. Munif al-Razzaz, a physician, formerly secretary of the party in Jordan.[39] Aflaq's replacement by Razzaz no doubt reflects the party's desire to accommodate the restless elements within the Ba'th who were somewhat weary of Aflaq's presence, and to ward off the charge that the Ba'th party was his personal domain. It should be stated here that Razzaz' rise to power had Aflaq's approval and blessings particularly since both men see eye to eye on most issues dealing with party policy and organization. Moreover, having Razzaz, a Sunni Muslim, at the helm of the party would refute charges that the Ba'th party is controlled by Christian elements, a fact that Aflaq was very well aware of. That he lasted for over two decades was due largely to his middle-of-the-road attitude and to his refusal to accept any responsible position outside the party. While staying out of the limelight, he could maintain his grip on the party. Knowing that he abhors extremism, the many factions within the party constantly used him as a referee. Although in public he rarely sides with either the left or the right, in actuality he generally tips the scales in favor of the right.

It is perhaps a weakness in Aflaq that he shuns responsibility, leaving the field open for those around him to vie for prominence and control. Thus factions are created around certain personalities factions that usually end in a party split, as has been the case with Abdullah al-Rimawi in Jordan, Fuad al-Rikabi and Ali Sale al-Sa'di in Iraq, and Akram al-Hourani in Syria.

In his writings about Arab nationalism Aflaq departs from the apologetic tradition of other Arab writers on this topic: "We do not proclaim that we are better but that we are different."[40] Arabs need not apologize for their nationalism, it needs no justification, it is a fact that must be accepted. The writings of Aflaq are of paramount importance to the Ba'th party. Only his writings and those of Bitar and Razzaz truly reflect the party line.[41]

In 1943 Bitar too ran unsuccessfully for the Syrian Parliament, as a deputy from Damascus. After that he devoted his time and energy to propagating and organizing the party and became totally involved in politics. After 1946 Bitar became an editor of *al-Ba'th*, the party newspaper, to which he is still a major contributor. He has been arrested several times: in 1945 by the Quwatli regime, in 1949 by Zaim, in 1952 and 1954 by Shishakli. In the latter part of 1962 he was sentenced to a one-month jail term which he was never made to serve. On that occasion he addressed an open letter to Nazim al-Qudsi, then president of Syria, in which he accused his government of reaction and of curtailing political liberties.

In 1947 and again in 1949 he ran unsuccessfully for a seat in the Syrian Parliament. He had better luck in 1954, when he became a deputy from Damascus. Since then he has been in the center of Syrian politics. He was foreign minister from June 15, 1956, until the formation of the U.A.R. In 1957 he gained international recognition as head of the Syrian delegation to the United Nations. During the lifetime of the U.A.R., he held the position of federal minister of state for Arab affairs, remaining in that office until the end of 1959, when all Ba'th ministers resigned in a collective withdrawal of confidence from the government of the U.A.R. In December, 1961, during the "secessionist" regime, Bitar ran unsuccessfully for a seat in the Syrian Parliament.

Since March, 1963, he has been a member of the National Revolutionary Council and several times premier of Syria. Following his criticism of Ali Saleh al-Sa'di, and the latter's role in the debacle that brought down the Ba'th regime in Iraq in November, 1963, Bitar gained the distinction of being the only prominent Ba'th leader ever to be expelled from, and later reinstated in, the party.[42] He owes his reinstatement to Aflaq, who called for an emergency meeting of the party which he had "packed" with his followers.

In his writings and speeches Bitar has less of a flare for the dramatic than Aflaq. But he is not as contradictory or vague.

More practical than his friend, he has been credited with being the party's tactician, Aflaq its philosopher. Bitar's writings, more than Aflaq's, are highly nationalistic. Whereas Aflaq frequently writes about socialism, Bitar rarely refers to it. His preoccupation is with nationalism; his writings are generously threaded with Ba'th ideology. He is an elitist: "The greatness of nations," he once wrote, "cannot be measured by the number of souls it has but by the number of geniuses and leaders" it produces.[43]

Throughout its history the Ba'th party has had to fight against difficult odds. Attempting to carry through a social revolution in a society where the shadow of the nineteenth century still lingers is by no means easy. The "balkanization" of the Arab would, and the party insistance on being Arab, rather than Syrian, Iraqi, or Jordanian, has had its effects on Ba'th methods and organization. Moreover, social conditions in each of the several countries where the party operates are by no means similar. Level of education, standard of living and social attitudes are indeed different in Lebanon and in Jordan. The gap is even wider between Lebanon and Saudi Arabia or Yemen. The various countries have different forms of government too. Jordan is a monarchy; Lebanon a republic; Saudi Arabia an absolute monarchy; Kuwait a sheikdom; Yemen a republic with the social conditions of the nineteenth century at best. Despite these differences, the Ba'th party preaches the same ideology throughout the Arab world. Because of this, it has had tremendous difficulties.

While the Ba'th party does not tailor its approach to fit the particular country in which it is operating, Ba'thist attitudes do vary subtly from place to place. In a country like Lebanon, for example, where there is a semi-stable democracy, one finds the Ba'thists more liberal than, say, those in Iraq, where the monarchist regime has forced opposition parties into taking rather rigid positions. That the 1963 Ba'thist experiment in Iraq lasted less than a year was a result of the Iraqi Ba'thists' inability to compromise on even the simplest issues. Indeed, Iraqi Ba'thists are perhaps the most militant of all. This is no doubt a reflection of their long and bitter underground activities against the monarchy until 1958 and later against their extremely harsh treatment at the hand of Abdul al-Karim Qasim.

In Jordan the Ba'th drew its main support from malcontents in Palestinian refugee camps and to a small degree from the intelligentsia. The Ba'th party there reached its zenith in 1958 and 1959 when Rimawi opened the ranks of party membership. (In the opinion of some this action diminished the quality of the party.) While the Ba'th party still has remnants of strength in Jordan, it was severely weakened in 1959 when the party expelled the Rimawi faction in a dispute over the proper place of the party *vis-à-vis* Nasser. Since then the vigilant Jordanian police, coupled with economic expansion and a rise in the standard of living, have further weakened the Ba'th. Further, the threat -admitted privately by some party leaders but denied publicly – that any drastic change in the regime in Jordan might result in Israeli intervention has limited Ba'th activities. All of these factors have tended in recent years to put Jordan in a peculiar position with regard to Ba'th party activities.

Iraq, in the eyes of the Ba'th party, is not in a peculiar position as are Jordan and Lebanon and thus is a prime target for Ba'th activities. The reasons for the 1963 Ba'th failure in that country will be discussed later; for the moment, suffice it to say that neither the socioeconomic conditions in Iraq nor the leaders of the Ba'th there were ripe for the drastic changes the party visualized.

The Ba'th activities in, and relations with, the U.A.R. will be discussed in great detail subsequently. For the moment, in Egypt, as in some other Arab countries, whatever Ba'th strength there is lies in a few cells of students that have a long way to go before they can achieve any degree of effectiveness.

The Ba'th party has had to contend with varying degrees of hostility from the governments in power throughout the Arab world, ranging from repression as in Jordan, Saudi Arabia, Kuwait, and Egypt, to a semi-enlightened approach as in Lebanon, where, while illegal, certain activities of the party have been tolerated. These include the publication in Beirut of a Ba'th newspaper, *al-Ahrar* (The Freemen). At the moment Ba'th activities in these countries are restricted to distributing propaganda from Damascus, and even this is curtailed by various repressive measures. It would seem unlikely that the Ba'th party will be able to change the status quo substantially in any of the Arab countries where it has cells and branches; nor is it willing to try at the moment. An exception to this statement is Iraq, for reasons discussed below. As has been stated previously, the Ba'th party does not at present have the strength to effect any considerable change in the Arab world. This is as evident in Egypt as in the Maghrib. The peculiar positions of Lebanon and Jordan place them out of the pale of any serious attempts by the party. It is also doubtful whether the Ba'th is in a position to effect change in the sheikdoms and principalities of the Arabian peninsula, in which the party's following is small and with which Syria, the headquarters of the party, has no common boundaries, and whose social and political conditions the party recognizes to be unready. For the moment this leaves only Iraq, where the Ba'th party once succeeded and might succeed again.

The fact that the Ba'th party was able to dominate Iraq briefly in 1963 is a sign of its strength there. The party claims – perhaps rightly – that its failure there was more a reflection of ineffective and divided leadership than of the party's lack of appeal among the masses. It is likely that the party will continue its attempts to overthrow the Aref regime. As the Ba'th in Syria is viewed with strong suspicion and hostility by its neighbors, it feels isolated and weak. Thus it is quite understandable that it continues its attempts to get a foothold in Iraq. The party's Pan-Arab plans for unity will ultimately depend upon its strength and durability in Syria. The latest *coup d'état*, in February, 1966, no doubt weakened the party's image not only within Syria but in the rest of the Arab world as well. Intellectuals and the uneducated masses alike will question the ability of a party to unite the vast and diverse Arab world if it is not able to achieve unity within its own ranks. The struggle between the different factions within the Ba'th is by no means ended. The left-wing military and civilians won a round in February, 1966 – only one round, one battle; the war will go on. The present ruling Ba'thists are by no means secure in their positions, and the right wing of the party, the followers of Aflaq, Bitar, Razzaz and former President Hafiz, are by no means eliminated.

It is very likely that a counter *coup* led by the right wing will soon occur. This is evidenced by the fact that in the last party Congress held after February, 1966, only 65 delegates of 137 who ordinarily attend such gatherings participated in the choice of the new leadership.[44] There is an Arab proverb that says while the two foxes were fighting, the chicken ran away! This may happen in Syria as it did in Iraq when President Aref ousted the two quibbling factions. Yet while this may occur, it is unlikely. History does not repeat itself: certain events only resemble one another on the surface. The situation in Iraq in 1963 differed greatly from that in Syria in 1966. The major difference, and the one which brought about the Ba'th debacle in Iraq, was the presence of a capable man like Aref at the helm. Aref was not – and has never been – a Ba'thist. No such person existed in Syria to effect the same change. This would make apparent the conclusion that the Ba'th – whether left or right – is here to stay, and this seems very likely at the moment, for there does not seem to be another effectively organized group or party which could take over in Syria were the Ba'th to leave.

Left, right, or center, the Ba'th party whether in or out of power has left an impression not only on Syria but on the entire political thinking of the Arab world, and perhaps its influence extends beyond these boundaries. The Ba'th party emerged as a result of the impact of Western civilization over traditional societies. It is not an isolated incident. Arnold J. Toynbee, in an insightful passage, states that "our Western know-how has unified the whole world… and it has inflamed the institutions of War and Class."[45] More particularly, Bernard Lewis relates that the people of the Orient "awoke to a disagreeable reality in which their countries, their resources, their civilizations, even their very souls were menaced by a West that was so rich and powerful."[46] The old conflict between the rich and the poor has been revived. This time it is more serious and deadly and has had a new element introduced into it: ideology. This new element gives the old struggle new fervor and adds to it the flavor of a moral crusade. Everywhere in Asia, Africa, and the Middle East the same revolution is apparent. Ba'th social nationalism is only a scion of a much larger phenomenon. The expectations released and those which have arisen will not be put down easily.

The new ideology, "modernizing nationalism" as Paul Sigmund calls it, is a by-product of the West's impact on traditional societies.[47] Whether it be called African, Arab, or Asian, it is a hybrid of Western and traditional cultures and attitudes. This new Afro-Asian socialism, including that of the Ba'th party and other brands of Arab socialism, corresponds to our definition of it as a new hybrid. It picks and chooses at will from Western democratic thought, Marxism-Leninism, and native culture. This new hybrid of socialism gives the leaders and parties that advocate it room to maneuver between East and West.

The Ba'th party, like many other Socialist parties in the developing world, is primarily a nationalist party. Socialism gives its political program the sinews necessary to bring about the changes advocated by the party. Arab unity is of prime importance to, if not the most important goal of, Ba'th socialism. Were the Ba'th party operating in a vacuum without adverse forces, it is quite likely that its program would find wide appeal among the Arab masses. But it does not operate in a vacuum; the various Arab regimes republics, sheikdoms, and monarchies are hostile to it. Vested interests are not likely to give up easily to this new Pan-Arab movement that advocates their overthrow. The Nasserite movement, a Socialist movement very much like the Ba'th in its program, which should cooperate with the Ba'th party, is extremely hostile toward it. The Ba'th's insistence on collective leadership both politically and intellectually precludes effective cooperation with the Nasser regime. The latest efforts of the rightist forces in the Middle East to counterbalance and offset the Socialist reform tendencies found expression in the Islamic Pact advocated by King Faisal of Saudi Arabia. While the aim of the Islamic Pact, in the words of King Faisal, is for "Moslems to come together and support one another in their every need,"[48] the truth is closer to the Turkish newspaper *al-Jamhuriyyah's* explanation of it as "an attempt to strengthen the conservatives in the Middle East against the revolutionaries."[49]

Nasser's reaction to an invitation to attend the conference was stated in the Cairo newspaper *Akhbar al-Yawm* which pondered, "How can President Gamal Abdel Nasser sit at the same table with the Shah of Iran…, Israel's most beloved Muslim?"[50] The Ba'th's reaction was quite similar to that of Nasser, and former President Hafiz remarked that the proposed pact will serve only "reaction and imperialism."[51]

The conservative regimes, it seems, are attempting to counter organization with organization. Thus the kings of Jordan, Saudi Arabia, and Morocco, the Shah of Iran, the presidents of Tunisia and Turkey, and the Sheikh of Kuwait are attempting to combat the revolutionaries in the Middle East. This cooperation between regimes, never before attempted, is likely to affect the activities and effectiveness of the Ba'th party. The Ba'thists and Nasserites are already getting anxious about their adversaries' proposed cooperation. The obstacles were formidable enough to begin with, and will surely become more so. And this is by no means the only difficulty facing the Ba'th; the Ba'th must solve internal problems too.

2 The Advent of the Arab Ba'th Socialist Party

The establishment of the Arab Ba'th Socialist party in Syria in 1943 by a small circle of young intellectuals was largely inspired by their desire to see the conditions of the Arab world ameliorated. This would be, they hoped, a party to resurrect the Arabs.

This handful of men included Aflaq, Bitar, his cousin Dr. Madhat Bitar, Dr. Razzaz, Dr. Ali Jabir from Beirut, Dr. Abdullah Abdul Daim, Dr. Wahib al-Ghanim, Dr. Jamal al-Atasi, Dr. Musa Rizik, Badi' al-Kasm, Sami al-Droubi, and Abdul Birr 'Iyun al-Sud. Salah al-Bitar and his cousin Madhat were the organizers and tacticians of the party from its inception. Salah later became more prominent as Madhat faded into the background.[1]

Since its establishment, the party has brought new concepts into Arab politics. Although it originated in Syria, it refused to recognize the national and "artificial" frontiers drawn by "foreigners." That it is an Arab rather than a Syrian party has been emphasized from the beginning.[2] Almost from the start, it was viewed with suspicion by the authorities. These were not the ordinary Arab politicians that the authorities knew. These were young men with intense emotions and with a deep sense of responsibility to "save" the Arabs.

They agitated against the French almost from the first day the formed the party. Until 1945, when the French left Syria they agitated relentlessly against their presence by making speeches and distributing leaflets and pamphlets. When they saw the need for it, they even backed "traditional leadership," as when they backed the national government of Quwatli formed in 1943. At that moment they thought the country needed all its forces united against the French.[2]

When the French dissolved the Lebanese Parliament and jailed the president of the Republic, Bisharah al-Khouri, and his entire cabinet, the party waged an all-out anti-French campaign. It distributed leaflets in the streets calling for strikes and demonstrations.[4]

After that episode the activity of the party seems to have subsided, to resurge in 1945. With Syrian independence almost in view, the party waged a strong campaign warning any future government of Syria against negotiating a treaty of alliance with France.[5] Anticipating French resistance to the granting of independence, the party called for the people to organize militia formations to fight the French.[6] The party hoped for fulfillment of the Greater Syria Plan – unity of Iraq, Palestine, Syria, and Jordan – as soon as independence was achieved. Thus when President Quwatli early in 1945 made a speech in which he agreed to this scheme, provided the other nations have a republican form of government – Jordan and Iraq did not – the party issued a statement saying, "It is strange to hear such excuses from a regime whose main characteristic has been to trample on liberties."[7] As a result of this statement, Bitar was imprisoned. Dr. Ali al-Khalil, a prominent leader of the Ba'th in Lebanon, later wrote that the party opposed the Greater Syria Plan in 1945 on two grounds: (1) that it would enhance a Syrian, rather than an Arab, nation; (2) that it was suspected by the party of British backing.[8] This does not correspond with facts and only manifests the party's embarrassment at having backed a Syrian, rather than an Arab, unity plan. Since then the party has stood firm in its opposition to this scheme.[9]

Since its formation, the party has objected to the Arab League's Covenant: "The Covenant is only an admission and a legalization of the present disunity in the Arab world. It is not only a short step toward unity but also the wrong step."[10]

After Syrian independence, the party assumed the role of opposition to the government. In a speech by Aflaq to party members in November, 1946, he commented on the newly formed government, saying, "The truth is that this regime is inflicted with a disease; it is not faithful to its constitutional principles." Later the party opposed the famous Decree No. 50, which restricted the freedoms guaranteed to the people by the Constitution by investing the minister of interior with sole authority to determine the extent of freedom to be enjoyed by the public and giving him the power to license political parties, newspapers, societies, associations, and public meetings and to ban any activity or party. According to the party, it caused such agitation that the Parliament was forced not to pass this law.[11]

In accordance with its nationalistic point of view, the party has always carried on a propaganda campaign against the loss of Alexandretta District to Turkey. Alexandretta was part of Syria until 1939, when the French mandate government ceded it to Turkey in an attempt to get Turkey on the Allied side in the impending struggle. On December 20 of each year, the party issues a statement denouncing the act and calling for return of the district.[12] The party has never ceased agitation over this issue; characteristic is its demand that all Arab League members sever diplomatic relations with Turkey until it returns the district.[13]

Starting in 1946, two years before the establishment of Israel, the party carried on a propaganda campaign against its anticipated establishment. It cautioned Arab governments to prepare themselves for the coming struggle and called on all Arabs to stand firm in their opposition to such a scheme.[14]

In 1947 the party fought the scheme of Jamil Mardam, prime minister of Syria, for indirect elections. It led and incited demonstrations and strikes until Parliament finally passed a direct election law.[15] In accordance with its principle of universal suffrage, the party also called for a law permitting women to vote. This was indeed an innovation in the traditional and conservative politics of Syria. During this year, the party also carried on an anti-foreign aid campaign. Commenting on President Truman's speech on the occasion of giving aid to Greece and Turkey, the party paper said: "Any foreign aid to a weak nation will shortly be transformed into political influence in that country. Let the Arabs look to each other for assistance and they will discover that their freedom is at home, and not in London, Washington, or Moscow."[16]

The First National Convention of the party was held in Damascus around the beginning of April, 1947.[17] It was during this Convention that the party's Constitution and Internal Rules were discussed, written, and approved. With some changes over the years, these basic documents have remained almost unaltered. The numerical strength of this party at the time was very much out of proportion to its influence on Syria's politics. Aflaq, the first speaker at this Convention, said: "No other party in the Arab world faced the difficulties that the Ba'th faced in its attempt to grow. During the first three years of its existence, our membership did not exceed ten."[18]

Considering the numerical weakness of the party and the fact that it did not at the time include in its ranks one prominent Syrian politician, the statement issued at the end of this First Convention was quite different from statements issued by other

Arab political parties. It was different in its comprehensiveness. In foreign policy it planted the seed of neutrality which it came to advocate strongly. The statement said the Arabs should be friendly only with governments friendly to them, that the Arab world is viewed similarly by both the Soviet Union and the United States. From this First Convention, we note the anti-Western attitude of this party. Arabs should not be friendly to Britain, which occupies the Nile Valley, Palestine, Jordan, Iraq, Libya, and the Protectorates. They should not be friendly with France, which occupies Algeria, Morocco, and Tunisia, nor with Spain, which occupies parts of Morocco and Er Rif. The party reiterated its anti-Turkish attitude and demanded the return of Alexandretta and Kelikia districts. It also warned against friendship with Iran, which took the Ahwaz District, and with the United States, whose interference in the Middle East was detrimental to Arab interests.

The party demanded that the Arab League take immediate steps toward achieving unity in the Arab world by combining the armed forces, foreign policy, and representation and by abolishing the need for passports between Arab lands.

In the sphere of domestic politics, the party demanded government protection of local industry, gradual termination of foreign business and investment in the country, application of progressive income taxes, inheritance taxes, reform of labor laws, supervision of domestic and foreign trade, price-fixing to combat exorbitant prices, better educational facilities, irrigation schemes, and high excise taxes. The Convention also agreed that strict limits should be placed on private property and that the party should adopt socialism as a slogan and as an ideology.[19]

Clearly this was a party which took it upon itself to discuss the problems of all the Arab-speaking lands from the Atlantic Ocean to the Persian Gulf.[20] Three days after this First Convention, Aflaq further clarified his position on the two power blocs in the world: the Anglo-American and the Soviet.

"Aligning with either," he wrote, "will do nothing but harm to the Arabs."[21] Thus another basic decision for the party was made; it was to be the first Arab party to advocate nonalignment. The party during this period carried on a frenetic propaganda campaign on the Palestine issue. It blamed the Arab governments for failure to propagandize the Arab point of view in the West. Bitar recommended that the Arabs use economic pressure on the West by putting a stop to the sale of oil to them:[22] he further recommended their withdrawal from the United Nations, "a tool for Zionism and the Western Powers."[23]

Considering the small membership of the party at the time and indeed at the present, it was presumptuous to discuss the problems of the entire Arab world. Clearly this was a party that thought and acted, even at this early stage, as a vanguard of the Arabs. It thought of itself as the awakening "conscience" of the Arabs in the mid-twentieth century. And while its propaganda statements at the time made little headway among the masses, it did attract a number of intellectuals, particularly among students.

When Aflaq and Bitar proclaimed their candidacy for office in 1947, they began their campaign by making accusations against the government, which they claimed might resort to fraud to prevent their election, and by demanding a neutral government to conduct the elections. In the heat of the election campaign, the government closed down *al-Ba'th* and Bitar was later fined and sentenced to a six-month jail term.

The Ba'th party actively participated in the Palestine War. It sent volunteers, collected money and weapons, and Bitar, Aflaq, Wahib al-Ghanim, and others were in the front lines.[24]

The defeat of the Arabs in Palestine gave the Ba'th party its first real plunge into the inner current of Arab politics. The Ba'th had been warning Arab governments since 1946 to prepare for the coming struggle. In 1947 and 1948 it had warned against relying on the United Nations to solve the problem: "The solution of the Palestine problem is in Palestine, not at the United Nations."[25] The shock of defeat was great for the Arabs, even though the party had foreseen defeat and warned against it.

The Ba'th had warned the Arabs not to expect justice from the West or from any of its "tools," such as the United Nations. It warned that the West pays no heed to the Arab's just desires and causes. Even milder Arab nationalist sympathizers such as Albert Hourani advocated that the Arabs should rely on themselves and become powerful and modernized. Hourani states: "The Western powers in deed if not in word treated the Arab countries as if the desires and wishes of their inhabitants were matters of minor importance."[26]

No one in 1948 could have presaged the tremendous effects of the Arab defeat in Palestine. Constantine Zurayk, later analyzing effects of the Palestine War, said: "The defeat of the Arabs in Palestine is no simple setback or light passing evil. It is a disaster in every sense of the word and one of the hardest of the trials and tribulations with which the Arabs have been afflicted throughout their long history." Calling for an end to apologetics, he prompted the Arabs to strengthen themselves. Strength is what counts in politics; the defeat was a shame and a disgrace. And finally Zurayk, not considered an extreme nationalist by the Arabs, asked for an "internal revolution" that would lead to strengthening the Arabs internally as well as externally.[27]

The deep frustration felt by the Arabs at the defeat in Palestine found vent in extremist movements later on. Indeed, this defeat caused the Arabs to reevaluate their entire mode of living and their "philosophical and political ethics" as well.[28] From then on, Arab politics was never to be the same. A leftward movement had started. Traditional Arab leadership had completely failed,[29] and the need for a new type of leadership had arisen. Razzaz writes that the outcome of the Palestine War was a result of the actions of governments that should not have been in power in the mid-twentieth century. It was the bell toll for the "bankrupt" Arab governments and it ushered in a new era – an era of revolution.[30]

Change did indeed take place. Within seven years of the Palestine defeat, the Ba'th, which in 1947 was composed of only a handful of followers, was at the helm of Syrian politics and had become a major movement in Jordan and Iraq as well. By 1955 it had branches in almost every Arab country. Change took place on the government level too. By 1955 there had been three *coups d'état* in Syria, a change of regime in Lebanon, a revolution in Egypt, a revolution in Algeria against the French, the assassination of King Abdullah in Jordan, and the assassination of lesser political figures in the Middle East. The Ba'th certainly capitalized on the failure of traditional Arab leaders to conduct a better campaign in Palestine. While the tribulations that shook the Middle East, and Syria in particular, between 1948 and 1955 were not all the result of Ba'th agitation, Ba'th helped arouse the feelings.

The Ba'th prepared the people for Syria's next phase. In four years, from 1949 to 1953, Syria was to undergo three *coups d'état*, twenty-one Cabinet changes, and two military dictatorships. It began with the *coup d'état* of Husni al-Zaim, who at first was backed by the Ba'th party. He was hailed as a new hope for Syria, especially when he attempted some sweeping reforms such as his campaign against the high cost of living, introduction of a civil code, revamping of the army, and emancipation of women.

When Zaim attempted to promulgate a new constitution written exclusively by civil servants and to require civil servants to take an oath not to join political parties, the Ba'th came out in open opposition. No one could dissuade Zaim from doing exactly as he wished; as a result, the Ba'th issued a small pamphlet denouncing his regime as restrictive of human liberties and demanding the formation of a new government from those parties in opposition to the "old regime."[31] This act did not please Zaim, who proceeded to ban all political parties in Syria and imprison the Ba'th leaders.

Zaim's regime lasted until August 14, 1949, when it was toppled by Colonel Sami al-Hinnawi. The role of the Ba'th party in executing the *coup* against the Zaim regime is not clear. What is clear is that the party accepted a share in a coalition government under Hashim al-Atasi "due to the need for national solidarity at the time."[32] Aflaq became minister of national education, a post he held for approximately three months when he resigned on the occasion of his third failure to be elected to the Syrian Parliament.[33]

Colonel Hinnawi ruled Syria for approximately six months, during which time parliamentary elections were held. These elections gave substantial gains to the People's party of Atasi, who with Hinnawi advocated the Fertile Crescent Scheme. This scheme calls for the unity of Jordan, Syria, Lebanon, and Iraq and for many years has been advocated by the Syrian National Socialist party.[34] Only three Ba'th candidates were elected. Aflaq and other Ba'th candidates lost because of alleged fraudulent practices by the reactionary and feudal elements in Syria. The party did not accuse the government itself of fraud.[35]

By 1949 the party had reversed its earlier stand on unity. Whereas previously it had cared little about the form of government in countries with which Syria would be united, now it took a definite stand against union with monarchical Iraq because it would mean sacrificing Syria's republican form of government. This stand put it in direct opposition to advocates of the Greater Syria Scheme.

Shishakli, the third military man to rule Syria, deposed the Hinnawi regime on the morning of December 20, 1949. Initially Shishakli chose to govern as a strong man behind the various governments that followed. Ba'th's attitude toward his regime was that of a wait-and-see policy until 1951 when he dissolved the Parliament, deposed President Atasi, and began concentrating power in himself. Conveniently, Shishakli discovered various "plots to topple the regime."[36] After a Ba'th leaflet was distributed in the streets of Damascus on January 26, 1952, and printed in *al-Ba'th*, Shishakli banned the paper.[37]

On December 28, 1952, Shishakli arrested seventy-six army officers who had been "deceived by the words of some extreme parties."[38] Next day Aflaq, Bitar, and Hourani were arrested, only to escape five days later to Lebanon where they resumed attacking his regime by various means. In April, 1953, Shishakli banned all political parties and pressed the Lebanese government to ask the Ba'thist leaders to leave. They left Lebanon for Europe in June, 1953, and did not return to Damascus until October, by which time Shishakli had assumed the presidency of Syria. During their absence, Shishakli had allowed a limited measure of freedom; he had allowed the existence of political parties and had organized his own Liberation Movement, a state party.

The Ba'thist leaders were not satisfied with these gestures of leniency and limited freedom. In September, 1953, before the elections to be held the next month, the Ba'th organized strikes and demonstrations against the regime. They also called for the Homs Pact, by which the Ba'th agreed with the People's party and the National party to boycott the coming elections. Shishakli's Liberation Movement won 72 out of 82 seats in Parliament. The election results further angered the opposition parties, and strikes and demonstrations broke out in various parts of Syria. The Ba'th party was most active in distributing leaflets and pamphlets denouncing the regime.[39] Shishakli responded by arresting Aflaq, Bitar, and Hourani again on January 25, 1954. Ba'th influence was penetrating into the army, which rose against Shishakli in Aleppo in northern Syria. Later the *coup* swept into Damascus, forcing the ouster of Shishakli later. On March 5 the Arab Ba'th party of Aflaq and Bitar and the Arab Socialist party of Hourani were united.

The Ba'th party had two major grounds for opposing the Shishakli regime. On the domestic level, the party objected to his conservative economic policy, the limitations on freedom, and the concentration of power in his own hands.[40] On the foreign-policy level, the party objected to his pro-Western attitude and charged that he was "working to participate in the Middle East Defense Scheme and had agreed to the settlement of Palestine Arab refugees on Syrian territory."[41]

3 Drift to the Left, 1954–58

Before the Ba'th merged with Hourani's Socialist party it had contented itself with assuming the role of "preacher" in Syrian politics. After the merger it decided to enter the political arena in full force. The decision to merge the two parties was no doubt prompted by the strength and popularity of Hourani, at least in his own district and city, Hama. It was an opportunistic step on the part of both parties to strengthen themselves despite their differences, which were later to cause their separation.

Akram Hourani was born in Hama, Syria. He has a law degree from the Syrian University and thus differs from Aflaq and Bitar in educational background. A brilliant speaker, he has always been more interested in office than in principles or ideology. Walter Z. Laqueur describes him as an opportunist who has been distinguished "by the most determined effort to gain power, whatever the means, and by a willingness to ally himself with all and any individual." Laqueur adds that Hourani during the 1930s and 1940s stood for an orientation toward Germany, Britain, and the United States, in that order.[1]

Hourani was a member of the Syrian Parliament from 1943 until the union with Egypt in 1958. In 1949 he was minister of agriculture; in 1950, minister of defense; in 1957, speaker of the Syrian Parliament; and from 1958 until his resignation at the end of 1959, a vice president of the U.A.R.

Hourani founded his Arab Socialist party in 1950. The Constitution of this party reflects the influence of the Ba'th on the course of political thinking in Syria.[2] Hourani, perhaps sensing the trend in Syria, almost copied the Constitution of the Ba'th party, with minor changes. Like the Ba'th Constitution, it defies national boundaries and treats the Arabs as one nation (Arts. 2 and 10). It proclaims deep faith in Arab nationalism as a force of human mission to spread "love and peace" among mankind (Arts. 8 and 9). It also calls for a republican parliamentary regime (Chap. IV, Art. 2) and a comprehensive social and economic program (Chaps. II and III). In foreign policy, it calls for an "independent Arab policy," independent of any foreign influence (Chap. V, Art. 1).

The Arab Socialist party, however, differs in organization from the Ba'th. Whereas the Ba'th has adopted the cell as a basis for organization, the Arab Socialist has adopted the branch system.[3] They also differ in geographical distribution and type of membership. Ba'th backing and membership thus far has come from pockets of intellectuals dispersed throughout Syria. The Arab Socialists were mainly bourgeois elements concentrated in the Hama district. Different also were the character and temperament of the respective leaders. Aflaq is an intellectual who shuns political maneuvering and political office. Bitar is the tactician of the party and lacks the effervescent character and political adroitness of Hourani. Hourani was to be the politician of the party but was less principled than Aflaq and Bitar. Hourani's socialism "promised everything [to] everybody."[4] The triumvirate – the philosopher, the tactician, and the politician – was thought to be advantageous to both parties. As will be seen later, it did not work well.

Hourani managed to survive the various changes of power in Syria with surprising agility. He managed to work well under the French, the "old regime" from independence until 1949, the various military *coups d'état*, and with the Shishakli regime at first. Only after Shishakli began concentrating power in himself in 1951 did Hourani quarrel with him and move over to the opposition.[5] Only then did Hourani begin to think of merging with the Ba'th. Hourani adopted the Ba'th principles and organization without any hesitation.

With Shishakli out of the way, the Arab Ba'th Socialist party resumed its activities. The party's newspaper resumed publication on April 8, 1954, and the party began an antifeudalist, antireactionary campaign on the domestic level. It organized rallies, distributed leaflets, and led demonstrations against the new government, which was beginning to "deviate" from the expected path.[6] With elections coming up in October, 1954, the party charged that the incumbent government could not be trusted to conduct elections honestly. In its effort to win popularity, the party became extremely nationalistic, even attacking "Nasser for compromising with the British over Suez."[7] It also charged that the days for military dictatorships were over and that the military regime in Egypt should relinquish its powers. The party charged Nasser with lack of "national consciousness" in reference to a remark he was alleged to have made to the Syrian Ambassador in Cairo: "I don't care if Syria unites with Iraq or Jordan, or even with Turkey, as long as that conforms with the wishes of the Syrian people."[8] It charged that Nasser's equation of Syria's unity with an Arab country to its unity with Turkey showed ignorance of Arab history and lack of understanding of Arab goals.

In the 1954 elections the Ba'th party won 16 out of 140 seats in Parliament. Eleven (11.4) per cent of the seats of Parliament were to dominate it later on. The increase in Ba'th strength in Parliament from 3 in the 1949 election to 16 four years later was due to several factors. First was the added strength of the

Hourani group. In the 1954 elections Hourani's entire list was elected in Hama.[9] Second was the general dissatisfaction with the old political parties, who were increasingly losing their appeal, especially to the younger generation. Third, the party gained from the general mood of anti-Westernism which it helped create. By adopting extreme nationalistic slogans, it was able to capture the imagination of many. Fourth, as Laqueur states, "there is reason to believe that the election campaigns were at least partly financed from unspecified army funds."[10] However, such a charge was never proved; nor was any mention of it made in any other source.

The election of 1954 proved vital to the history of Syria. The new Parliament was "weak, inseparably divided, and utterly lacking in direction."[11] It proved easy prey for such a tightly knit, well-organized group as the Ba'th party. And the influence exercised by this small group in the new Parliament was certainly out of proportion to its size.

H. A. R. Gibb, the noted Orientalist, attributes the unrest and instability of the Middle East to these three basic factors: (1) political problems, especially the issues dealing with foreign policy and the State of Israel; (2) economic instability – the attempt to build a new, viable, and efficient economic structure; (3) social factors where many of the weaknesses of the Arab world stem from the failure to recognize and meet adequately the problems of a prolonged social crisis.[12]

The Arab world between 1954 and 1958 was a hotbed of crises. During this period, the Western powers, particularly the United States, were attempting to bring the Arab governments into some kind of defense scheme. To many nationalists, such a scheme was unthinkable. As the West attempted more pressure to further its schemes, many less extreme nationalists joined ranks with the Ba'th party. For these nationalists, the Ba'th symbolized intense hatred for a "deceiving" West and stood for a radical social program internally. In the international sphere the Arabs were frustrated in their quest for a powerful ally. For their pet project – "getting rid of Israel" they could find no powerful ally. No one would even sell them weapons. Internally, while the need for modernization and social change was apparent, the traditional instruments of change were unable or unwilling to effect it.

During this period can be discerned an anti-Western, leftist movement not only in Syria but in many other countries in the Arab world as well. The Jordan Parliament in 1954 passed a law giving political parties, denied legal existence by the government, the right to appeal to the High Court of Justice. Under this new dispensation, the Ba'th party became legal, and Jordanian politics entered a new era.[13] Ba'th, however, had maintained illegal existence in Jordan since 1948, when young graduates of Syrian schools returned home. In 1950 two Ba'th candidates won election to the Jordan Parliament. As in Syria, these two members of Parliament assumed the role of "permanent leaders of Parliamentary opposition."[14] J. B. Glubb states that much of the extremist bitterness injected into Jordanian politics since has been due to the Ba'th party.[15] Indeed Jordanian politics has not been the same since the coming of the Ba'th to Jordan. After the 1954 election a left-wing government was formed in which the Ba'th joined with the National Socialists. Rimawi, the leader of the Ba'th in Jordan, became minister of foreign affairs. Glubb Pasha, Commander of the Jordan Army, was dismissed in March, 1956, and the 1946 Anglo-Jordanian Treaty, giving preferential treatment to Great Britain, was terminated in March, 1957.[16]

The leftist movement in Egypt culminated in the nationalization of the Suez Canal in 1956. In Iraq this provoked anti-Western demonstrations. In Lebanon it triggered the 1958 anti-Chamoun revolution. Chamoun was the only Arab politician whose policies were clearly pro-Western and who accepted the Eisenhower Doctrine.

In the first few months of 1955 the party spoke out against alliances and pacts with the West. A vehement anti-Iraqi campaign was carried on by the party to protest Nuri al-Said's pro-Western policy and his signature and adherence to the Baghdad Pact. *Al-Ba'th* vehemently denounced Iraqi adherence to the past and an Iraqi Regional Ba'th statement distributed in the streets and reprinted in *al-Ba'th* called on the people to overthrow the Said regime and abrogate the Iraqi-Turkish Pact.[17]

The rise of the Ba'th fortune following the downfall of Shishakli in Syria caused the rightist parties to unite against it. Verbal and physical clashes between the Ba'th and its opponents became frequent. A fist fight was reported on February 27, 1955, between Ba'th and Syrian National Socialist party members in Deir al-Zour; another on March 5 in Harem in souther Syria; and a third on March 6, in which two people were killed and thirty wounded. Clashes with the National Liberation Movement in the Hama district in which several people were injured or killed were reported on April 17. This series of fights culminated in the assassination of Adnan al-Malki, a deputy chief of staff of the Syrian army and a prominent Ba'thist, by a member of the Syrian National Socialist party.[18]

The assassination of Malki caused many to sympathize with the Ba'th. It ushered in a new era in which the Ba'th was relentlessly working to destroy its rightist opponents. "Taking a page from the Communists, Ba'thist partisans within and without the army methodically discredited their opponents by a series of treason trials that left the mass of Syrian politicians cowed."

The trials for the assassination ended in the demise of the Syrian National Socialist party.[19]

Ba'th technique during this period was to outbid their rivals in nationalistic declamations and to infiltrate the army with their propaganda. In Jordan the Ba'th so successfully infiltrated the army that a Ba'thist, Ali Abu Nuwwar, became commander of the Jordan Army.[20] In Syria Ba'th's principal ally in the army was Colonel Abdul Hamid al-Serraj, chief of the security and intelligence department.[21] To achieve its end of discrediting rightist opposition, the Ba'th in both countries cooperated with the Communists.[22] In Parliament Ba'th members outbid all others in their demands for a better society to be achieved through a comprehensive Socialist program.[23] No other party, except perhaps the Communists, could demand more.

In its internal drive for supremacy over other parties in Syria, several factors bolstered the rise of the Ba'th to power during this period. Among these factors was its rapprochement with Nasser. Until 1955 the Ba'th was unsympathetic toward Nasser. It objected to his "personal dictatorial" regime, his "enclosed provincialism," his cooperation with "dictatorial regimes" in the Arab world, especially Shishakli's, and his "link" to "imperialist powers" made apparent, the Ba'th party claimed, in the Anglo-Egyptian agreement concerning the withdrawal of British troops from the Canal Zone in 1954.[24] As the Nasser government took on a more anti-Western line, coupled with an emphasis on the Arabism of Egypt and a policy of more involvement in its neighbors' affairs, Ba'th's attitude began to change. The joint Syrian-Egyptian hostility to the Baghdad Pact brought the Ba'th to look with more favor on Nasser. Egypt's Czechoslovakian "arms deal" was hailed as a further step in the liberation of the Arabs from Western monopoly of weapons in the Middle East.[25] The "arms deal" was acclaimed as breaking the Western monopoly as well as strengthening the Arabs in their struggle against Israel.[26] The Syrian-Egyptian rapprochement culminated in the Tripartite Arab Agreement by which Syria, Egypt, and Saudi Arabia agreed to a unified economic policy, common market, uniform currency, unified army, and one external policy based on bringing out "an independent Arab policy," meaning neutral policy.[27]

The deterioration of relations between the Western powers and the Arabs went into a downward spiral that ended in the Suez Canal affair. By this time the West was morally "completely discredited in the eyes of the Arabs. It [was] regarded as a predatory imperialist… a rabid warmonger… The Western monopoly of culture had been broken." Militarily, the Western powers had by this time lost a number of their important bases in the Arab world, while this can be contrasted to the size of Soviet armies near the region.[28] Having lost some of their bases in the area, the Western powers began to place emphasis on alliances and pacts – bilateral, as in the case of Jordan, or multilateral, as in the Baghdad Pact arrangement; hence the pressure on Syria to join the Baghdad Pact. The Ba'th party interpreted the Baghdad Pact as an attempt to bring the Arabs into an anti-Soviet coalition, at the same time protecting Israel since the Arabs under the terms of the pact could not engage in independent activities. "Pacts to the Arabs mean their control by the imperialist powers."[29]

A second aspect of the downward plunge of Western esteem in the Arab world is that connected with the "rigidity" of American foreign policy in this region and its attempt to "hang on" to every advantage while at the same time maintaining the status quo.[30] This was in direct opposition to Ba'th and nationalist aspirations that demanded change internally by adopting Socialist programs. Such Socialist programs, however, in the Ba'th view could not be adopted unless unity were achieved. This meant that certain regimes should be overthrown. Also repugnant to the Ba'th was the American policy of semi-guaranteeing the frontiers in the region (meaning the State of Israel) and the semi-official adherence to such policy since the Tripartite Agreement of 1950 with Great Britain and France.

The anti-Western trend was further aided by a change of policy in the Communist propaganda of the Soviet Union. During the 1930s and 1940s international communism banned cooperation with the "national bourgeoisie," branding them traitors and collaborators. Even the Mahatma Gandhi was classified as a British "agent." However, by 1955 Soviet experts were indulging in self-criticism and admitting their fault on this score. Henceforward, cooperation with the entire national movement was recommended.[31] The Soviet Union was able thus to appear as a benefactor of Arab nationalism. Its task was "greatly facilitated by the successive pressures of the West on the Arabs, for example, the Baghdad Pact, the Suez Canal invasion and the Eisenhower Doctrine."[32] It was early in 1955, after Shepilov's visit to the Middle East, that the new line became evident. The new line became a formal policy after the Communist party's Twentieth Congress in February, 1956.[33] And while neutrality was considered almost heresy by the West, particularly by Dulles, it was considered a gain by the Soviet Union and was encouraged. The Czech-Egyptian "arms deal" and the Soviet promise to send "volunteers" to the Middle East during the Suez Canal crises, no doubt enhanced Soviet prestige in the Middle East and strengthened the position of those parties that called for a more positive attitude toward the "Socialist," i.e., Communist bloc.

The Ba'th party assumed the role of opposition to the government of Faris al-Khouri, formed on November 1, 1954, "due to its vagueness on foreign policy."[34] Until June 2, 1956, when it entered a coalition government formed by Sabri al-Asali, its activities were influenced mainly by foreign policy. By April, 1956, the Ba'th began advocating unity with Egypt and calling for rallies and demonstrations in favor of it.[35] What shape the party thought unity should take was not clear at this time. The fact that both countries (or Regions, in the parlance of the Ba'th party) were "progressive" was the most important basis for unity and thus its shape was not important.[36] The fact that the Ba'th participated in the new ministry in June, 1956, made the party's policy of unity with Egypt a government policy. The two Ba'thist ministers, Bitar and Khalil Kallas, held the important portfolios of foreign affairs and national economy. The party agreed to participate in the coalition government only on "condition that unity with Egypt, at least on a Federal basis, be adopted as government policy."[37]

It was not long afterward that the Syrian Cabinet made a decision to form a committee to negotiate unity on a federal basis with Egypt. The mood in Syria was overwhelmingly pro-unity and the Parliament approved the Cabinet's decision unanimously.[38] Sentiment for unity was growing and there was no way of stopping it. No one in Syria wanted to stop it, nor did anyone dare come out against it for fear of public reprimand. Politicians contended for recognition as being most in favor of unity. Even the Communists, persecuted by the Nasser regime, did not dare to come out against unity.

Union sentiment was so strong among the Ba'th party membership and among the Arab masses that the party seemingly would have welcomed any union regardless of form and without serious study. This was, indeed, the case. This lack of serious study as to what type of union should be concluded with

Egypt cost the party dearly. It is indeed odd that a party whose major concern was unity did not, when the time came, have the vaguest notion about what kind of union it demanded.

The months that followed the nationalization of the Suez, Canal in July were months of ferment, anxiety, and heated debate in the Arab world. The Ba'th party was outspoken in its denunciation of the "imperialists," in its backing of Egypt's action, and in its call on all Arabs to prepare for the coming struggle with the "imperialists." The Ba'th party was sure the West would not let this action by Egypt go unpunished and thus demanded that the Arab people should prepare themselves.[39] The attack on Egypt in October, 1956, enraged the Ba'th party and convinced the Syrian public of the imperialist nature of the West. In 1957 the leftist movement gained more momentum.

The party began the year 1957 with an anti-Western propaganda campaign. In January the Regional party in Jordan issued a statement declaring the Eisenhower Doctrine an outright interference in the internal and external affairs of the Arabs. It gave the United States the right to defend the Middle East, which was not acceptable to the Arabs, who felt that the protection of the Middle East was carried on with an eye to American interests only. The statement also noted that the Eisenhower Doctrine confirmed and guaranteed the existence of the State of Israel.[40] A later editorial in *al-Ba'th* warned that the Eisenhower Doctrine might "warm" the cold war.[41] The protestations of the Ba'th party continued to appear in the party newspaper throughout 1957.

Ba'th influence was not confined to Syria; it extended to Jordan as well. Both Syria and Egypt were pressing Jordan to expel its army's British commander in chief, J. B. Glubb, which it did in March, 1956. To rid Jordan of any British influence whatsoever, Syria, Egypt, and Saudi Arabia were pressing that country to terminate its treaty with Britain. Jordan, having no financial or economic resources on which to stand in 1956 and 1957, could not well afford such a move without assurance that the subsidy paid by the British under the terms of the Anglo-Jordanian Treaty would be forthcoming from some other source. To this end, on January 19, 1957, the governments of Syria, Egypt, and Saudi Arabia signed what was then called a Mutual Defense Agreement, by which the three governments would provide the equivalent of the British subsidy to Jordan. Two months later, in March, 1957, the Anglo-Jordanian Treaty was terminated.

The Ba'th party was in ascendancy now in Syria. Following his Ba'thist inclinations, Bitar, then minister of foreign affairs in Syria, carried on a full propaganda campaign for positive neutrality. Positive neutrality means "cooperation with all nations regardless of their economic, political, or social order."[42] Bitar added that while the Arabs appreciated the United States' help during the Suez crisis, they could not ignore its vigilant backing of Israel. When the Nabulsi leftist government in Jordan was toppled – King Hussein demanded its resignation – the Ba'th condemned this action and blamed it on American interference under the Eisenhower Doctrine.[43]

Economic agreements with the Soviet Union were hailed by the Ba'th party as victories in the Arab struggle against Western imperialist nations, which refused to make such agreements without "many strings attached." The new economic agreements were seen as a triumph for the principle of positive neutrality, especially at this time when Syria was surrounded by unfriendly neighbors, Israel on the south and Turkey, which was carrying on maneuvers on Syria's north border.[44] There is no doubt that a definite pro-Soviet attitude was taking shape in Syria in 1957. Internally the Communists were gaining strength they had never before enjoyed in Syria. This was partly due to the general mood in the country and partly to the cooperation with the Ba'th. It was also due to the growing prestige and influence of the Soviet Union in Syria, which was enhanced by Soviet loans, technical assistance, and arms.[45]

Communist sympathizers or opportunists were taking responsible positions in the Syrian army and government, On August 17, 1957, Afif al-Bizri, a Communist fellow traveler, was appointed army chief of staff. Another opportunist and fellow traveler, Khalid al-Azim, was minister of defense and successfully concluded a very favorable loan and aid agreement with the Soviet Union.

By the end of 1957 the Ba'th party seemed entrenched in Syria. To all appearances, it had gained all it wanted. It held the two important portfolios of foreign affairs and national economy. Abdul Hamid al-Serraj, chief of the Army's Security and Intelligence Department, was its ally and Hourani was speaker of the Syrian Parliament.[46] But a struggle was going on between the Ba'th and its ally the Communist party. The Communists – the Afif Bizri-Khalid al-Azim coalition – hoped for closer ties with the Soviet Union that would ultimately bring them to power. By now the Ba'th realized it had been used by the Communists, who were in powerful positions in Syria.[47] Just as it thought it was on the threshold of power, the Ba'th discovered that its ally and collaborator the Communist party was getting strong – too strong for the Ba'th party alone to fight. To avert a Communist takeover in Syria, the Ba'th clamored for unity with Egypt. By uniting with Egypt, the Ba'th would frustrate Communist designs and bring about the most cherished hope of the Arabs in modern history: unity. The price was the surrender of Syria's independence and the party's dissolution in Syria.[48]

While the Ba'th party has always advocated unity as a general principle, it was not until February, 1956, that it began advocating unity with Egypt specifically.[49] Egypt fulfilled all the requirements demanded by the Ba'th. It had "progressive" leadership, and by this time it had begun taking a more active role in Arab affairs, and its new constitution declared for the first time that it was an Arab rather than an Egyptian state. Moreover, by mid-1957 the party was beginning to worry about the rising fortunes of the Syrian Communist party. The Ba'th was worried about the November municipal elections, and with all the power it could muster it postponed them indefinitely, to the Communists' chagrin.[50] Following a speech by Aflaq on April 17, 1956, in which he advocated unity with Egypt, this became the official line of the party. From then on the party's newspaper and other publications were filled with the call for unity with Egypt. When, by the middle of 1957, the party found itself the lone opponent of the Communist party – other parties cowed or discredited – it stepped up its pressure for unity with Egypt. Late in 1957 official visits were exchanged between Cairo and Damascus. On November 1, 1957, Aflaq visited Nasser in Cairo. On November 18 an Egyptian parliamentary delegation met with the Syrian Parliament in a "joint session" and unanimously agreed on a federal union. Bitar visited Cairo on January 16, 1958, for unity talks. On January 26 the Syrian Cabinet approved the unity steps with Egypt: two weeks later Aflaq hailed the Syro-Egyptian union, now called the United Arab Republic (U.A.R.), as a guarantee for "revolution of the Arabs" and a great step.[51] The Union was to be open for any other Arab state that wished to join. Only Yemen chose to establish loose ties with it. The Ba'th party had realized its dream of unity and defeated the Communists for the moment.

The first Cabinet of the U.A.R. had four Ba'th ministers. One of the four vice presidents of the U.A.R, was a Ba'th member too. The Ba'th and its ally Shukri al-Quwatli (then president of Syria) seemed satisfied with the result.

4 Ba'th and the U.A.R

Upon formation of the U.A.R. the Ba'th seemed to have reached the height of its ambition. The first actual union of "dismembered" Arab nations became a reality mainly through the party's efforts. Nasser, the hero of the Arabs and the Ba'th, was lauded as a progressive national leader for all Arabs. The Ba'th party built a great image of Nasser who

> as every day's experiences untold proves that he plans with a constructive scientific mind, works with a revolutionary zeal that ignores hesitation and fatigue. Abdel Nasser understands that he leads a nation and is building a comprehensive and greater one.[1]

So great was the party's faith in Nasser that when he insisted that political activities of the Ba'th and other parties be halted before he agreed to the proposed union, the Ba'th – perhaps naively – assented. When Nasser, insistent that no political parties be allowed to exist within the newly formed nation, proposed a one-party state, the National Union, the Ba'th yielded.

The Ba'th party aspired to dominate the political scene of the newly formed nation, to wield a high degree of influence on the course of events. Individual Ba'thists thought of themselves as potential leaders. Aflaq stated:

> We hoped that the party would have a basic and responsible share in the governing of the new nation which we helped to create. We hoped our role would be both practical and theoretical since it was we who began preaching Socialist ideas at least fifteen years before Nasser assumed power.[2]

Nasser, it seems, had other ideas. From his point of view, the Ba'th was forced to unite with Egypt or submit to a Communist takeover.[3] Nasser saw no reason to allow them any extra privileges. Deluged by their own propaganda, the Ba'thists began to believe that the union was made of their own volition. Nasser, who until the beginning of 1958 had opposed haste and called for more comprehensive studies and plans for the proposed union, rushed into union in the second half of January, 1958, seriously fearing a leftist takeover in Syria.

His fears were not unfounded. No sooner had the union been proclaimed than trouble began brewing in Syria. Nasser should have heeded the former president of Syria, Quwatli, who upon the proclamation of the U.A.R. remarked, "You have acquired a nation of politicians; fifty percent believe themselves to be national leaders, twenty-five percent to be prophets and at least ten percent to be gods."[4]

Immediately after the formation of the U.A.R., Nasser began ridding Syria of Communist influence while at the same time attempting to effect mild economic reforms along the same lines as those in Egypt. His first major act was to dismiss General Afif al-Bizri, Syrian Army chief of staff, which caused the first serious dissension between Egyptian and Syrian officers.[5] In this measure, and in his stand against the Communists, Nasser was accorded full backing by the Ba'th party, which then and throughout the years 1958 to 1961 was waging an anti-Communist campaign.

While the Ba'th party had some serious reservations concerning the management of affairs in the new nation from the outset, it aspired to cooperate with Nasser in every way possible. The Ba'th hoped that eventually it could influence Nasser to extend more liberties to the party. From the beginning the problem of liberty was a constant source of friction between Nasser and the Ba'th. While the Ba'th agreed that the new state would be "unitary" rather than "federal," it had not envisioned the ever-tightening grip of Nasser's centralization measures. Nor were the Syrian businessmen and bourgeois elements any happier with Nasser's economic and political measures. Syrian disappointment with Nasser's style was bound in the end to be reflected in the Ba'th party's attitude.

The first real sign of Syrian-Egyptian strain appeared when Syrian customs authorities decided to increase the tariff on certain import items. President Nasser promptly summoned his two Syrian vice presidents, Hourani and Sabri al-Asali, to Cairo to inform them that such matters should be left to central legislation.[6]

By September, 1958, Nasser had introduced land reform measures in Syria similar to those applied in Egypt. These measures provided compensation for landowners whose estates were to be taken over and redistributed.[7] The Ba'th party, more doctrinaire in its approach to agricultural reform, considered such compensation a compromise with the feudal landlords.[8]

Nasser's centralization measures began with a decree combining the separate emergency laws of Syria and Egypt into one law.[9] A week later Nasser announced that a single central cabinet would replace the two existing cabinets for the new republic. Not long afterward, Nasser relieved Hourani of his duties in Syria, keeping him as a vice president but moving him to Cairo. This move, viewed with disfavor by the Ba'th party, was clearly an attempt by Nasser to tighten his grip on Syria.

Following the dissolution of all political parties in Syria, Ba'th party headquarters was moved to Lebanon, where it began publication of the newspaper *al-Sahafah*. The paper made no reference to the growing discontent between the Ba'th and Nasser. In fact, it operated largely as a propaganda sheet for the U.A.R. and carried on an anti-Qasim, anti-Communist Campaign throughout the years 1958 and 1959. The quarrel between Nasser and Qasim, which culminated in open hostility, led the Ba'th party to support Nasser. The paper accused Qasim of being a member of the Communist party, of conspiring with Israel against Arab nationalism, and finally, of conspiring with Britain the imperialist against the Arabs.[10] Yet as Nasser attempted to increase centralization and tighten his grip on Syria, the rift between the Ba'th and Nasser could not be concealed for long.

A succession of events led to the break between Nasser and the party. By 1959 a number of zealous Ba'thists began to feel that since there was so much agreement between the Ba'th and Nasser – their view of socialism, their view of unity, and their demand for neutrality in foreign policy – the Ba'th as a party should dissolve itself throughout the Arab world. These Ba'th partisans argued that the party should devote itself to the service of the U.A.R. and President Nasser. Abdullah al-Rimawi, secretary general of the party in Jordan, held such a view. However, by mid-1959, Rimawi's position on this issue stood outside the main stream of party opinion. The National Command of the party in Beirut, disturbed by Rimawi's support of Nasser at a time when Nasser clearly was working against the Ba'th, demanded that Rimawi proceed to Beirut to explain his activities. When he refused to attend the party's inquiry, declaring it illegal, the National Command expelled him from the party.[11]

The Rimawi affair was the first serious split in the party's history. He was a very popular leader in Jordan, particularly among the Palestinian refugees. He was a prominent opposition leader to the successive conservative governments of Jordan from 1950 to 1956, and a one-time foreign minister of Jordan in the Nabulsi government. Added to that, Rimawi had strengthened his own position within the Ba'th party by slackening membership requirements and swelling its ranks with his own people.[12]

There is no doubt that Rimawi's expulsion from the Ba'th tremendously weakened its ranks in Jordan. A popular figure in his own right, he was also a Nasser advocate and rallied around him those unionist forces that were not Ba'thist. His expulsion also alienated Nasser, who perhaps took it as a personal affront. With his characteristic speed of action, two weeks after Rimawi's expulsion Nasser dismissed Riad al-Maliki, minister of national guidance of the Northern Region and a prominent Ba'thist.

Nasser had decided to get rid of his Ba'th allies earlier in 1959. Only six months after the formation of the U.A.R, the Cairo government interfered in the elections of the National Union, a body which purported to replace Parliament. Out of 9,445 seats allotted to the Northern Region the Ba'th party won only 250.[13] Aflaq lost the election, while all other Ba'th leaders were elected. While the Ba'th was extremely displeased with the results of these elections, publicly they never admitted their dissatisfaction, saying that the Ba'th really did not lose since 90 per cent of the seats had been won by Socialists anyhow.[14]

By October, 1959, Nasser was disturbed that the old parties were clandestinely resuming their activities in Syria. He was also distressed over the slow progress of his industrial and agrarian program in that country. Thus he dispatched his right-hand man, Abdul Hakim Amer, to Syria and gave him "full powers .

.. to carry out his policies there." Amer was placed in authority over the Syrian Cabinet and administration and was responsible to Nasser alone. Soon afterward four Ba'th ministers resigned their posts over a dispute with Amer. The Ba'th ministers, given high-sounding titles, had no real power and they resented the mistrust shown them by Nasser and Amer. They also objected to the National Union as a substitute for Parliament. One week later Khalil al-Kallas, minister of economy of the Northern Region and the last Ba'thist in the U.A.R. government, resigned.[15]

Outwardly the Ba'th party maintained the fiction of full backing for President Nasser and his regime. It insisted that the mass resignation of Ba'th ministers was not a party policy, and that each minister resigned of his own volition because of his "personal feeling" of disagreement with the policies carried on by the Nasser government. The party added that it would not attempt to work against the U.A.R. but would continue to support it.[19] In fact, however, by this time the party had become completely disenchanted with Nasser and his regime, while it never actively worked for the break-up of the U.A.R., withdrawal of party support was one of the major reasons for the eventual downfall of the republic.

Before any discussion of the reasons for the break-up of the U.A.R. and the party's major disagreements with Nasser can be meaningful, a brief historical sketch of the party's activities in Iraq is necessary for two reasons: (1) a split occurred within the party in Iraq over disagreements on the party's stand on Nasser; (2) the party came to power in Iraq on February 8, 1963.

The growth of the Ba'th party in Iraq parallels its growth and development in other regions of the Arab world with two important differences. First, it suffered constant repression under the monarchical regime from its establishment until July 14, 1958, when the regime was overthrown. With the exception of a short period, it also suffered severe repression under the Qasim regime from 1958 to February 8, 1963. The second important difference lay in its organization, which was much tighter and was forced to be clandestine because of the Iraqi government's hostility toward the party.

The Ba'th party was brought into Iraq around 1949 by some Palestinian refugees and Iraqi students studying in Syria and Lebanon.[17] It concentrated on preaching its ideology while refraining from activity until 1952, when it led some anti-government demonstrations. This was the first time the Ba'th appeared as a major "street power" in Iraq. While it maintained close connections with the "Mother Ba'th" in Syria, it was not recognized as a full-fledged Region of the Ba'th until 1954. The two most prominent Iraqi Ba'th leaders were Fuad al-Rikabi and Feisal Khaizuran. By 1954 the party was strong enough in Iraq to issue statements and distribute them in the streets. It opposed the Nuri al-Said policies in Iraq on the national and international level. Said represented reaction, feudalism, and corruption on the domestic level and subservience to Great Britain on the international level. He was, in the party's words, a British "agent and stooge."

When the Iraqi government signed the Iraqi-Turkish agreement in 1955, later to be known as the Baghdad Pact, the party went into a frenzy of activity against the government. In a statement distributed in the streets of Baghdad in January, 1955, the Ba'th called on the Iraqi people to overthrow the Said government.[18] The greatest boost to the party's popularity in Iraq came, however, after the Suez Canal crisis. By this time the party had become a major "street power" in Baghdad and was distributing its literature throughout Iraq. In 1956 the Ba'th entered the National

Front composed of the National Democratic, Communist, and Istiqlal parties. This Front organized a boycott against the 1957 parliamentary elections. These elections, according to the party, were only tools in the hands of the reactionary government to perpetuate the status quo.

In the first months of 1958 the party opposed union between Jordan and Iraq, which came as a Hashemite answer to the formation of the U.A.R. When the July 14, 1958, revolution took place, toppling the monarchy, the Ba'th was one of the major forces that backed the new Qasim regime. In fact, the party, at least Rikabi, its secretary general in Iraq, knew in advance of the coming revolution. This is evident since Rikabi was a member of Qasim's first Cabinet.[19]

Aflaq states that Rikabi's participation in the government was strictly personal. He also says that while the Ba'th was well aware of Rikabi's participation in the government, it neither condoned nor condemned it.[20] This ambivalent stand taken by the national leadership of the party in Damascus is important because of subsequent differences between Qasim and the Ba'th and between Rikabi and his own party which resulted in another significant party split. While Rikabi's participation in Qasim's first Cabinet was not party policy, the party did acquiesce. Such a stand was no doubt prompted by the hope that the Qasim regime would be a "unionist" one – a regime that would bring Iraq into the U.A.R. Three months later, when Qasim's intentions were made clear, the party demanded that Rikabi resign his post. By October, 1958, it became evident that Qasim had no desire to join the U.A.R. and that he intended to rule Iraq his own way.[21] In fact, he was beginning to checkmate the nationalist elements, clamoring for unity, with the aid of left-wing and Kurdish elements. The pro-Nasser Colonel Abdul Salam Aref was arrested and tried, and by the beginning of 1959 the Ba'th party was carrying on a full-fledged anti-Qasim campaign in Iraq.[22] The Nasser-Qasim quarrel was in progress, and the party aligned itself with Nasser.

Like Rimawi, by the beginning of 1960 Rikabi saw no reason for the separate existence of the Ba'th party. He argued that the similarity between the Ba'th party and Nasserism was so great that there was no need for a separate Ba'th movement. Instead, he urged the Ba'th to dissolve itself and become a wing of the Nasserite movement. It should be recalled that by 1960 the Nasser regime had eliminated its Ba'th allies in Syria and thus the Ba'th party there was adamantly opposed to the stand taken by Rikabi.

By August, 1961, Rikabi was rallying his own forces within the Ba'th party in preparation for a split. He charged the Ba'th with cooperation with the Communists, Qasim, imperialism, and even the British.[23] Constant warnings to Rikabi to cease his antiparty activity were to no avail, and the party's National Command in Beirut finally expelled him. His expulsion represents the second significant split in the party. As in the case of Rimawi, Rikabi's expulsion did not have a drastic effect on the party in Iraq or in the rest of the Arab world. Again, this split was caused by Rikabi's stand *vis-à-vis* Nasser.[24]

There were other reasons for the expulsion of Rikabi. A very ambitious man, he thought that regardless of the differences between Nasser and the party on the issue of liberty, for example, the party should forego its separate existence. On ideological grounds, too, he differed from the majority of his party. He condoned the use of violence and assassination. In fact, without the knowledge of the Regional Party Command in Iraq or the National Command in Lebanon, he participated in the plot to assassinate President Qasim in September, 1959.[25]

When Qasim accused the Ba'th of leading this plot, the party hastened to defend itself, saying:

> The party's condemnation of political assassination throughout its historical struggle . .. is based not only on its respect for the individual... but also on its faith in the people who can achieve their goals... Political assassination shows weak faith in the people to achieve their goals.[26]

Rikabi never wavered from his belief in violence and in political assassination if necessary.[27]

Despite the extreme repressive measures taken against the Ba'th by the Qasim regime, the party grew stronger in Iraq. With its strong machine, it was able to dominate a number of trade unions and the influential Iraqi Students' Organization. It was able to publish four official underground newspapers: *Wa'yy al-Ummal* (Workers Consciousness), *Al-Ishtiraki* (The Socialist), *Al-Ittihad al-Watani Li al-Talabah* (The National Union for Students), and *Hisab al-Jamahir* (Mass Judgment).[28]

By infiltrating the armed forces and the students' organizations, the Ba'th party was able, on February 8, 1963, to stage a coup that toppled the Qasim regime. For several months in late 1962, the party had been preparing for the coup and conditioning the public to it. A long student strike, which lasted from December 27, 1962, until the day of the Revolution, made Iraq ready for change.[29]

And a change of government took place on February 8, 1963, with the Ba'th party at the helm in Iraq. Military units of the Iraqi army sympathetic to the Ba'th toppled the Qasim regime. The dictator surrendered and, although the Ba'th party avowedly condemns violence, he was executed immediately in accordance with a sentence passed previous to his surrender.[30]

5 The Break-up of the U.A.R.

On the morning of September 28, 1961, when a group of army officers and conservative politicians carried out a *coup d'état* that was to end the union between Syria and Egypt, the Ba'th party did not resist. This was not surprising in light of events within Syria from 1959 to 1961. In fact, a sizable wing of the party, led by Hourani in Syria, welcomed the break and worked with the conservative regime that took over. The split of Hourani's wing from the party and the aftermath of the split will be considered in more detail later. Here only the major reasons leading to the break will be discussed.

Perhaps much of the blame for the break between Syria and Egypt is to be placed on the distinctly different temperaments of the two peoples. The Syrians are a volatile, independent people. They are individualistic in their enterprise whether in the cities, where they tend to be small independent businessmen and artisans, or in the countryside, where each peasant tills his own small plot of land. The Egyptians, on the other hand, have traditionally been more amenable to a strict central authority, perhaps owing to their dependence on the Nile as the sole source of their irrigation system – a system so intricate that it necessitates strict central regulation. Karl Wittfogel includes Egypt among what he terms the "hydraulic societies" – those societies largely dependent for their livelihood on an irrigation system supplied by a main river. He lists among the characteristics of such a society the trait of atomization. Individuals do not possess any "corporate organization that could negotiate on equal terms with, and obtain legally established rights from, the ruler."[1] The strict centralization measures taken by Nasser did not please the Syrians, who were unaccustomed to such regulations. Natural disaster was to give further reason for the break. During the three-and-a-half-year period of unity, Syria had a severe drought, which people blamed on the Nasser regime.

In addition the Syrian business community was extremely unhappy with Nasser's Socialist measures. The Socialist laws he passed in the summer of 1961, a few months before the *coup d'état*, only added to the rapidly rising discontent. These laws were aimed at considerable socialization of private enterprise in the U.A.R.[2] It was not only the conservative elements that were displeased with these Socialist measures. Although the Ba'th party issued a statement on June 22, 1961, referring to the laws as a stride in the Arab march toward socialism, a circular letter distributed only to party members revealed that the party was just as displeased with these measures as the conservatives, only for different reasons. The letter stated that these laws should be viewed only as measures to stem the tide of popular discontent and to deprive the progressive movements" in Syria (i.e., the Ba'th party) of some of their weapons. These laws, the party stated, should be viewed as a transfer of authority to the bureaucracy and an indication of the "bureaucracy's desire to move from a defensive to an offensive position only." The aim of the government was to placate the people only.[3]

The union, hastily concluded, could not stand under pressure of provincial interests, personal jealousies, and ideological differences. Within the army Syrian officers were complaining of the highhanded manner assumed by both their Egyptian superiors and equals. The Syrians had believed they would have a fair share of responsibility in the government, but now they felt they did not.[4] Many Syrians, even party members who later split with Hourani, felt that Syria was increasingly becoming a mere market for Egyptian goods and they were chagrined by the Egyptian monopoly over trade regulations on imports and exports.[5]

There were several other differences leading to the break-up of the U.A.R. Chief among these was Nasser's reliance on police methods to rule Syria. In the mistrust and increasing trouble and dissatisfaction he encountered in Syria, Nasser increasingly relied on Colonel Abdul Hamid al-Serraj, chief of the army intelligence division. Serraj's sinister influence in Syria and his police methods made Syrians feel they were living in a police state.[6]

Nasser's use of the principle of divide-and-rule among the "progressive unionist elements" no doubt helped in lessening Syrian support of the government of the U.A.R. Soon after the proclamation of the new nation, Nasser put an end to Communist influence in Syria by means of the nationalist elements, among them the Ba'th. Having eliminated the Communists, Nasser ousted his former allies the Ba'thists. This "liquidation" of the Ba'th and other Syrian national elements left only the ineffectual "independents." Weak and unorganized, these were no match for the forces of conservatism which – chagrined by Socialist measures – had allied with traditional elements and certain army officials.[7]

Added to countering one group in Syria with another was Nasser's ban on political parties. This left a political vacuum in the country that could not be filled by the ineffectual one party state, the National Union, set up by Nasser.[8] The Ba'th accepted the ban on political parties in the hope that political restraints would later be relaxed. But instead the reverse occurred, and the issue of freedom remained a point of disagreement between

Nasser and the party. In the words of one of its prominent leaders in Lebanon, the Ba'th hoped that a democratic regime would soon evolve and the party would fill the vacuum.[9]

Nasser's socialism was pragmatic. The Ba'th was more doctrinaire in its approach and felt that since Nasser had no framework of ideology for his socialism, he was more compromising than the party liked.[10] They differed on application of the agrarian reform law in Syria. The Ba'th party also opposed the 1961 nationalization of banks and insurance companies and their replacement by a Joint-Stock Company of which 50 per cent would be owned by the state.[11] The party charged that such a step was a transfer of capital from private hands to bureaucrats. This amounted to nothing more than state capitalism and in the eyes of the party could not be called socialism. Such laws placed the economy in the hands of bureaucrats and made the state the sole mover and mainspring of the society.[12]

There are also obvious differences between Nasser's socialism and the Ba'th in terms of the origins of each movement. Whereas the Ba'th has always been restricted largely to civilian elements, in Nasserism the military elements lead the civilians. The Ba'th party, based in the people, claims to be a mass party. The Nasserite movement originated with a group of army officers at the top and no organized popular movement at the bottom. This still holds true, despite Nasser's repeated efforts at organizing such a movement. Nasser's remains a group at the top that has "no real faith in the people."[13]

Hafiz adds that the "Egyptian revolution," having no faith in the people and no framework for a Socialist ideology, depends on the principle of "trial and error" in its application of Socialist measures; and its Socialist program thus resembles a succession of "raids" rather than a sustained, full-fledged advance.[14]

The Ba'th party preaches and practices equality among its members. It calls for close consultation between the members and leaders, whereas Nasser believes in dictating. Nasser believes he is the sole leader, whereas the Ba'th preaches the principle of collective leadership.[15] Nasser's, insistence on being the sole leader caused the Ba'th to complain of the "numerous mistakes of individualist [as opposed to collective] leadership during the period of the union."[16]

In addition to the above, it should be mentioned that the hasty manner in which unity was proclaimed did not make for a proper basis for a perpetual union. Geography, no doubt, was part of the reason for the final split between the two countries. In the words of one astute observer:

> What union means between two countries which are divided from each other by the sea and by Israel, and which lack any material reason for integration, is doubtless... baffling.[17]

What this observer failed to see was the force of union sentiment, among other things, which was strong enough to bring about the U.A.R.

The separatist *coup* of September 28, 1961, ushered in a new era in Syria's turbulent history. The separatist elements were predominantly conservative in attitude. They were composed of merchants, landowners, and capitalists who saw in separation the only means of preserving their interests.[18] The military *coup* that made Syria an independent state once more confronted the Ba'th party there with a dilemma. The party simultaneously condemned the authoritarian rule of Nasser and blamed it for the separation. At the same time, it condemned the separatist rightist elements that had supported the *coup*.[19] The dilemma of the party translated itself into a split within the party membership and leadership in Syria as to the proper stand vis-*à*-vis the Nasser regime. This resulted in the Hourani faction's split from the party. The Ba'th party's continual insistence on union even with Nasser – a more practical union not so hastily arrived at as the last-caused yet a fourth major split in the party's ranks, this time in Lebanon in 1962.

The troubles between the Ba'th party and the government of the U. A.R. began shortly after the formation of the republic in 1958. The party agreed to comply with President Nasser's wish to dissolve itself within Syria, thus rendering a supreme sacrifice at the expense of its byword unity. The party agreed to dissolution knowing that there was no real justification for it only the desire of President Nasser.[20] There were those within the party who welcomed dissolution from the outset in the belief that the membership of the dissolved party would eventually become the spokesman of the United Arab government. When Rimawi and Rikabi expressed such views,[21] both were expelled from the party. There were also those who objected to dissolution from the start.

As the second year of union came to a close, it was evident that the government of the U.A.R. was working against the Ba'th party. This became obvious in the elections to the National Union, during which fraudulent practices were applied against the Ba'th.[22] Still the Ba'th party welcomed the results of the elections, stating that they, the newly elected, were Socialists and thus it made no difference under what label they were elected. Holding fast to its anticipation of reconciliation with the Union government, the Ba'th discouraged open struggle. The second major break between the party and the Nasser regime came about because of the closing down of the newspaper *al-Jamahir*. This paper, edited by Doctor Jamal al-Atasi, a prominent Ba'thist, was receiving government subsidy until the summer of 1959 and after the elections of the National Union. The paper pointed out the discrepancies in government policy in Syria and criticized the methods as well as the results of the elections. Government subsidy was withdrawn, thus forcing the closing down of the paper. The Ba'th party took this as a second affront.[24] The third major event was the resignation of the Ba'th ministers from the government. While publicly continuing to back the Nasser regime, the party considered the resignations the final break with it.[25]

In view of this background, the stand taken by Hourani in 1961 is understandable. Since his resignation in 1959, Hourani had advocated a full fledged attack on U.A.R. aimed at damaging Nasser's image. In his words, the union between Syria and Egypt was not a true union but a process of "Egyptianizing Syria."[26]

Thus, when the military *coup d'état* which was to break the union took place on the morning of September 28, 1961, Hourani immediately welcomed it and was one of the signatories of the "declaration of separation."[27] Hourani described the officers who led the coup as "good, honest and dashing youngsters."[28] He called Nasser a "dictator" who consented to resettle the Palestinian refugees in the Arab countries and who consented to Israel's scheme for the diversion of the River Jordan.[29] One week later he accused Nasser of attempting to liquidate the Palestine question under the guise of Arab unity and of "implementing [the] American policy verbatim."[30] Hourani was clearly and vehemently anti-Nasser in his policies and actions. His views, however, were not representative of the entire party. Later the National Command expelled him.

When the *coup* occurred, the National Command of the party met in Beirut to formulate its stand *vis-à-vis* the new situation.

The party's lack of good communications was evident at this time. The Syrian Region of the party a few days after the *coup* sent word to the meeting in Beirut, stating the breakup to be a reality which was to be accepted. The party was to reorganize itself in Syria and begin a new call for unity on a democratic, Socialist, and popular basis. The Regional parties of Iraq and Jordan each issued its own statement condemning the break-up and demanding an immediate return to union on a new basis, while a sizable wing of the party in Syria, led by Hourani, welcomed the break-up immediately.

The party organizations in Iraq and Jordan called for an immediate return to union. This stand was prompted by the fact that both of these organizations were operating under severely repressive regimes and were receiving a great deal of sympathy and assistance from Nasserite elements.[31] The party organization in Lebanon, while agreeing with Hourani on all his views regarding the Nasser regime, would not accept Hourani as their leader. They regarded him as a "traditional political leader interested only in furthering his own ambitions."[32] The Ba'th organization in Lebanon issued its own views on the break-up of the union one month after the meeting of the National Command in Beirut. In June, 1962, the Regional Command of the party in Lebanon met and issued a statement to the National Command rejecting the latter's stand. It called for reestablishing unity with Egypt while at the same time working "internally": i.e., within the united government, to bring about more democratization and liberalization of the regime. On September 16, 1962, the Regional Command in Lebanon again met and decided to sever all its connections with the National Command of the Ba'th party for the above-stated reasons. The Regional Command in Lebanon accused the National Command of "ideological deviation" and of harboring within its ranks "Nasserite agents" who called for a return to union under Nasser.[33]

The National Command of the party, on the other hand, issued its own statements calling for a return to union even under Nasser. It called on its members to work toward this end. At the same time it pointed out the several errors committed during the existence of the U.A.R., stating that what had failed was not unity itself but the way in which it was applied. It also stated that the mistakes of the Nasser regime were not adequate reason for the break-up of the U.A.R. It called for a return to union based on the principle of collective leadership, an end to the ban on political parties, more democracy, and a federal union instead of a unitary government.[34]

Differences between the majority of the Ba'th party and a sizable wing under Hourani's leadership led to major splits within the party in Syria in 1961 and in Lebanon in 1962. Both were caused by differences of opinion concerning the Nasser regime and the advisability of cooperating with it. The dissidents in both Syria and Lebanon believed such cooperation to be not only improbable but impossible. They viewed Nasser as an absolute dictator and any cooperation with him a compromise of the party's traditional slogans of freedom and democracy.

The split in Lebanon was prompted by the National Command's call for a return to unity with Egypt. In May, 1962, the National Command demanded such a return on a new basis. The new proposal called for a federal union between Syria and Egypt. It was clearly fashioned after, and similar to, the Constitution of the United States. To signify the supposed equality of both regions, the president and vice president were not to be from the same region.[35] The federal government was to be in charge of defense, external relations, fiscal and monetary affairs, development, and planning; the federal cabinet to be composed of both regions aided by consultative councils pertinent to each ministry; the legislative branch to be composed of two houses: an upper house with equal numbers of representatives from each region and a lower house elected in proportion to the population of each region. Laws were to be approved by both houses. In case of difference, a joint committee of both houses would be called to reach a compromise. The proposal called for a federal court to pass on the constitutonality of laws and judge disputes between the federal and regional governments. Each region was to have its own governmental apparatus to administer the internal affairs of the region. The new proposal was contingent on the recognition of differences between the two regions – differences that could not and must not be ignored if the new scheme for unity was to operate effectively. [36]

The Ba'th party did not confine itself to preaching reunion among its membership. On May 25, 1962, the Beirut office of the party issued a statement calling on the Syrian government to negotiate union with Egypt. While this statement criticized the Nasser government as "autocratic" and as the cause of the 1961 separation, it condemned the "secessionist" government and described the *coup* that brought it about as an "imperialist reactionary conspiracy."[37] In June the prime minister of Syria, Khalid al Azim, declared that Syria would welcome a federal union with Egypt.[38] Still the Ba'th party continued its propaganda attacks on the government. These attacks resulted in the government's decision to close *al-Ba'th* and later to sentence Bitar to a one-month jail sentence which was never executed. The jail sentence was passed after Bitar issued a memorandum to the president of Syria, Nazim al-Qudsi, accusing his regime of reaction and of curtailing political liberties.[39] The Ba'th party condemned the Syrian government's decision to suspend the July, 1961, Socialist measures passed by Nasser.[40] Despite the ban on its newspaper, the party continued its attack on the Syrian government by issuing antigovernment leaflets.

The period from September 28, 1961, to March 8, 1963, was difficult for the Ba'th party. It experienced two major splits in Syria and Lebanon and was under attack from its dissident wings. It was also under bitter attack from Nasser sympathizers all over the Arab world. The Egyptian newspapers charged that it had led the secessionist movement, especially since two of its prominent leaders signed the "separation document."[42] Also, prominent Egyptian writers attacked the Ba'th party.[43] The party was also under severe attack from the Syrian government itself, which banned publication of *al-Ba'th* and encouraged other newspapers to attack the party. Syrian authors who attacked the party received the government's blessing and encouragement.[44] Despite these handicaps, the party was able to reorganize and act effectively. Its organization and propaganda were very successful in this period; it was able to stage a *coup d'état* that toppled the Qasim regime in Iraq on February 8, 1963, and another exactly one month later that toppled the government of Syria. For the first time the Ba'th party was to come into complete control of government, not in only one country but in two at the same time. A new era for the party had begun.

6 The Ba'th Party in Iraq, 1963

The principal event facilitating the Ba'th party's accession to power in Iraq on February 8, 1963, was the Iraqi students general strike that began on December 27, 1962. The strike was prompted by an insignificant incident at al-Sharqiyyah (Eastern) High School in Baghdad – an incident that could have been averted had high-handed methods not been employed to quell the students. A quarrel broke out between the son of Fadil Abbas al-Mahdawi, chief of the High Military Court,[1] and another student. When school officials attempted to discipline both parties, Mahdawi intervened on behalf of his son. This touched off a strike in the high school which spread to all the high schools of Iraq, then developed into a general students' strike that included students at the University of Baghdad.[2]

The Ba'th party cooperated with the Iraqi Students' Union in increasing the scope of the strike to include all the students of Iraq and sustained a tremendous effort to keep the crisis at a high pitch. Success came in February, 1963, several months after it had begun planning to overthrow the Qasim regime.[3] The new government formed by the Ba'th party after Qasim's demise included independents as well as non-Ba'thist ministers. In fact, the new president, Aref, was a non-Ba'thist. The Ba'th party in Iraq, composed mainly of young and inexperienced men, decided that the choice of Aref for president would enhance its chances of remaining in power. But the choice turned out to be unfortunate for the party in Iraq.[4] A few months later, taking advantage of a serious split among the Ba'th's Regional Command in Iraq, he was to organize his own *coup* and oust the party.

The assumption of power by the Ba'th party in Syria, too, followed a crisis. The Syrian Cabinet issued a decree dismissing thirty government teachers, many of whom were members of the Muslim Brotherhood. The minister of education refused implementation of the decree and three Hourani ministers finally resigned in mid-February, 1963, to be followed by the resignation of the three ministers representing the Muslim Brotherhood.[5] During this crisis, which lasted throughout the month of February, the Ba'th party was outspoken in its denunciation of the "criminal separatist" regime.[6] It was also outspoken in hailing the new "revolutionary regime" in Iraq.

The pressure put on the Syrian government by the Ba'th party was so great that its foreign minister was finally forced to issue a statement calling for a federation between Syria and Iraq. Indeed the pressure can be understood only if it is remembered that the Syrian government at the time was anti-Ba'th while the new "revolutionary" regime in Iraq was Ba'thist. The Iraqi Ba'th government also aided in undermining the position of the Syrian government. At the invitation of the Iraqi government, on February 17 a delegation of the Ba'th party, headed by Aflaq, arrived in Baghdad to discuss a "suggested union with Iraq."[8] The invitation of the Ba'th delegation to discuss such an issue while the Ba'th in Syria was in opposition was indeed aimed at undermining the existing Syrian Cabinet, headed by Khalid al-Azim. The Syrian government could not withstand the pressure from within, applied by the Ba'th party, and from without, applied by the new Iraqi Ba'th government. It was easily toppled by the March 8, 1963, Ba'th-engineered *coup d'état.*

The new Ba'th government of Syria was composed of twenty ministers, ten of whom were members of the Ba'th party. The new Cabinet, headed by Bitar, held the "reactionaries, imperialists and their tools" responsible for the breakup of the U.A.R. In its statement it pledged itself to work for unity, socialism, and positive neutrality in world affairs and to struggle against "imperialism."[9]

The differences between the Ba'th-dominated government in Syria and the Ba'th-Aref government in Iraq *vis-à-vis* the issue of unity were apparent at this time. Aref, a non-Ba'thist, wanted cooperation among the Arab governments along the lines of the European Economic Community (Common Market), to be followed by a political and legal union.[10] The Syrian Ba'th government, on the other hand, was advocating immediate union between the "revolutionary governments" of Syria, Iraq, the U.A.R., Algeria, and Yemen. The new Ba'th plan called for a federal union with "collective leadership."[11] A Syrian delegation was dispatched to Cairo to negotiate the terms of the new union; it was joined by a delegation from Iraq.

The unity talks between the delegations of Syria, Iraq, and the U.A.R. continued until April 17, 1963, when they reached an agreement. The main points of difference were the issues of the presidency and the existence of political parties. The Iraqi delegation acted as mediator between the Syrian and Egyptian delegations. The Syrian delegation, composed mainly of Ba'thists, was insistent on a "collegiate presidency," maintenance of local autonomy, and freedom to organize political parties.[12] President Nasser, however, demanded that the people decide by a plebiscite whether the presidency should be collegiate or individual.[13] Certain of his popularity among the masses in Syria and Iraq, Nasser insisted on this point and a deadlock seemed inevitable.

Recalling the inferior status they were relegated to by Nasser for the duration of the U.A.R., the Ba'th in Syria were adamant in their insistence on a federal form of government, collective leadership, and local autonomy. The Ba'th party had no personality comparable to the charismatic Nasser. Thus it was insistent on including constitutional and institutional safeguards to protect its interests in the proposed union.

The deadlock was circumvented by the presentation of a new draft by the Iraqi delegation. The Iraqi plan called for a federal union that would eventually evolve into a unitary state with one president. It stated that initially democratic liberty would be guaranteed to all political associations advocating unity and socialism. This meant that "traditional" and Communist parties would be denied this right. As the federal union gradually progressed into a unitary state, party strife would be curtailed by formation of a national front similar to that in Algeria. The Iraqi plan further stated that the new union should adopt socialism as a basis and that it should be open to Algeria and Yemen, should they wish to join.[14]

Five Nasserite ministers in the Syrian Cabinet attempted to pressure the government into a union following the lines of the draft submitted by Nasser. When the Syrian government resisted this pressure, they threatened to resign and public demonstrations ensued. By declaring martial law, the government was able to withstand the pressure and adhere to its proposals.

The three governments finally agreed on the formation of a federal union with one president and a federal council. The conclusion of the union agreement, called the April Seventeenth Agreement, combined the efforts of the three nations to bring other Arab countries into the union. The first major target was King Hussein of Jordan. The radios of Cairo, Damascus, and

Baghdad called on the Jordanian people to revolt and overthrow the monarchical regime. Riots and strikes ensued in Jordan; the government retaliated by declaring martial law but to no avail. The city of Nablus, on the western bank, declared its secession from the Hashemite Kingdom of Jordan and the formation of the Jordanian Arab Republic.[15] In the Jordan Parliament, 32 out of its 60 members spoke in favor of joining the new proposal for union and the government of Samir al-Rifai was forced to resign. The new "tough" premier was Sherif Hussein Ibn Nasser, the King's uncle. Despite his severe measures to restore order, the planned *coup d'état* against the King was averted only after the United States and Britain took "military precautions," intervening with the U.A.R., Syria, and Iraq to stop the propaganda attack on King Hussein.[16] Western intervention and a developing dispute between the Ba'th and Nasser were instrumental in averting the overthrow.

A new dispute between the Ba'th and President Nasser developed soon after the party assumed power in Syria. Nasser interfered in the formation of the new Syrian government headed by Bitar. He pressed Bitar into accepting more non-Ba'thist, pro-Nasser elements into the new Cabinet. He also pressed the Syrian government into including more non-Ba'thists in the delegation that came to Cairo to negotiate the unity terms in mid-March, 1963.[17] From the beginning the Ba'th party was unhappy about this interference in its internal affairs but felt obliged to yield in its efforts toward reconciliation with Nasser.

Throughout the unity talks Nasser challenged the representative character of the Syrian government. He maintained that any valid agreement on a future union must be made by a government in which other "unionist," non-Ba'thist elements were represented. The Ba'th party was also chagrined by an editorial in the influential Egyptian newspaper *al-Ahram*. Muhammad Hasanein Haykal, its editor and unofficial spokesman for Nasser, jibed at the Ba'th with reminders that Bitar was first among those who signed the declaration of separation in 1961. The party felt that these interferences and jibes were attempts on Nasser's part to undermine it.

The dispute was sharpened when 47 pro-Nasser officers of the Syrian Army were dismissed or pensioned off late in April. The Ba'thists believed a plot had been engineered to oust their regime. On May 2 the five Nasserite ministers tendered their resignations. The Nasserites demanded equal representation with the Ba'thists in the Cabinet and in the National Revolutionary Council. The National Revolutionary Council was formed immediately after the *coup d'état.* It was composed of 21 members; 11 of these were Ba'thist, while the remainder included members of the Arab Nationalist Movement, the Arab Union Front, and the Socialist Unionist Front. These three groups supported the Nasser regime in various degrees. Cairo retaliated by postponing indefinitely the talks on military unity that were scheduled to begin on May 12.

On May 8 the Syrian government crushed an attempted pro-Nasser revolution in the northern town of Aleppo. On the same day the Syrian government banned publication of two pro-Nasser newspapers, *al-Wihdah* (Unity) and *Sawt al-Jamahir* (The Voice of the Masses). The government decree charged they were "doing harm" to the cause of unity.[18] Pro-Nasser demonstrations in Damascus and other Syrian towns forced the resignation of the Bitar ministry and his replacement by Dr. Sami al-Jundi, a man believed to be more sympathetic to Nasser and a former member of the Socialist Unionist Front. The Iraqi government, too, felt the pressure of pro-Nasser elements and was forced to resign. A new government, more sympathetic to Nasser, was formed by Premier A. H. al-Bakr.[19] Jundi's Cabinet in Syria lasted exactly two days; then a new Cabinet, more sympathetic to Nasser, was formed, this time by Bitar. The new Bitar government, composed only of Ba'thists supposedly sympathetic to Nasser, proclaimed in its statement "a sincere wish to cooperate and reconcile with all the unionist forces in Syria to bring about the fulfillment of the April Seventeenth Agreement for union."[20]

The rift between the Ba'th party and Nasser increased when new attacks by Haykal were made in *al-Ahram*. The new attacks attempted to differentiate between the Ba'th in Iraq and in Syria. It stated that the Ba'th in Syria was suffering under a "power-complex," that it wished to "hoard" all the political power for itself. Haykal then added, "I do not think that the United Arab Republic... can cooperate with the leadership of the Ba'th party in Syria, not even to peacefully coexist with it."[21] Still the Ba'th government hoped for reconciliation with the Nasser regime. On May 20 Bitar, leading an all-Ba'th government, repeated his offer of a week earlier to give the Nasserite elements half the seats in the Cabinet and the National Revolutionary Council. The Nasserite elements rejected the offer, claiming they held a majority over the Ba'th and thus should be given more than half the seats.[22] On May 25 the government of Iraq uncovered a plot to overthrow the regime engineered by pro-Nasser elements.[23] The patience of the Ba'th in Syria seemed to have run out and propaganda warfare soon developed between Cairo and Damascus. On June 14 *al-Ba'th* charged that Nasser was sympathetic toward the Barzani Kurdish revolt in northern Iraq. On June 17 the paper demanded that Nasser deny the claim made by Jalal al-Talbani, a prominent leader of the Kurdish revolt in Iraq, that had received a promise for aid from Cairo.

By the beginning of July both Cairo and Damascus were convinced of the futility of attempting to fulfill the unity agreement. Each, however, was blaming the other for the breakdown. The Ba'th in Syria, unsure of its hold on the Syrian masses, organized the National Guard on July 1. The aim of this National Guard was to protect the "revolution" from its internal and external enemies. Only those who believed in the aims of the revolution, i.e., either Ba'thists or Ba'thist sympathizers, were to be allowed to join.[24]

In a last effort at reconciliation with Nasser, on July 18 the Syrian government dispatched a delegation to Cairo for further talks concerning fulfillment of the Unity Agreement. On the same day a revolt was crushed in Damascus. Later evidence revealed by the Syrian government pointed to the fact that Cairo was an accomplice in the plot. Twenty participants were court-martialed and shot in al-Mazzeh prison in Damascus on July 20. Seven more participants were sentenced and shot two days later. On July 23, 1963, the anniversary of the revolution in Egypt, Nasser vehemently attacked the Ba'th party and called it a "Fascist movement."[25] The proposed Tripartite Union between Egypt, Iraq, and Syria thus met its demise.

For failure to effect the April Seventeenth Agreement, Nasser and the Ba'th blamed each other. Clearly each side was suspicious of the other and each was attempting to strengthen itself by undermining the other. This was a major cause for the failure of the Tripartite Agreement.

7 Syria, the Ba'th Party, and the Loss of Iraq

President Nasser's speech of July 23, 1963, the anniversary of the Egyptian Revolution, was construed by the Ba'th government in Syria as a withdrawal from the Tripartite Unity Agreement of April 17, 1963. The Ba'th party denounced Nasser for his attacks against them. Such attacks, the party stated, would "cause a dangerous schism in the Arab Camp, which is an enemy of colonialism, reaction, and Zionism; Cairo should be blamed for the schism."[1] Even in its denunciations of Nasser, the Ba'th party left room for future reconciliation. Even after Cairo's implication in the July 18, 1963, attempt to overthrow the Syrian Ba'th government, the latter could not, and would not, carry its feud with Nasser so far as to preclude rapprochement. Even then Nasser had a strong following in Damascus.

The minister of propaganda, Jundi, one week after the attempted *coup d'état* stated, "I am still a Nasserite; I am still ready to go to prison for Abdel Nasser's sake. But I feel deep bitterness for Abdel Nasser's withdrawal" from the Tripartite Unity Agreement.[2]

In its official statements the Ba'th government kept insisting that any meaningful unity agreement must include Nasser. In fact, however, the rift between the Ba'th and Nasser became wider. The Syrian government closed the Egyptian Middle East News Agency's office in Damascus and deported all its employees. Cairo called the Ba'th party "traitorous" and "Fascist" while the Ba'th called Nasser a "dictator" and "separatist."[3]

Damascus turned to Baghdad. A Syrian delegation proceeded to Baghdad for "an exchange of views with responsible Iraqis." More specifically, the Syrian delegation was to negotiate an "economic cooperation" agreement with the Ba'th regime in Iraq.[4]

The rift between the Ba'th and Nasser lifted the pressure from King Hussein's regime in Jordan. The Jordanian government found in the split between Nasser and the Ba'th an opportune moment to arrest prominent Ba'th leaders.[5] In its move to placate Nasser, the Jordanian government further allowed Egyptian newspapers and magazines into Jordan and released Suleiman al-Nabulsi, a prominent Nasser sympathizer who was under house arrest. On his part, Nasser refrained from attacking King Hussein. He was attempting to isolate the Ba'th regimes by allying with his former adversaries. The Ba'th party condemned the "alliance" between "reaction" in Jordan and the "fakers" of "Socialist slogans" in Egypt.[6]

A last-minute attempt by the Ba'th party to stave off a complete break with Nasser did not succeed. On August 21, 1963, President Aref of Iraq headed a delegation to Cairo in an attempt to reconcile Nasser and the Ba'th and to stop the Egyptian propaganda campaign against the party. Cairo made it evident that its reception of Aref did not mean recognition of the Ba'th as the legitimate "ruler" of Iraq or of Syria. Aref asked that the propaganda campaign against the Ba'th be stopped. This was not done. Instead, the editor of *al-Ahram*, Haykal, addressed an open letter to Aref – still in Cairo – in which he stated his doubts concerning the role Aref was playing as mediator. Haykal then added that any cooperation with the Ba'th party in either Syria or Iraq was not possible.[7] The propaganda warfare subsided while Aref was still on his official visit to Cairo, only to resume full force soon after his departure.

The rapprochement between Jordan and Egypt naturally brought the Syrian and Iraqi regimes to closer cooperation. They concluded an agreement on economic unity in September, 1963, calling for an Economic Planning Council which would regulate economic affairs, growth, and planning in the two countries. The delegations of Syria and Iraq also agreed on the necessity of close cooperation between their armed forces in preparation for complete unity. Only two days later the Economic Planning Council held its first meeting. Military unity, combining the Syrian and Iraqi armies under one command, was declared on October 9, 1963. On September 17, 1963, the date designated by the Tripartite Agreement for a plebiscite to put the agreement into force, the National Command of the Ba'th party met in Baghdad and issued a statement calling for a union to be concluded between Syria and Iraq. The National Command agreed that Aref was to be the first president of the union and Bitar its first prime minister.

The Ba'th party expected more trouble to develop with Nasser. It charged that an "autocratic regime" like Nasser's would not tolerate any opposition or criticism. The Ba'th was justified in its fears. For the drama of the Ba'th party's troubles with Nasser has continued. Only two days after his verbal attack on the party, on the eleventh anniversary of the revolution, his *protégé* Abdullah al-Sallal, president of the Yemen Republic, attacked the Ba'th party and its leadership. Sallal ridiculed the idea that Arab unity should be advocated by the Ba'th party. How can the Ba'th fulfill such a goal when it is led by a man whose name is non-Arabic? He was alluding to Michel Aflaq.

And he added, "What a strange name. We are genuine Arabs, what do we have to do with Michel?"[8] This jibe against the party, so sensitive about its image as advocate of Arab unity and Arab heritage, did not go unnoticed.

Nasser's attacks continued. He charged the Ba'th with being antireligious. The Ba'th vehemently denied the charge and stated it was a "demagogic" and "reactionary" attempt to destroy it.[9] Indeed this was a tremendous blow to the party. Among the Arab masses, religion is still a very important social and political force. The Ba'th is very sensitive to the charge that it is anti-religious, a charge that can be construed to mean anti-Muslim, especially since Aflaq is Christian.

The leadership of the Ba'th – specifically Aflaq – were portrayed as semiliterate and as poor public speakers. This was done by publishing the minutes of the meeting that led to the April 17, 1963, agreement for unity. In the minutes published by Cairo, Aflaq somehow never finished a sentence without stuttering and using semiliterate language.[10] The Ba'th party charged that Cairo did not print the complete text of the talks, that certain passages were deleted, and that words were clipped from passages attributed to Aflaq to give his speech the appearance of stammering.[11] Later Nasser acknowledged publicly that the unity talks as published were not complete.[12]

The friction between the Ba'th and Nasser took a serious turn when an anti-Ba'th campaign was launched in the Lebanese newspapers. The gist of the campaign was that the Ba'th party was planning – rather was going to plan – the annexation of Lebanon in its coming Sixth National Conference scheduled for October, 1963. The Lebanese government, always sensitive to the issue of Arab unity, increased its border patrols along the Syrian border; an incident between Syrian and Lebanese patrols resulted in the death of four Lebanese soldiers. Pro-Nasser Lebanese newspapers charged that the "murder" of the four soldiers was part of a master plan to annex Lebanon. The Ba'th party and the Syrian government hastened to deny the charge and to voice their respect for Lebanese independence and integrity.[13]

This tension even reached the Arab Students' Organization in the United States. At their Twelfth Annual Meeting, at Fort Collins, Colorado, the friction became apparent in the election of officers. The Ba'th party charged that one night before the election, the Egyptian cultural attaché in Washington brought Egyptian and other pro-Nasser students from all parts of the United States to participate in order to secure a pro-Nasser leadership.[14]

The practical reasons for President Nasser's withdrawal from the Tripartite Agreement were varied. Internally, such a union would limit his personal authority by the Ba'th's insistence on collective leadership. Nasser also felt that the three countries – Egypt, Iraq, and Syria – were far from prosperous. To accomplish any real development in the new union would necessitate seeking outside loans and financial assistance, which he was reluctant to do.[15] He felt that he could not retreat from carrying out a Socialist program that would put him face to face with the foreign-owned oil companies in Iraq. To nationalize these companies would mean another major crisis with the British, which he clearly did not want. Failure to nationalize them would diminish his prestige in the entire region. The proposed tripartite union would mean Nasser's control over Iraq's oil supplies and its pipe lines through Syria. This, he felt, in addition to his authority over the Suez Canal, would compel the Western powers to retaliate.

In Iraq the situation was complicated. The Iraqi Ba'th regime was carrying on a bitter anti-Communist purge. If Nasser were to continue such a purge, this would mean an open affront to international communism. Furthermore, there was the Kurdish problem in Iraq. Should Nasser grant local autonomy to the Kurds, as they demanded, his prestige would be greatly reduced in the Arab world. To refuse to grant such autonomy meant the continuance of military operations in the mountainous country of northern Iraq and the involvement of the Egyptian army. Besides, the Egyptian army was already supporting the republicans in Yemen.

Nasser had further reasons. Such a union would push his frontiers in the north and east to Turkey and Iran. Both were members of the Central Treaty Organization (CENTO), formerly called the Baghdad Pact. In the south his frontiers would be pushed to the Persian Gulf and its rich oil resources. This would place him face to face with British interests and their navy in that area. Nasser felt, perhaps rightly, that a union between Iraq, Syria, and Egypt would bring about the downfall of King Hussein's regime in Jordan. This would involve Nasser in guarding the frontiers of Israel and confront him with a possible Israeli attack should the Jordanian regime crumble.

On the basis of these factors plus personal jealousies and his hatred of the Ba'th party, Nasser decided to withdraw from the proposed union, to blame the failure of the union on the Ba'th party, and to attempt to bring about the downfall of the Ba'th regimes in Syria and Iraq.

The Sixth National Convention of the Ba'th party, held in Damascus from October 5 to October 23, 1963, was a major event in the history of the party. It was preceded by regional conferences in both Syria and Iraq. Both regional conferences elected new leadership and sent recommendations to the coming national convention. Chief among the recommendations was the desire to conclude union between Iraq and Syria, to unify the Ba'th party's organization in the two countries, and to attempt to clarify the vague points of the party's ideology.[16]

This convention was attended by some 120 delegates from every country in the Arab world and from students' organizations in Europe and the United States. The most important decisions of the Convention were: establishment of a federal union between Syria and Iraq, the economic policy of which would be based on Socialist principles emphasizing collective farming and a policy of austerity; backing of the Algerian and Yemeni revolutions; establishment of a Progressive Arab Front; organization of a Palestine force to resist forcefully the diversion of the River Jordan. The convention further agreed on accepting Nasser as a future partner in the new union and on the necessity of having Egypt as a part of any proposed union. Finally, it agreed on the principle of positive neutrality coupled with an attempt at strengthening the ties with the "Socialist camp."[17]

The Sixth National Convention was a landmark in the ideological evolution of the party. The tone and text of its decisions pointed left. The party's newly elected leadership were of the younger generation, more dogmatic in their views than the party's older, and perhaps more mature, leadership. Of the new thirteen-member National Command only five were between the ages of forty and fifty; the rest were closer to thirty. The more rightist elements within the party were put aside. Men like Bitar of Syria and Talib Shabib of Iraq, known for their moderation, were not elected to the new command.[18] By all outward appearances, the party was moving far to the left. In fact, however, this was not the case because Aflaq maintained his grip on the party by having himself elected its secretary general once again.

Soon after the convention wound up its business late in October, 1963, pro-Nasser newspapers charged that certain "secret" decisions made at it had gone unpublished. Chief among these was the convention's supposed decision to annex Jordan and Lebanon by 1965.[19] Such plans were strongly denied by spokesmen of the Ba'th party in both Iraq and Syria.[20] The governments of Syria and Iraq proceeded to implement the recommendations of the Sixth Convention. The two governments agreed on the principles of economic unity and were preparing to unify their citizenship and police regulations and to abolish all passports between the two countries when a new crisis developed within the regional leadership of the Ba'th party in Iraq. The split within the top leadership gave Aref the opportunity he obviously had been waiting for to purge the Ba'th party and to carry out a successful *coup d'état* in which he assumed political power. The new *coup* against the Ba'th party put an end to its schemes for political unity between Syria and Iraq.

The ouster of the Ba'th party in Iraq was a direct result of the *sub rosa* struggle within the wings of the party from the time it took over the government in February, 1963. The strong man of the party in Iraq and the one most responsible for its Strict organization, Ali Saleh al-Sa'di, became minister of interior after the *coup*. Sa'di was the leader of the wing in the Regional party in Iraq that advocated immediate socialization and opposed reconciliation with Nasser. He was skeptical about the success of the negotiations for a tripartite unity between Syria, Iraq, and the U.A.R. When these negotiations did apparently succeed, and the agreement of April 17 was signed, his wing in the party suffered a blow. Following the signature of that agreement, Sa'di was demoted from minister of interior to minister of guidance. The rightist wing, led by Shabib, minister of exterior, and Hazem Jawad, the minister of interior who succeeded Sa'di, was in the ascendancy. The wing favored reconciliation with Nasser and advocated a slow process of applying the Ba'th Socialist program in Iraq. It was supported by Aref and had Aflaq's sympathy as well.[21]

Events of July 18, 1963, in Damascus, proved Sa'di unmistaken in his "tough" attitude toward Nasser, and he was quick to seize on this opportunity to oust his opponents Shabib and Jawad from the leadership of the Regional party in Iraq. In the elections to the National Command at the Sixth National Convention in October, Sa'di's wing secured 3 out of the 5 seats allotted to Iraq.[22]

Upon their return to Baghdad from the Sixth National Convention, Sa'di's opponents proceeded to rally their own forces. The rightists issued a call for an emergency Regional Convention to be held in Baghdad on November 11 to elect a new Regional Command for the party. At this convention, held at the appointed time and packed with anti-Sa'di partisans, Sa'di lost the election. Upon his denial of the legality of the proceedings and the results of the election, his opponents arrested him and his four most important aides and exiled them to Spain. When news of Sa'di's failure to be elected to the Regional Command and his exile to Spain reached his partisans that same day, they poured into the streets of Baghdad in protest demonstrations. Air Force units attacked the presidential palace and the Ministry of Defense. The Iraqi radio called on the National Command of the party to proceed to Baghdad to solve the crisis. The National Command met in Baghdad on November 14, 1963, and for a while it seemed to have the crisis under control. It began by exiling Shabib and his right wing to Lebanon in an attempt to be fair to both disputant wings. It then declared unconstitutional the Regional Convention and the elections held on November 11. It vested itself with the authority to direct the party's affairs in Iraq until the election of a new Regional Command. By exiling both wings of the party, the National Command in essence jettisoned the real leadership that had effected the Ba'th takeover in February and left the field open for Aref and the military.[23]

Aref was quick to seize on the opportunity. On the morning of November 18, 1963, he placed the National Command of the Ba'th party under arrest and took over the government of Iraq.

Aflaq, Amin al-Hafiz, president of the National Revolutionary Council in Syria, and other members of the National Command were not to be released until all resistance to the new *coup d'état* had subsided. The new regime headed by Aref was clearly anti-Ba'thist and pro-Nasser from the outset. Cairo immediately recognized the new regime and warned the Syrian Ba'th government that any military operations against the new regime in Iraq would bring U.A.R. forces to the aid of the country.[24]

The rightist wing of the party, led by Shabib and Jawad, declared their support of the Aref *coup* while the National Command of the party was still being held hostage by Aref. The following day Aflaq, Hafiz, and the others were released and sent to Damascus. They held a meeting and immediately expelled Shabib, Jawad, and their supporters from the party for their "ideological deviation from party principles and conspiracy with reactionary elements to destroy the party."[25]

The reasons for the failure of the Ba'th party in Iraq are varied. As a movement in Iraq since the late 1940s, it had been operating under severely repressive regimes and was forced to function secretly. When it came to power it was unable to operate as efficiently as it had underground. On this point, Professor As'ad Rahal states: "Ba'th has always been in opposition. Like most opposition parties in the Middle East, the party never thought it would gain power so quickly. They came to the governing chairs with no positive program of action."[26] Fawaz Tarabulsi, leader of a small dissident wing of the Ba'th party in Lebanon, concurs in this opinion.[27] Even the most ardent defenders of the party admit to this charge. The party was surprised to find itself in power: it had no program for applying socialism in Iraq, nor was it prepared to handle the Kurdish problem, the oil industry, or peasant conditions.[28] This Ba'th partisan added that the secrecy under which the Ba'th operated in Iraq caused the rise of personal rivalries and tendencies and the abandonment of the principle of collective leadership. Radi al-Shagrah, an Iraqi Ba'thist, states that the leadership that took over the government in Iraq was inadequate. They assumed important roles in the first days of the revolution in February while the real leadership was still is prison. Shagrah adds that the reversal was caused by the assumption of power by such people as Shabib and Jawad, who were unprepared for positions of authority.[29]

The Ba'th party in Iraq, as in Syria but to a lesser degree, was composed of and led mainly by the younger generation. For an opposition party concerned with embarrassing the government and appealing to the masses, such a composition was suitable. But these young leaders, experienced only in underground operations, had neither the necessary talent nor the experience to operate a complex modern government.[30]

The split among the party leadership in Iraq was a further cause of its failure. Personal rivalries and jealousies were largely responsible. However, there was a more serious and less apparent split along ideological lines. Sa'di was accused of being an ex-Communist, but this charge could not be proved.[31] At the Sixth National Convention of the party, he succeeded in incorporating his Marxist goals in the decisions of that Convention – such goals as collective farms and closer friendship with the "Socialist camp." The rightist wing advocated a more moderate program of socialization. Socialism should be applied in stages and adopted as a long-term program. These rightists shuddered at Sa'di's Marxist leanings. To counter this tendency they succeeded in forcing upon the convention a plank stressing the importance of Egypt in any union and calling for reconciliation with Nasser.[32] The split in the top leadership of the party in Iraq was along Marxist-nationalist lines. The left looked to the Socialist camp; the right to Nasser.

As in the case of Syria and Egypt, there was a certain amount of provincial jealousy. The Syrian intellectual "trusteeship" over the Ba'th party no doubt aroused some resentment in Iraq. This, coupled with the *de facto* assumption of the Syrian Ba'th party in the role of "big brother" to its Iraqi counterpart, deepened Iraqi resentment. That the National Command had conducted Iraqi affairs during the November crisis did not please sensitive Iraqi elements, particularly the army officers. Damascus became the center of activity, while Baghdad was pushed into a secondary role.

The Iraqis, more traditional than Syrians in their religious outlook, and led by Aref, himself a devout Muslim, were not pleased with the Sixth National Convention's adoption of "scientific socialism" as a party policy. Aref himself and the Cairo authorities, aware of Iraqi sensitivity toward religion, hastened to stress the religiousness of the new government. *Sawt al-Arab* (Voice of the Arabs), Cairo radio, hailed Aref immediately for saving Iraq from the "criminal, agnostic and anti-Arab and anti-Islam Ba'th gang." Throughout the coming months, Baghdad was to capitalize on Aref's religiosity and piety.[33]

The National Guard, created on the first day of the February, 1963, Ba'th *coup d'état* in Iraq, was one of the immediate reasons for the Ba'th debacle in Iraq. Created for the purpose of "protecting the revolution from within and without," it soon began thinking of itself as an elite group with special privileges. This alienated many people whom the Guard sometimes treated badly, as well as the regular armed forces, jealous of the privileges the Guard had assumed for itself.[34] The Ba'th party in both Syria and Iraq was aware of such shortcomings connected with the National Guard. This was evidenced by the Sixth National Convention's admonition that no member had more rights than the ordinary citizen.[35] The Convention specifically warned that National Guard offenders would be strictly disciplined. The sixty-five thousand Ba'thist National Guardsmen in Iraq were an immediate cause of the Aref *coup d'état* against the Ba'th, Aref was aided by regular army officers and troops chagrined by the National Guard's "smugness and outrageous activities."[37]

The purge against the Ba'th succeeded and Aref proceeded to seek rapprochement with Nasser. From the first day of his move against the Ba'th, he called for Nasser's assistance and praised him. Two weeks after the purge, the new government of Iraq released the frozen assets of Rikabi, the former Ba'th leader who had advocated that the party dissolve itself as a separate movement and declare its allegiance to Nasser. Iraq turned to Nasser, and the Syrian Ba'th government stood alone among hostile neighbors.

King Hussein of Jordan, President Aref of Iraq, and President Nasser of the U.A.R. were attempting to form an axis that would eventually bring about the downfall of the Syrian Ba'th regime. An agreement between Iraq and the U.A.R. for the purpose of coordinating the efforts of the two nations was eventually concluded. The agreement called for the establishment of a presidential council whose primary objective was to coordinate the major policy issues of the two nations. It was viewed as a first stage in the development of complete unity between the two countries.[38] King Hussein of Jordan was in harmony with the rapprochement between Egypt and Iraq; in fact he had been instrumental in bringing it about.

Instead of fortifying itself against both internal and external forces coalescing against it, the Ba'th party in Syria was weakened by leaders intriguing against one another. The seemingly never-ending drama of party rifts continued with renewed vigor.

Early in January, 1964, Bitar criticized Sa'di, attributing to him the downfall of the Ba'th regime in Iraq. In a press conference unauthorized by the party, Bitar recommended the condemnation of the Sa'di group. He said the party had been witnessing its infiltration by this group, prone to employ Stalinist methods to attain power. According to Bitar, the Sa'dis were demagogic and dogmatic and discounted the democratic principles for years valued by the party.[39]

The Regional Command of the Ba'th party in Syria, highly. influenced by the Sa'di group, was quick to retaliate. On January 24, 1964, this Command met and approved Bitar's expulsion from the party.[40] Bitar's expulsion was indeed a serious incident. After all, he was one of the founders of the party and perhaps its most familiar figure, both internationally and domestically. The moderate wing of the party, led by Aflaq, was frightened into action and retaliation. Aflaq used his influence to call for a Regional Convention in Syria. The Convention, packed with Aflaq sympathizers, succeeded in unseating the pro-Sa'di Regional Command. But Sa'di was not to be outmanoeuvred. This time it was he who called for an emergency National Convention, which met in Damascus. Again, Aflaq succeeded in controlling this Convention by packing it with his followers. Sa'di was not expelled, but he was not reelected to the National Command.[41] Once more Aflaq had defeated Sa'di.

The Sa'di crisis did not end here. Using his influence, Sa'di and his group called for an Emergency Regional Convention in Lebanon. The Lebanese Regional Convention was held on February 23, 1964, and was attended exclusively by Sa'di followers. The outcome of the deliberations of this convention was a complete rejection of the Aflaq wing of the party and its principles. The Convention denied the legality of the Seventh National Convention which

Aflaq had summoned and which was to assemble a few weeks later. It withdrew its confidence from the Regional Command in Lebanon and elected a new Regional Command, composed chiefly of Sa'dis. Finally, it affirmed its support of the decisions of the Sixth National Convention and asserted that Aflaq's call for a Seventh National Convention was a rightist conspiracy to rescind the decisions of the progressive Sixth Convention.[42]

The National Command in Damascus attempted to reconcile with the Sa'di group in Lebanon, but its efforts were fruitless. There was too much of a gap between the Sa'dis and the Aflaqites – the leftists and the rightists – to be bridged easily. Sa'di as a militant Marxist could not help but clash with the moderate Socialists of the party led by Aflaq. Sa'di's vigorous youth, militant idealism, insistence on immediate socialization, "tough" attitude toward Nasser, charismatic personality, and perhaps brash adventurism stood in stark contrast to the characteristics of his rightist colleagues. These, led by Aflaq and Bitar, were characterized by a mild approach to socialization, timidity *vis-à-vis* Nasser, lack of charisma, and a practical and perhaps more humane approach to the problems of a changing society. These qualities alienated the Sa'dis, impatient with the slowness of the party in tackling its problems. The National Command finally expelled Sa'di from the party altogether. So far no one has been able to gauge the impact of the Sa'di split. In Syria and Lebanon, the party consolidated itself once more and seems to have overcome the recent division. In Iraq, where Sa'di was most popular, the effects of the split are totally unknown. Sa'di proceeded to form a new party which he called *al-Hizb al Thawri al-Ishtiraki al-Arabi* (The Arab Socialist Revolutionary party), which is based on the same Ba'th principles and ideology but visualized replacing the slow and moderate methods of Aflaq with more revolutionary methods. Sa'di is sure of his popular image and support in Iraq.[43] However, with the anti-Ba'thist, anti-Sa'di attitude of the Aref regime in Iraq, no one thus far has been able to measure the effectiveness of this new movement. Sa'di, however, is sure of one source of support: Moscow.

On March 5, 1964, *Pravda* attacked the expulsion of Sa'di as a hypocritical move by the "rightists" who expelled Sa'di for his "leftism" while themselves brandishing "leftists" slogans.[44]

The difficulties of the Ba'th regime in Syria have been varied. Aside from difficulties and divisions within the party itself, there have been both internal and external enemies conspiring for its overthrow. Chief among Ba'th troubles have been deteriorating economic conditions in Syria. The Ba'th regime, like Nasser's before them, inherited a country that for the preceding decade and a half had been the target of its neighbors' ambitions and torn with political instability. This instability eventually reflected itself in the economic situation, which by 1964 had become critical. Domestic as well as foreign investments had become almost nonexistent. Foreign capital rests on political stability, and in Syria there was none. Domestic capital, for fear of nationalization, was deposited in foreign banks. The value of the Syrian pound deteriorated and exports dropped off, while unemployment rose steadily.[45]

In a country like Syria, attempting to modernize, the economic situation was desperate. Syria was practically undergoing an economic blockade by most of its neighbors. Exports to Jordan, Iraq, and the U.A.R. had stopped. Only Kuwait agreed to give the Syrian government a loan in 1963, and that was considered the price of Ba'th recognition of Kuwait's independence.[46] The Syrian business community, composed mainly of small, independent enterprises, was suffering from financial difficulties at home and abroad. The Syrian government was desperately seeking a market for its products. Outside of Kuwait only Saudi Arabia agreed to conclude a commercial agreement with Syria. Negotiations with the Saudi Arabian government have been in progress since early February, 1964. The Commercial Agreement with the Saudi government exempted from customs duties all Syrian natural resources and manufactured goods entering Saudi Arabia.[47] This of course gave Syria a tremendous advantage in the Saudi Arabian market. But for political considerations, the Saudi Arabian government, fearing the entente between Egypt, Iraq, and Jordan, concluded this generous agreement.

By 1964 the business community in Syria had become totally dissatisfied with this deteriorating situation. As the target of any nationalization schemes, they were naturally against any Socialist program. Their opposition to the Socialist measures of July, 1961, took the form of a *coup d'état* ending the union between Syria and Egypt. The Ba'th party, a Socialist party promoting the welfare of the working class, found only weak support for its policies in the major cities of Syria. The paradox of Ba'th weakness in the cities can be explained in terms of the general weakness and lack of organization of labor. On the other hand, the "haves" were well organized into professional and business organizations and had the means to influence the course of events. The Damascus Chamber of Commerce, for example, issued a statement that indicated the business community was withdrawing its support of Ba'th policies.[48]

The business community was looking for an excuse to begin its struggle to topple the Ba'th regime. While being investigated in the jail at Homs, a Communist was killed. The merchants of Homs took this opportunity to stage a strike against the cruelty of this act, although the Ba'thist minister of interior hastened to deplore the murder and pledged to punish the responsible people. The government dealt severely with the "destructive elements" trying to "foment trouble," and five hundred people were reported arrested. A delegation of merchants from Homs went to Damascus to discuss the "economic situation" in Syria. Next day the governor of the District of Homs was relieved of his duties.[49] This was evidently done after the complaint by the Homs merchants against the governor's highhanded attitude and was an attempt by the government to reconcile the merchants.

Indeed, the government was attempting to placate the business community. A more serious step toward this end was the attempt, by Hafiz, to form a coalition government of Ba'thists, "people from the center," and "capitalists." Hafiz also attempted to bring Hourani into this coalition. Clearly, the attempted cooperation with "capitalists" meant that the party was moving away from its traditional hostility to capitalism in an attempt to placate the business community and keep itself in power. Both Hourani and the business community fixed a high price for co-operating. Among other things, Hourani demanded that all "Hourani officers" be returned to their posts and that the government dissolve the National Guard.[50] The negotiations continued.

In April, 1964, the Ba'th regime was to survive one of its most serious crises while in power. A merchants' strike which began in Hama spread to Homs, then to other Syrian towns, and finally to Damascus itself.[51] The Syrian Lawyers' Union also joined the strike in sympathy with the merchants.[52] A general strike against the Ba'th regime developed and most outside observers thought the end of the Ba'th was near. The Syrian government was able to withstand the strike, which lasted only a few days and was followed by a period of precarious stability.

The price the Ba'th paid to placate the business community amounted to a partial rejection of its Socialist ideals. The emphasis now lay in cooperation between the public and private sectors of the economy. In a speech at Latakia, Prime Minister Bitar emphasized the idea of cooperation between these two sectors of the economy. He stated, "I tell you the government will never be more than a partner in the private sector."[53] Such a statement stands in sharp contrast to earlier Ba'th Socialist slogans.

It was no accident that the changes of government in Iraq and in Syria ushering the Ba'th party into power were aided and in fact executed by the military. The downfall of the Qasim regime in Iraq and of the Azim regime in Syria came about as a result of *coups d'état* engineered by the Ba'th party and carried out by the military.

In both Iraq and Syria the role of the military was of central importance. In fact, without it the Ba'th party would not have succeeded in coming to power. Very few details are available concerning the events leading up to the collapse of Qasim's regime. The entire operation was planned in secrecy and consummated on the morning of February 8, 1963. Ba'thist, Nasserite, and independent officers alike cooperated in executing the *coup d'état*. Ba'thists were in the majority and this composition was later reflected in the first Iraqi cabinet formed after the coup.[54]

In Syria cooperation between the civil and military wings of the Ba'th party prior to the 1963 *coup d'état* is much more clearly defined. The month of February, 1963, preceding the "revolution," witnessed a bitter struggle between Ba'thist and other "unionist" army officers on the one hand and Khalid al-Azim, premier of Syria, on the other. Azim wanted to reconvene the previously dismissed Parliament and these officers objected.[55] Parliament was finally reconvened despite the efforts of the Ba'th and other officers. During this entire month, charged with an air of crisis and emotion, the Ba'th party was outspoken in its attacks on the

Premier. The party's position was greatly strengthened, at least morally, by the Ba'th takeover in Iraq. Civilian and military Ba'th leaders made a tremendous effort to keep the crisis at a high pitch.[56]

The difference between the Ba'th takeover in Syria and that in Iraq is that in Syria the civil wing of the party is known to have played a major role in executing the *coup*, whereas in Iraq, mainly because of the need for secrecy, the role played by civilians is not quite clear. In both cases, however, the takeover would not have been accomplished without the military, which, being aware of the situation, demanded its price.

The price was an uneasy cooperation and coalition in which there were frequent clashes. In Iraq the situation was further complicated by Aref's presidency and his eventual *coup* against the Ba'th party. In Syria the highest post, that of president of the National Revolutionary Council, went first to Luayy al-Atasi, commander of the Syrian army. It is in Syria that one can readily observe the relationship between the civilian and military wings of the party. Such a relationship can best be described as an uneasy one in which both factions find it convenient, at times, to cooperate. The two factions are, in a sense, forced to cooperate. To illustrate this point, it is necessary to recall the events leading up to the ouster of Atasi and his replacement by Hafiz, president of the Revolutionary Council from July, 1963, to February, 1966. It should be recalled that on July 18, 1963, a *coup d'état* sympathetic to Nasser and against the Ba'th party in Syria was attempted. The Military Court in Damascus passed a death sentence on three of the leaders of this *coup*. This decision was referred to the National Revolutionary Council for final approval. Atasi, the president of the Council, and a man suspected by the Ba'th party of harboring sympathy toward the Nasserites, objected to the sentence. The party by this time had despaired of any reconciliation with Nasser and thus sided with Hafiz, who voted for the execution of the three men.

With the civilian members of the party on his side, Hafiz managed to get enough votes for execution, and Atasi, thus overridden, was forced to resign his post.[57] With the ouster of Atasi from the most responsible position in Syria, the civilian wing of the party initiated cooperation with Hafiz, who was later to assume the post of president of the National Revolutionary Council. A man heretofore unknown in Syria and elsewhere, Hafiz owes his rise to power, in large measure, to the fact that the civilian wing of the party voted for him and backed him.[58] This is precisely what the party had been looking for: a military man whom it could help to assume position and as a result receive his cooperation. To the party, Hafiz owes his position as well as his loyalty. He recognizes his need for the civilian wing of the party as an ideological frame for his activities. He also recognizes his need for the political acumen of men like Bitar and until February, 1966, he managed to cooperate with the "civilians" as far as possible.[59] It is perhaps accurate to describe Hafiz as the strong man of the Ba'th regime since 1963. It should also be stated that both the civilian and the military wings of the party recognize the necessity for cooperation in order to remain in power, if not to survive.

It is perhaps appropriate at this moment to attempt a brief discussion of the role of the military in general terms. Whereas a military takeover in Europe and to a large extent in Latin America has meant the ascendancy of rightist and reactionary tendencies, in the Arab world military takeovers invariably have meant introduction of a leftist tendency. For in the Arab world – Syria, Iraq, and Egypt included – there has been no military tradition along the lines of that in the West. The armies of the

Arab countries are staffed mainly with what we shall call the proletariat for lack of better terminology. Enlisted men and officers are for the most part the sons of workers and peasants,[60] the lower classes rather than the aristocracy. Thus their tendency has been not to preserve the status quo but to change it. Syrian politics and armies since independence attest to this fact, and the socialism we are witnessing today in Syria could perhaps be called military socialism in the sense that it reflects the influence of a civilian ideology on certain Syrians who happen to be wearing an army uniform. For it is perhaps accurate to describe most Arab armies as being made up of workers, peasants, and civil servants in uniform.

It is hoped that this background may throw some light on the confused role of the military in the Ba'th takeover in Syria. The marriage between the military and the Ba'th party in this light becomes more meaningful and has stronger bonds than a "marriage of convenience," whereby the party would function merely as a front for actions decided upon by the military. Indeed, in this light it is difficult to pinpoint what is a "military" action and what is a "civilian" action.[61] Accordingly any conflict that may arise between the military and civilian wings is more in the nature of a clash of personalities than a clash of ideas. In this context, particularly since the Iraqi-Ba'th debacle in 1963, the emphasis has been placed on cooperation between the two wings of the party.

Recognizing the need for a better liaison between the military and the civilian, the Ba'th party in 1963 paid particular attention to this problem. Thus Decision Thirteen of the Sixth National Convention in 1963 dealt specifically with the "ideological education in the armed forces" (see Appendix A). To implement this decision a special office dealing with the armed forces was set up at the national headquarters of the Ba'th party in Damascus.

Furthermore, a new department of ideological guidance (*al-Tawjih al-Ma'nawi*) was established in the army. In the words of its head, Colonel Ibrahim al-Rifai, it is "a meeting point between the military and the civilian.

It aims at educating and keeping the army in line with the party's policies."[62] So far the marriage between the two has worked well. This is largely due to two important factors: (1) the heed paid by the military and civilian wings to the lesson of Iraq; (2) the personal attributes of Hafiz as representative of the military. Hafiz has not attempted to create for himself a distinct role and personality aside from that of the party.[63] For it is the habit of the Ba'th, in the words of Michael Abu Judeh, an astute Lebanese newspaperman, to "swallow" its "strong men" if they attempt to stray too far afield.[64]

8 Ba'th Ideology

The Ba'th Constitution provides the skeleton of Ba'th ideology, while the writings of its leaders, mainly Aflaq and several others, amplify and explicate it. Indeed, the greatest difficulty in undertaking a study of Arab socialism is its lack of a manifest theory. "Asia is aquiver with utopianism"[1] and the Arab world is aquiver with the excitement that precedes and accompanies change. Everywhere in the Arab world people speak of socialism, while few understand its implications.

The paucity of literature on Socialist doctrine in the Arab world gives the impression that Arab socialism has no theory at all. According to Hans Tutsch, "socialism in this part of the world is merely a label covering all sorts of government intervention. There is hardly any serious study of socialist doctrine."[2] While this statement appears accurate, it should be regarded as a hasty condemnation and a superficial observation.

For this lack of elaborate Socialist theory was, until recently, a source of pride among Arab intellectuals.[3] Muhammad A. Hatim, a one-time United Arab minister of state, concludes that "one of the great characteristics of our intellectual and spiritual experience has been [the fact that]... we did not get involved in theories searching for our life, but... in life searching for theories."[4] In another publication, Hatim further extols the lack of theory, stating that there is a similarity between Arab and British socialism in that the practice of both originated with need rather than dogma.[5] Ahmad K. Abu-al-Majd warned against basing Arab socialism on dogmatic theories, particularly those imported from the West. Arab socialism, he states, must reflect the reality of the Arab present while taking into account its heritage. It must be pragmatic to fit the situation as it arises.[6]

The Arab Ba'th Socialist intellectuals, led by Aflaq until recently, conformed to the above description. To theorize on the problems of society was considered useless by Aflaq. "Society is a living organic being and not a dead mechanical [creature]," he wrote; thus it defies abstract analysis. Aflaq attacked abstract thinking and theoretical definition as stripping reality of its essence. The true "idealist is not the opposite of the realist. For the realist is not the one who surrenders to the present but who understands it." The true idealist then, in Aflaq's thinking, is the one who understands his surroundings and attempts to change them.[7] Abstract thought, a trait of European knowledge, teaches that "all nationalisms evolve along shared and fixed axioms." According to Aflaq, such a view "disfigures" our Arab personality, forces us to forget our present problems, and gives us the false hope that the mere imitation of certain European ways will help us attain their level. The greatest danger in abstract thinking is its ability to give the impression that by changing the composition of certain elements, reshuffling some figures, the desired effect can be produced.[8] Aflaq then asserts that Arab nationalism is not the product of thought but gives rise to thought. "It is not the slave of art, but its mainspring and spirit. There is no contradiction between it and liberty, for it is liberty if it pursues its natural course and fulfills its capabilities."[9]

A more plausible explanation for the lack of theory is that advanced by another Ba'thist intellectual, Muhsen Abu Maizer. According to him, Arab socialism is an experiment not yet completed. To try to confine it to a theory in advance of its realization would contradict its nature as a "realistic and live experiment comprising all aspects of Arab society."[10] Abu Maizer, however, adds that the goals of the society – and only the goals – should be identified.

Aflaq rejects abstract theory completely on the ground that abstractions tend to limit the actions of those in power. A theory not realized is nothing more than a projection into the future of the will or desire of the philosopher. It is impractical since it does not take into account the realities and circumstances under which the theory might have to operate in practice.

It is perhaps more accurate to say that Aflaq, the anti-Western nationalist that he is, could not help but take such a stand. After all, the idea of socialism is a product of Western thought. Thus while rejecting theorizing, Aflaq is also rejecting Western socialism. His insistence on practicality, the pragmatic approach, taking into account the "present in which we live" is an attempt to show that Ba'th socialism is something indigenous to the Arab world and not imported from Europe.

A later generation of Ba'th intellectuals, perhaps more sophisticated than Aflaq, attacked his stand that Arab socialism is something unique and new. Atasi, later a minister of interior in the Ba'th government, said that Aflaq's insistence on "Arab" socialism is merely a sentimental reaction against the internationalism of Communist doctrine, and only compounds the vagueness of Ba'th doctrine. This approach to Socialist theory should be abandoned, for while each nation has unique qualities and needs, it can benefit from some aspects of the heritage of other nations. "Arab" socialism should mean socialism as adapted to the peculiar circumstances of the Arab world.[11] It should not mean total rejection of theory and of Western socialism.

The above criticism of Aflaq's thought by other Ba'thists should be viewed as the coming of age of a new brand of nationalists in the Middle East – a brand that has the fortitude and maturity not to be embarrassed by accepting foreign thought. Also, Aflaq's rejection of abstract thought can be dangerous in practice. To eliminate all theory leaves those in positions of authority with no frame of reference on which to rely. This can endanger their program, as has happened in Iraq. Further, it places no limits whatsoever on the power given the government. While Aflaq fears, justifiably, that a manifest theory might become rigid and unworkable, he should not reject theory completely. To do so might give rise to unrelated, unsuccessful experiments justified only by pragmatism.

Exposed to new problems, searching for new beginnings, and lacking influential intellectuals, Arab socialism has had to rely on the pragmatic approach. The Arabs suddenly awoke to find themselves in the twentieth century a century not particularly pleasant for the weaker nations.[12] They have had little time to produce theories; they are still learning. With the exception of Aflaq, there are few Arab intellectuals who command attention in the Arab world. Practice of socialism there has preceded doctrine.[13] Manfred Halpern is perhaps correct in his conclusion that Arab socialism came out of necessity rather than reasoned conviction.[14] On the other hand, the Arabs thus far have resisted the temptation of adopting a totalitarian regime to achieve their objectives.[15]

Upon reviewing the available literature on Arab socialism, one comes to the conclusion that the movement was an alternative method of attack on the problems of modern society, a middle way between capitalism and communism. Such is the view of socialism in the Arab world. This, however, leaves the relation between Arab socialism and Western socialism rather ambiguous.

The reasons for the rejection of Western Socialist thought by Arab Socialist intellectuals will be discussed later. For now, it seems that "history and circumstances have conspired to make Asiatic socialism a Third Force in the effort to find a path between capitalism and Stalinism."[16] Arab Socialists, intent upon finding an ideology they could claim as their own and not associated with either of the two great power blocs, hit upon socialism. According to Ahmad I. Khalaf-Allah, "There was only one door by which the developing nations might save themselves from the capitalist or communist imperialist octopus. . . This [door] is the human, democratic, cooperative socialist."[17]

Sir J. B. Glubb's remark that the terms "socialism" and "left wing" are of European origin and mean little in studying Arab politics, including that of the Ba'th party, has some truth in it.[18] Glubb, however, does not explain the reasons for this phenomenon and merely states that intense nationalism is of greater importance for a study of Arab politics. What he is suggesting is that socialism in the Arab world is nothing more than an expression of nationalism. The Ba'th party adopted "Unity, Liberty, and Socialism" as its slogan. Note the order of words: unity first, socialism last. Why?

In the Arab world socialism as an ideology remained a wing of the nationalist movement[19] which would develop as soon as independence was won. Unlike Communist ideology, nurtured by Moscow, there was no outside help in the development of socialism in the Middle East. The nationalists, such as the Ba'th party, who fought for political independence from foreign rule subjected their Socialist ideas to a secondary role until that independence was won. Socialism evolved as part of the nationalist revolution.

Ba'th ideology explicitly emphasizes nationalist goals over Socialist ones. In justification of such a view, Gebran Majdalany, a prominent leader of the Ba'th in Lebanon, maintains that

British or French Socialists have no problems of national unity and thus are able to concentrate their efforts on social ideas. But Arab Socialists must solve nationalist problems, such as unity, first.[20] Aflaq agrees with such a view, writing that "unity takes precedence [in our principles] over socialism." In another passage he adds that Arab Ba'th nationalism is a guarantee "of its humanity [that it is a humanitarian movement]… Our socialism thus is a means to resurrect our nationalism and our people and is the door through which our Arab nation enters history anew."[21] Socialism thus, as seen by Aflaq, is a means by which Arab glory can be regained.

In linking socialism to nationalism and unity, Ba'th intellectuals have found a way of accomplishing two aims at the same time. They can fight a revolution on two fronts. They can combat their "colonial" adversaries in the international sphere who do not wish to see the Arabs unite, and the domestic problems of an underdeveloped society. Bitar identifies the enemies of Arab unity as colonialism and Israel. Later he adds Communists, capitalists, and reactionaries. Thus the struggle for Arab unity is a struggle for progress and against colonialism.[22]

Unity is necessary before socialism can be achieved.[23] The Arab countries individually are considered too poor to achieve any real economic advancement. Bitar states it is obvious that individual Arab countries are unable to achieve "real economic and social progress without unity."[24] Elias Murkos, another Ba'thist intellectual, adds that "socialism cannot be achieved except in a large country with huge complementary resources,"[25] while Aflaq concludes that "neither the liberation nor the Socialist struggle can succeed as long as the one nation is divided."[26]

That socialism is an expression of nationalistic aspirations in Ba'th ideology cannot be denied. Ba'th intellectuals stress this point. They take pride in their so-called ideological neutrality. They reject both approaches: capitalist and Communist. They do not admit that capitalism in the classic sense is no longer in existence.

Aflaq says Arab socialism is "independent… does not follow a particular doctrine… but benefits from all theories and experiments of other peoples while it attempts to condition itself to the circumstances and desires of the Arab nation."[27] Bitar was more explicit in his doctrine of a neutral ideology between capitalism and communism. Capitalism entails injustice, the exploitation of the majority of the people by a minority. It cannot secure social justice for Arab society. On the other hand, communism with its repressive methods prevents the exercising of individual initiative.[28]

In the internal sphere, the local capitalist system has failed to secure any social or economic advancement for Arab society. Moreover, local capitalists allied with "imperialist" powers in exploiting Arab lands. Murkos states that while Arab capitalism has failed to partake of the first "industrial revolution," the world today is on the verge of a second industrial revolution brought about through automation. Since a capitalist system has failed to benefit from the first, then only in a Socialist system is there hope for real progress. Socialism is the only hope for salvation from poverty and the only means to social justice.[29]

Imperialism, a synonym for capitalism in the parlance of the Ba'th party, cooperated with communism to crush the nationalist aspirations of the Arabs.[30] The imperialist powers also cooperated with reactionary local capitalists to retard social progress. Often the most influential private enterprises in the Arab world were controlled by foreigners. Local capitalists were closely allied with and/or dependent upon these enterprises and the foreign powers behind them. "Hence," as Manfred Halpern writes, "acts of nationalization are above all declarations of national independence."[31] Since the Ba'th calls for complete independence, economic as well as political, it has often demanded nationalization of all foreign companies in Syria.[32]

In the international sphere, the Arabs were disillusioned with their maltreatment by the West, which culminated in the creation of the State of Israel in 1948. Since they sided with the West in two world wars, they see as unjust the division of their lands into mandates and protectorates after the First World War and Western creation and sustenance of the State of Israel. "Arab liberalism," according to Morroe Berger, "never more than a tender shoot... finally withered just after World War II in the white heat of the West's insistence upon maintaining its special position in the Near East and the creation of the State of Israel in 1943 and the ensuing War."[33]

To this may be added that the humiliating Arab defeat by Israel explains why Ba'th Socialist doctrine stresses national strength. It also helps explain the rejection of Western ideas and thought. Clovis Maqsud clearly points out that the "Arab Left was not a political force of import until the Arab defeat in Palestine when the traditional leadership failed."[34] The implication is obvious. The creation of the State of Israel was blamed on the West, and thereafter the Ba'th party, intensely nationalistic, could not accept anything Western.[35]

As strongly as Ba'th ideology claims independence of Western influence, it also claims independence of Marxist doctrine, Perhaps its rejection of Marxist doctrine rests on more solid ground than its rejection of Western influences. Taking Marxist doctrine at its word, Sa'dun Hamadi, minister of agricultural reform in Iraq during the Ba'th regime in 1963, writes that communism in the West came as a result of industrial capitalist advancement and as a reaction to the socioeconomic and political conditions brought by the Industrial Revolution. In the Arab world, he states, socialism came as a result of socioeconomic and political retardation. The Arab world was still under the agricultural, feudal order of the Middle Ages. Thus, Hamadi concludes, the Arab world is not yet ready to accept Communist doctrine.[36] Hamadi here is obviously ignoring the fact that Communist accession to power in many parts of the world did not follow classic Marxist doctrine.

Just as the West was equated with colonialism, so Marxism was equated with the Soviet Union and its activities. The distinction between the Soviet Union and Marxist ideology was not made until much later in Ba'th history. The Soviet Union was anti-Arab nationalism; in the United Nations it voted for partition of Palestine.[37] It was considered just as wicked as the West. The charge that Communist parties in both the Arab world and the Soviet Union were and continue to be opposed to Arab unity and nationalism has appeared in Ba'th literature since the creation of the party.[38]

In addition to the idea of nonalignment in world affairs, an idea the party has expounded since 1948 – perhaps the first Arab party to do so[39] – the Ba'th charges that Communist doctrine is too cruel. Communism "treats disease with disease."[40] Atasi, another important Ba'th writer, denies that the Soviet Union has a Socialist system. Soviet postponement of Socialist aims during the period of the "dictatorship of the proletariat" has created the worst kind of cruel and bureaucratic police state.[41] Socialism, avowedly an ideology aimed at the economic and political liberation of man, has been distorted to fit the Soviet regime. Furthermore, the Soviets by postponing the idea of "the withering away of the state" have created a new directing class, a new bureaucracy that is ever more efficient in its totalitarian police methods. What the Arabs want is not only nationalization of the means of production but the means to rule as well.[42]

Communist doctrine was also rejected on ideological grounds. Primary among these is the desire for an indigenous ideology. Aflaq wrote that "communism is the daughter of European thought." "The Arabs are not like any other nation of secondary" importance. Thus they cannot accept an alien doctrine; they cannot imitate: they must create. Aflaq objects to Marxism as a "materialistic internationalistic message," which denies the existence of nationalities as well as of spiritual values. Communism is destructive, he says, because it comes as a "revelation" that promises "Heaven on Earth" – a Heaven that follows the destruction of the present society. It is also destructive because of its desire to bind Arab destiny to that of the Soviet Union.[43]

Ba'th socialism objects to the Marxist doctrine of economic determinism, arguing that to explain history in terms of economics alone is a denial of the spiritual values cherished by the Arabs.[44] To attribute everything to one factor is to distort the meaning of life and progress.[45] While Marxists believe socialism to be the inevitable result of dialectical materialism, Ba'th ideology preaches that socialism will come about as a result of the conviction of the majority of the people, that socialism answers the need for a moral and just order in society.[46]

Ba'th insistence on a brand of socialism resulting from the Conviction of the majority of the people amounts to denial of the Marxist principle of class struggle. Aflaq rejects the idea of representing any one class. "In the West," he says, "injustice touches only some classes [in the society]. .. [All] the East represents nothing but an oppressed people."[47] Ba'th socialism as a "cooperative movement believes that the majority of the people – not one class" – has an interest in changing the existing order.[48] While Ba'th socialism recognizes that throughout history there has been class friction, it believes that this principle has been exaggerated and that history, so far, has proved its in-validity. It clearly rejects the international labor movement.[49] Rather than champion the interests of one class against the rest, the Ba'th wishes to level the differences between classes and to narrow the gap between wealth and poverty.

Communist insistence on economic determinism has caused disregard of the individual and his liberty. It has permitted the rise of a totalitarian regime that "suffocates the liberty of man."[50] It also ignores the wish of men to own and to inherit private property.[51] Further, while the Ba'th party claims to be secular, it objects to the Marxism's total denial of religion as an essential factor in society.[52]

Rejection by the Ba'th party of many Communist party principles has not prevented it from cooperating with the Communists when such cooperation was propitious. In Jordan the Ba'th party worked with the Communists after 1954 for the purpose of ridding that country of British influence, and of Glubb, the commander of the Jordanian army.[53] In Iraq the Ba'th cooperated with the Communists until the time of, and during the fall of, the monarchical regime in 1958, in an effort to embarrass the regime and bring about its downfall. Only after the Qasim regime came to depend too heavily on the Communist party did the Ba'th break away from it.[54] In Syria cooperation between the Ba'th and Communist parties commenced after the Shishakli takeover. Because of the cooperation between the two parties in Syria, Khalid Bakdash, secretary general of the Syrian Communist party, became the first Communist to be elected to Parliament in the Arab world. The Ba'th used its cooperation with the Communists to discredit and destroy its rival political parties in Syria. Thus it reduced the power of the Syrian National Socialist party (PPS);[55] and by so doing, was able to dominate the Syrian political arena from 1954 to 1958, when unity with Egypt was accomplished. The Ba'th call for union with Egypt in 1957 was partly due to its fear of rising Communist influence.[56]

Just as vehemently as it rejects Communist ideology, the Ba'th also rejects Fascist and Nazi socialism. These two movements permit colonialism in the name of superiority of certain races over others. Internally, they rest on the superiority of one individual over another and because of this they permit the rise of an autocratic regime. Ba'th socialism does not seek imperialist expansion, nor does it preach the racial superiority of Arabs. It only calls for the erection of a "just economic order" in the Arab world alone and demands an end to the exploitation of certain nations by others.[57]

Arab socialism and Western socialism have several similarities. Both movements refute the Marxist claim of the inevitability of scientific socialism, the theories of class struggle, and the dictatorship of the proletariat. Both movements have similar economic programs, placing special emphasis on the degree of nationalization they advocate. Since most Arab Socialist intellectuals either received their education in the West, or received a Western-oriented education, a trace of liberal democracy lingers in Arab socialism. Both movements emphasize improving the conditions of the working class. Arab socialism, however, gives more emphasis to the problems of the peasantry and is more nationalistic than Western socialism.

The difference between the two movements lies in the kinds of problems they face in domestic and foreign affairs. Internally, Western Socialist theories emerged in the wake of the industrial advances made in the nineteenth century.[58] They emerged as a reaction to economic class stratification following the Industrial Revolution. Emphasizing the element of class struggle that transcends national boundaries, they aimed at improving conditions of the working class the world over. In economically under-developed countries, socialism emerged as a result of the social consciousness of nationalists, clamoring for independence, and, in the Arab world, for unity.[59] Since Western industrialization hardly spread to the Arab world, there was no large proletariat there that a Socialist movement might defend. Socialism thus remained merely a wing of nationalism. In essence, it might be considered the social content of nationalism. In this light, Arab nationalism may be considered a constructive force.[60]

In the Arab world, where problems of industrialization are not so acute, socialism is less class conscious than in the West. Furthermore, owing to the presence of a large peasant population, Arab socialism naturally pays more attention to peasants' problems. It places great emphasis on land reform and on the problems of agricultural workers.

The strong link between nationalism and socialism in Ba'th ideology is justified in terms of the problems the Arabs have to face. Aflaq thus advances the theory of "battle on two fronts": externally to "struggle against imperialism" and for unity; internally to "struggle against internal maladies." Lack of unity, blamed on the West, and internal maladies have permitted "imperialism" to penetrate the Arab world.[61] Western Socialists are not confronted with problems of national unity.[62] Their independence and dignity are secure. Western influence, Socialist and otherwise, "was contaminated with political domination and with military occupation, suppressing those Arabs who found hope for the building of a new society in Western ideas."[63] Aflaq states that Western Socialists were just as imperialistic as anyone else when they assumed power in their own countries. The Léon Blum government in the 1930s did not give Syria and Lebanon independence. Israel was created while the Labor party was in power in Britain in the 1940s.[64] Moreover, French Socialists have supported the suppression of the nationalist movement for the liberation of Algeria. "Such action is not only anti-socialist but inhuman," states Khalil, the prominent Lebanese Ba'thist.[65] Western socialism is "too materialistic" and has "stood beside exploitation, injustice, reaction, expansion, and colonialism."[66] Maqsud states that Western socialism is at best a "progressive wing in a colonialist, capitalistic frame." The connection between the capitalist colonial interests and the Socialist parties in the West, he continues, have caused the latter to support the State of Israel.[67] Thus the Ba'th party approaches its understanding of socialism. In its eyes, and indeed in the eyes of most nationalists in the Arab world, the West is morally discredited.

The final point to be made concerning Arab *vis-à-vis* Western socialism is in terms of the evolution of these movements. In Asia socialism evolved after, rather than before, the formation of Communist parties.[68] Therefore, unlike Europe, where communism emerged as a reaction to the slow progress of socialism, in Asia socialism emerged as a reaction to Communist doctrine.[69] This is of the utmost importance in understanding the implications of social development. Examination of the ideological differences between Ba'th and Communist theories reveals the complete rejection by Ba'th socialism of the "cruelty," "inhumanity," and "dogmatism" of Communist doctrine. This also indicates that Ba'th socialism might be a reaction to the infiltration of Communist ideology in the Arab world.

The Ba'th party's attitude toward the major ideological movements in the twentieth century manifests a series of negative attitudes. Frustrated nationalists that they are, the Ba'th intellectuals cannot bring themselves to associate with a West they consider imperialistic. Thus even in terms of ideology they insist not only on being neutral but on embracing only "Arab" Socialism.

9 Ba'th Socialism

Ba'th socialism, in the words of Khalil, "is more of a cause than a philosophy." Later he adds, "It is humanitarian as well as nationalist."[1] It is humanitarian since it aims at alleviating the lot of the underdog. In a speech at a labor rally in 1950, Aflaq said that socialism is an attempt to obliterate poverty, ignorance, and disease."[2] In another context Aflaq relates that socialism would bring about a better life for all. It means rejection of the "putrid present," where a few enjoy life while the rest go hungry. Without socialism the Arabs can never progress internally; nor will they be able to become a better nation – a nation equal to other great nations.[3]

According to Aflaq, the link between socialism and nationalism is clear. The appeal to link these two seemingly contradictory theories is made in the name of progress, humanity, and the "Arab mission." Without socialism the nation, under its present conditions, cannot possibly achieve industrialization and progress. Without these, it will not be respectable enough or strong enough to fulfill its mission and assume its rightful place among other nations. And it is self-respect, a feeling of equality, and mutual respect that the Arabs want in their dealings with other nations.[4]

Razzaz, secretary general of the Ba'th party until 1966, gives a more comprehensive definition. For him socialism is a way of life, not just an economic order. It includes all aspects of life such as "economics, politics, upbringing, education, socialization, health, manners, literature, science, history, and all aspects of life large and small."[5] Such a comprehensive way of life is designed "to free the capabilities of the [individual] Arab from his chains so he can produce, [re]build the civilization of his nation and that of the human society."[6] Atasi adds that the purpose of socialism is to transform scarcity to plenty, provide equal opportunity for all, and put an end to the exploitation of one man by another and of one class by another. The socialism advocated envisions collective ownership of the means of production and a society in which everyone works according to his capability and receives goods and services according to his needs.[7]

The above statements reveal that Ba'th socialism is more than an economic program. Rather, what these writers seem to demand is regeneration of Arab society – a renaissance of the Arab people to be accomplished through a new economic order accompanied by new values. Politics and economics are to be the means of effecting such a change. As Charles Malik once said, "In our study of the Near East we cannot stop with the political: we must press on to the deeper modes of human existence."[8] Indeed, a study of the Ba'th party must take full account of the social, economic, and political aspects of life.

That socialism is considered indispensable for the Arab people to achieve their potential can be seen in the Ba'th Constitution (see Appendix B). Articles 26 through 48 are the basis of the economic and social policy of the Ba'th party. They reveal the ethical tendency in Ba'th socialism, deeming economic measures insufficient. Social justice necessitates equality of income and dignity as well as the worth of each individual. Thus classes are abolished, along with titles and privileges.

The economic provisions of the Constitution include the just redistribution of property. All citizens are equal, thus exploitation of others is prohibited (Art. 28). Public utilities, large public enterprises, and transportation are to belong to the nation. Foreign companies should be banned (Art. 29). Agricultural ownership is to be limited according to the individual's capacity to run it without exploiting others (Art. 30). Ownership of small-scale industry will be limited so that owners will not be permitted to enjoy a higher standard of living than other citizens (Art. 31). Workers are to share in management, their wages and shares in the profit to be decided by the state (Art. 32). Ownership, but not the exploitation of rents in real estate, is to be guaranteed by the state. The state is to guarantee to its citizens minimum ownership of real estate (Art. 33). Private property and inheritance are natural rights guaranteed within the national interest (Art. 34). The government will abolish usury among citizens and will take over banking services and credit facilities (Art. 35). The government will direct the affairs of domestic and foreign commerce to abolish monopolies and protect domestic enterprises (Art. 36). A comprehensive economic plan will be drawn for the purpose of increasing national production (Art. 37).

The social commitments in the Ba'th Constitution include free health services and government responsibility to find appropriate employment for all citizens. The state is responsible for the livelihood of the aged. Working hours are to be limited and paid vacations guaranteed for workers. Unemployment and accident compensation are to be provided as well as retirement benefits. Workers are to be free to form trade unions. "National" education is a responsibility of the state. The state is responsible for abolishing the extremes of wealth and poverty.

This indeed is a comprehensive social program going beyond the idea of state welfarism. It is a socialism that does not call for dictatorship of the proletariat or of the "lower middle class," as Leonard Binder puts it.[9] It is a program aimed at complete change in the society. It is to level classes and create a one-class mass of people.

These Socialist principles of the Ba'th Constitution can be readily traced in the Syrian Provisional Constitution of 1964 (see Appendix C). For it is in this Provisional Constitution that the Ba'th party made its ideology the state policy of Syria, thus committing the government of Syria to its own program. Articles 17 through 30 of this Constitution are the basis on which rest the Socialist policies of the Syrian state. These articles are similar to the Socialist program of the Ba'th party set forth in the party's Constitution. This similarity is by no means an accident, since the framers of the state's Constitution drew heavily on the party's Constitution.

Article 17, Section 1 of the Provisional Constitution states that education is a right of every citizen – an education which is "national" in character and which imbues youth with a sense of honor and pride in its heritage. By the provisions of this Constitution the state assumes the duty of providing health services to the sick, the orphaned, the disabled, and the aged (Art. 19). The state also has taken upon itself the right to interfere in the family as a unit of society. Article 20 states that the "family is the basic unit of society and is under the state's protection." Thus the state shall undertake to remove social and economic impediments to marriage, including the frequently exorbitant dowry demanded of a prospective bridegroom. Such undertakings are indeed unique, the first to be introduced in any Arab country, and it is doubtful whether the economic resources of the Syrian government will be sufficient to fulfill such lofty aspirations.

On the labor front, the government undertook to protect the workers' right to organize on "the basis of the independence of unions, clarifying their responsibility in building the national economy" (Art. 18, Sec. 3). Nothing is mentioned about labor's right to collective bargaining, its freedom to strike or boycott. The state, however, undertook to protect labor, guarantee just compensation, limit working hours, guarantee social security and vacations (Art. 18, Sec. 2). It also should provide work to citizens (Art. 18, Sec. 1). All these privileges labor will automatically get from the state without having to bargain for them independently. In other words, labor unions are to be and to act as agencies of the state.

All "the products of the Fatherland as well as its energies [shall be placed] in the service of the people" (Art. 23). Articles 24 and 25 spell out in detail the means by which the collective ownership by the people shall be placed in the hands of the state as representative of the people. Curiously such articles, so clearly stating the manner and design of collective ownership, are followed by Article 26, which begins, "Private property is protected, [but] the law shall regulate its social function." In other words, if a certain sector of the economy is not in conformity with the nebulous principle of social justice, it is to be expropriated. The ambiguity in this phraseology must have been deliberate, to allow the government to define which property serves a social function and which does not. Again the Provisional Constitution of Syria, like that of the Ba'th party, adds another contradiction with the statement, "The right of inheritance is protected according to law." What law? What are the limits, the definitions of this law? How much inheritance is allowed? All that is left to the government to decide.

The Provisional Constitution does spell out a comprehensive Socialist framework for the Ba'th regime in Syria. This Constitution reflects the party's intention to put its ideology into practice, and indeed it has.

The insistence of the Ba'th party on tying socialism to nationalism is made for the purpose of effecting a better standard of living internally. Such a program will unleash the Arab genius to effect the "Arab mission."

Although the concept of national mission occupies a central position in Ba'th thought, it is the most difficult to analyze.[10] On this point Aflaq's romantic nationalism is shown at its best. "Nationalism, like every kind of love, fills the heart with joy and spreads hope in the soul, he who feels it would wish to share with all people this joy... He who feels its sanctity is led at the same time to venerate it in all people. It is, then, the best way to a true humanity."[11]

The most important slogan of the Ba'th party is "One Arab Nation with an Eternal Mission." And its constitution states that the "Arab nation has an Eternal Mission" (Third Principle). What is this mission and what does it aim for? The Constitution again says that the mission reveals itself "in ever and new related forms through the different stages in history. It aims at the renewal of human values, at the quickening of human progress, at increasing harmony and mutual help among nations" (Third Principle). Such an undertaking results in opposition to colonialism and support of all national liberation movements throughout the world.

"Nationalism is love before everything else."[12] Thus nationalism must have social content: socialism. Socialism will bring out the potential of the individual so that he can contribute to his nation. The greatness of his nation in all fields is a contribution to humanity. "A mission is what one part of humanity presents to the whole of humanity."[13]

The concept of mission emphasizes the role of the Arabs in history. It aims at the regeneration of the individual's self so he can participate in the regeneration of his nation. It calls for an Arab self similar to that during the "glorious period" in Arab history.[14] It attempts to bridge the gap between the individual and his society, and between the nation and all of humanity. The focus on the eternal Arab mission in Ba'th ideology causes it to emphasize the role of the individual. But not all individuals are capable of greatness; thus the concept of the vanguard arises.

In the youth lies the source of salvation for the Arab people. Traditional leadership has failed: it was too conservative and could not effect change. In 1943 Aflaq wrote, "The spreading diseases that are affecting our nation, and the deep maladies in its system, cannot be remedied by the clever tricks of the [old] politicians: it [the nation] needs a struggling vanguard that has faith."[15] The old politicians are basking in luxury, while the nation is suffering terrible maladies. Only a few, an elite, are aware of these maladies and can struggle to correct them.[16] This organic look at society where every part must play its proper role, and with the elite at the helm is further expounded by Bitar.[17] The elite, the vanguard (in Ba'th parlance, *al-Tali'ah*), are those who recognize these ills – the retardation and the backwardness – and have the will and faith to attempt change.

During the period of *inqilab* (complete change), the elite must lead the nation.[18] The role of the vanguard is to mobilize the nation behind the national idea and to lead it in fulfilling the "eternal mission." The elite are to set the perfect example of the Arab individual, in all aspects of life, struggling for the betterment of the Arab people according to the principles of the Ba'th party.[19] The *Internal Rules Manual* of the party specifies the following oath for would-be-members: "I swear upon my honor and belief that I will be faithful to the principles of the Arab Ba'th Socialist party, that I will keep its trust, follow its rules, and execute its plans" (Chapt. II, Art. 7).

The elitist spirit of the party is justified on the grounds of the "realities" of the majority of the Arab people. Writing in 1950, a Ba'thist intellectual suggests that "we must not forget the large scope of illiteracy and ignorance in most classes of our society, this compels us to insist on placing the leadership in the hands of those conscious" few. Aflaq adds that the need is for those who are "instinctively aware": those who can achieve regeneration of their "self" in a "moment's reflection," especially since "the time between us and the future is psychological," not chronological.[20] Thus what is demanded is a few individuals who are aware of the bad conditions surrounding them and who are psychologically ripe to lead the nation. These few are in the future and the present at the same time. They are in the present because they are aware of its conditions and in the future because they are the image of the true Arab for whom Aflaq is asking.

Without this elite the national idea cannot be achieved. The national task cannot be accomplished by ideas alone. The idea must be exemplified in individuals. It must personify itself in those individuals who can sacrifice for it. The idea not personified, and not fought for by individuals, will perish. Personalities are important, but only the right kind of personalities. The emphasis is on quality, not quantity.[21]

This unconstrained desire and clamor for the elite is not restricted to Ba'th party intellectuals. Many Arabs, humiliated by the West in the twentieth century and particularly after the Palestine War in 1948, propagandize for an elite that can unite the nation and lead it to glory. Men like Constantine Zurayk,[22] and Nabih Faris,[23] by no means extreme nationalists, seek an elite, as do nationalists in general.[24]

Almost all of these writers received a Western education. By and large, they are less involved in the traditional life of their society. The Ba'thists legitimize themselves because they feel that they possess within themselves the spirit of the nation they visualize an advanced, industrious, progressive nation.[25] They are revolting against the slumbering traditional society in which they have found themselves.

The vanguard is necessary, for the most important problem in the Arab world is that of leadership.[26] The Arabs need competent leaders who have faith and can change the existing order. The presumption of the party is that society, like an organic being, must maintain a certain balance among its parts in order to be healthy. As the "head," i.e., the leadership, has failed, new leadership must take its place. The appearance of Socialist doctrine therefore is viewed as an attempt to redress the balance. The vanguard is to take charge of the state. The state, from this point of view, is an expression of the vanguard. It is the political authority and must direct the affairs of society and maintain the balance of its organs.

In the economic sphere the state is to increase "national production… develop industry and agriculture, maintain a balance between imports and exports, encourage foreign trade, and protect national production and the interests of producers and consumers."[27] The state should direct its affairs for the welfare of "each individual."[28] The state must be democratic: its authority must come from the people and it must operate in their name and for their welfare.

The state is a necessity in modern society. Abdul Daim ridicules the Communist principle of the "withering away of the state" since it cannot happen in practice. He states that the problem is not whether the power of the state increases or decreases but in whose name authority is practiced and whether such authority is democratic. The Communists who advocated the "withering away of the state" created the worst kind of bureaucratic and autocratic rule. They created a new "class" and imposed a new "slavery" which replaced that of the "dictatorship of capital."[29] The state in the Ba'th Constitution is a constitutional parliamentary regime elected directly by the people (Art. 14). It must be decentralized (Art. 16).[30] The principle of decentralization is aimed at lessening the central powers of the bureaucracy and at sharing authority with the largest number of people.[31]

The interesting point of the Ba'th's treatment of the role of the state in society is that while it requires the state to take charge of directing a large segment of the economic and political affairs of the society, it does not visualize it as an all-powerful and domineering monolith that will be inimical to the liberties of the people. The state is viewed as the agent of the people, reflecting their desires and aspirations within the "national goal." Such a democratic regime is presumed to come after the period of *inqilab*, in which the vanguard are to lead. Yet nowhere in the Ba'th Constitution, or in any of the polemics of the Ba'th intellectuals, is a time limit placed on this period.

Aflaq does not indicate when this tutelage by the vanguard would end.[32] He is not fearful that this vanguard may turn into an instrument of repression and therefore he takes no measures to control it.

The social and political setting in which the Ba'th party operates should be recalled. After the First World War, most Arab countries adopted a parliamentary form of government. However, these regimes were parliamentary only in form; that is why there has been rebellion against "false parliamentary governments." The acceptance of governmental takeover in the economic sphere should also be viewed against that background. Historically the government has been the largest employer and the principal owner of capital. Arab governments after the First World War took charge of most public utilities such as telephone and telegraph, electric power, railroads, and several other municipal services. Thus, the practice of socialism in the Arab world antedates its acceptance as an ideology.[33] The Ba'th denies that this is state capitalism, arguing that in state capitalism the government uses "profit" as a yardstick for measuring the "healthy" activities of "capital." State capitalism does not abolish classes, nor does it end exploitation; it merely restricts them.[34] The Ba'th Socialist state means creation of a direct democratic relationship between the consumer and the producer. It eliminates profit as the sole measure of production. Thus it is not state capitalism.[35]

What the Ba'th party seems to demand is an economic as well as political democracy. As Abdul Daim said, what is needed is not only nationalization of the means of production but of the means to rule as well.[36] What he neglected to add, and what might be inimical to the principle of nationalization of the means to rule is the phrase "within the national interest," presumably defined by the party.

In their declamations and discourses on socialism, Ba'th leaders offer few concrete proposals concerning the means by which Arab society might be transformed into a Socialist one. Asked about the most important weakness of Arab society and the possible cure for it, Aflaq replied, "Our social backwardness… the cure [for which] lies in the education of the people."[37] While education is a necessary first step toward realization of a better society, Socialist or otherwise, it is hardly a panacea. However, upon closer examination of the Ba'th Constitution and other writings by Ba'th intellectuals, it becomes evident that the state is to become the instrument by which a Socialist society is to emerge.

Article 29 of the Ba'th Constitution states that "public utilities, extensive natural resources, big industry, and the means of transport are the property of the nation. The state will manage them directly and will abolish private companies and foreign concessions." Abolition of foreign concessions has been a repeated theme in Ba'th declamations.[38] In the decisions of the First National Convention, the party advocated state aid and protection for national industries. Since that first convention, the party has advocated the application by the state of a progressive income tax, inheritance taxes, minimum wages, high excise taxes on luxury items, and the reform of labor laws to abolish the dictatorship of capital over labor. The first duty of the state is to provide work for everyone with adequate compensation, guaranteeing a decent standard of living.[39]

Stating that labor alone gives the right to ownership, Khalil insinuates that the Ba'th position is similar to that of Pierre J. Proudhon. Khalil adds that the party program specifies that "industrial ownership should be limited depending upon the interests of the public and the citizens' prevailing standard of living, and that workers should become shareholders."[40] Like that of Proudhon, the party's program is intended to eliminate the monopolistic and exploitative features of ownership.[41]

Nationalization then is one means by which the state is to effect socialism. Since socialism is aimed at freeing man from want and enabling him to produce and realize his capabilities, nationalization must be practiced judiciously. The state may take direct control over some nationalized industries, or when desirable may relegate their management to cooperative societies.[42] Nationalization should be practiced in stages, with the more important enterprises nationalized first and the owners adequately compensated.[43] Depending upon the circumstances, the standards of efficiency required, and the end desired, nationalization does not always mean complete control by the government over all enterprises. Razzaz advocates government partnership in some enterprises, with the people providing the remaining capital. Complete nationalization has two drawbacks, he states. First, it gives the government a large burden which it might not be able to carry, and second, it converts the entire populace into public servants, which might inhibit private initiative and creativity.[44]

Workers and peasants form the basis upon which the Ba'th party rests, according to Murkos.[45] Therefore, the Ba'th pays particular attention to the problems of both. For the workers, it advocates better working conditions, fringe benefits, health services, a share in profit and management (see Appendix A). For the peasants the party demands land redistribution, land reform, an end to feudalism, and creation of cooperative societies and collective farms.[46]

Since the Arab world is basically agricultural, the Ba'th party pays particular attention to land problems. Until 1958 the agricultural pattern in Syria was feudal.[47] Article 30 of the Ba'th Constitution states that land ownership would be limited according to the owners' ability to manage the land without exploiting the labor of others. The extremes between large estates and sharecropping should be abolished. Murkos feels that "land should belong to whoever ploughs it."[48] For each man to own only what he can physically plough means the end to exploitation and absentee landlordism and the just distribution of land properties.[49] But to break up the existing order into small farms would result in inefficiency and would lower production. For this reason the party advocates the encouragement of existing cooperative societies in the countryside and the establishment of new ones. In addition to land redistribution and the creation of cooperative societies, the party has been advocating the creation of land banks to extend credit to farmers and thus combat usury. Finally, since 1963, when the party came into power in Syria, the idea of collective farms has been advocated for the confiscated, but not yet redistributed, lands.[50]

With few exceptions the stand taken by Ba'th intellectuals with regard to private property is quite clear. Unable to reject it or abolish it completely since Islam clearly condones it, Ba'th Socialists have compromised with it.

The goal of production, according to Razzaz, ought to be service, not profit.[51] Therefore, in order to provide services to all the people, a curtailment on the amount of property becomes imperative. Article 34 of the Ba'th party Constitution states that "property and inheritance are two natural rights. They are protected within the limits of the national interest." Believing in "individual liberty," says Khalil, "Ba'th socialism recognizes the individual's right to earn the worth of his efforts and qualifications."[52]

There are some Ba'th intellectuals who take issue with this line of the party. Abu Maizer,[53] and Yasin al-Hafiz,[54] more doctrinaire leftists, demand total abolition of private property if real economic freedom is to be achieved. Abu Maizer states that total nationalization is necessary. Otherwise, if partial nationalization, i.e., nationalization of major enterprises and utilities alone be effected, the state will turn into some kind of philanthropic organization whose task it is to alleviate the misery of the poor;[55] it will not be a true Socialist regime. This view, however, is not accepted by the majority of Ba'th party intellectuals; nor is it a party line. In fact, Hafiz was expelled from the party in 1964 precisely because of his extreme "leftist" leanings, bordering on communism.[56]

Rejecting capitalism, which uses profit to gauge effectiveness of production, Aflaq also rejects Marxism as too utopian in its total rejection of private property. Ba'th socialism, he adds, recognizes the strength of the instinct for private property; thus it permits it while at the same time placing some restrictions on it.[57] Abdul Daim states that the danger to the democratic socialism demanded by the Ba'th is not only from external factors but also from within. The problem is how to find a proper tie with democracy.[58]

The dilemma of the Ba'th Socialists in reconciling liberty with socialism is a problem facing Socialists everywhere. In 1951 the Socialist International, voicing the opinion of thirty Socialist parties, "adopted a program that specifically rejected the older doctrine of total nationalization."[59] Perhaps unconsciously agreeing with George Bernard Shaw's analysis that "individual liberty, with unrestrained private ownership… is irreconcilable with the common weal,"[60] the Ba'th party came to recognize that total nationalization too is inimical to individual liberty. But while the Ba'th party rejected total nationalization before the European Socialist International, its agreement in principle with Fabian socialism goes no further. Ba'th socialism admits that a certain amount of property should be allowed "within the national interest." But nowhere is the national interest defined. Nowhere is it possible to know to what lengths the party might go in defining it either. In power in Syria since March, 1963, the party has not yet nationalized all the means of production and it allows a certain amount of private property.

10 Ba'th Orientation

The Ba'th slogan, "Unity, Liberty, Socialism," is significant. Also significant is the order of the words. This slogan, which appears first in every party publication, on party stationery, and on the door to the party's headquarters in Damascus, has been adopted as its slogan by the present Syrian government.

As one broaches the problem of Ba'th socialism, the place of the individual and his liberties proves most difficult to clarify. In societies where individual liberties are not so carefully safeguarded as they are in the West, it might seem that they are not so highly valued. But the problem is not so simple. For while Ba'th writers may be anti-Western and reject or deny their indebtedness to the West, in reality some remnants of Western liberalism have survived in them. Yet while they preach that the individual and his freedoms must be safe-guarded, they see no contradiction in restricting them.

Observe what the Ba'th party does: The Constitution provides for the freedoms of speech, press, association, and religion "within the national interest" (Art. 41). These freedoms are too limited not by a clearly defined law but by the vague words "within the national interest."[1]

Perhaps Aflaq, more than any other writer, sees the ills of Arab society as a result of weakness in the Arab "self." Thus he demands an end to evasion of responsibility.[2] He deems necessary a regeneration of those noble values within each individual that once made the Arab nation strong.[3]

Until such regeneration becomes a reality, some liberties, indeed most liberties, may be sacrificed in the "national interest." Aflaq is very frank in his approach to the problem of personal freedom. At one point he is merciless in his treatment of those who do not accept the tutelage of the vanguard during the *inqilab* period. He says, in effect, he wants to force them to be free. "Our mercilessness has for its objective to restore them to their true selves which they ignore, to their hidden will which they have not yet clearly discerned and which is with us even though their swords are against us."[4]

According to Khalil, the Ba'th concept of liberty is moral. It is based on the liberation of the individual from economic, political, intellectual, and social restrictions, and on emancipation of his will, which allows him to realize his potential and to lead a better and more productive life.[5] Sa'dun Hamadi adds that liberty means the release of the inner capabilities of the individual from psychological, social, economic, and political bondage. It is a liberation aimed at the eradication of wickedness, evil, selfishness. Liberty alone means liberation of the humanitarian aspect of man.[6] The conclusion is that the "unhumanitarian" aspect, as defined by the party, may be restricted.

The Ba'th Constitution places emphasis on social equality as well as on political freedom (Prin. 1, Secs. 1 and 2). Liberty implies equality. Men cannot be free unless they have equal opportunity, and socialism provides it. The society demanded by Ba'th intellectuals is pluralistic within the framework of an accepted social goal.[7] Shibli al-Aysami, one-time minister of guidance during the Ba'th regime and former assistant to the secretary general of the party, is more specific on this point. He states that liberty will be extended to those individuals and associations that are in agreement with the aims of the Arab nation, i.e., the party.

"We do not object to criticism or to the formation of independent parties and associations provided they are in agreement with the goals we preach. They can differ with us on methods only."[8] Khalid Yashruti, an architect and a member of the Regional Command in Lebanon, says that the "enemies of the revolution, i.e., those who disagree on the goals we preach, will have no freedom to associate."[9] Within five days after its accession to power in March, 1963, the Ba'th banned demonstrations and took away the publication licenses of sixteen opposition newspapers.[10] At present political parties are not allowed to form in Syria; only the Ba'th party is legal.

In the Arab world the Ba'th party was one of the earliest to demand equality of the sexes. In 1947 it demanded that women be given the right to vote. This demand was incorporated in the decisions of the First National Convention.[11] Razzaz comments, "We have inherited from the Ottoman era a nation whose other half is dead and imprisoned behind walls... [and which] understands nothing of the meaning of life."[12] Clearly, any real liberty must include woman's emancipation and equality.

The Ba'th Constitution calls for a "parliamentary constitutional" regime (Art. 14). The Constitution also states that the people are to be the sole source of power and authority. Sovereignty should belong to the people (Art. 5). Emphasizing their democratic spirit, the Constitution also insists on a decentralized government (Art. 16). Decentralization is required to curb the power of the bureaucracy and secure more popular participation in government.[13]

Since the party came to power in 1963, there has been a major departure from its emphasis on parliamentary democracy. "False democracy," "false parliamentarianism," has been manipulated in the Arab world in favor of the "exploiting classes." The people are not free to vote so long as they are not economically free.

The Arab people have been living under these so-called democratic regimes which in reality are not democratic. This, however, should not mean abolition of democracy, but correction of its distorted features.[14] The Ba'th wants to replace the "traditional", "bourgeois parliaments" with a "truly" democratic regime that reflects the wishes of the people.[15] The new emphasis is on "popular democracy" – democracy from the bottom up, as Abdul Daim calls it.[16] This new democracy emphasizes collective leadership at the top and the principle of democratic centralism within the party and the state (see Appendix A, Decision I). In 1964 the Provisional Constitution proclaimed by the Ba'th regime called Syria the "Socialist Popular, Democratic Republic of Syria" (see Appendix C, Art. 1, Sec. 1). Popular democracy in Ba'th parlance is a pyramidal structure with the people at the bottom electing their village or city councils directly. These councils in turn elect district councils, then regional councils, then the national council. The higher councils are elected by the lower ones. Democratic centralism and collective leadership are two principles that should be strictly heeded.[17]

The kind of regime desired by the Ba'th has not yet been achieved. This is what the party hopes the present regime will become. Presently, the executive and legislative powers in Syria are vested in the National Revolutionary Council, a body thus far self-appointed. The Provisional Constitution of 1964 was proclaimed by this body, which places virtual control of the legislative and executive powers in itself and the Cabinet, an inferior body to be responsible to it. Until the Provisional Constitution is replaced by a permanent one, this will be the pattern of authority in Syria.

The issue of liberty in Ba'th ideology is of central importance. Like other ideologies that preach the economic and political liberation of man, Ba'thism is facing the paradox of how to reconcile liberty with socialism. Revolting against the existing forms of government in the Arab world, which though avowedly democratic in fact were not, the Ba'th adopted the idea of "popular democracy." The curious thing is that the Ba'th party, adopting popular democracy, never changed its adherence to parliamentary democracy in its Constitution. Also curious is the suddenness with which the party switched to the new principle. Perhaps the party visualizes popular democracy as a first step toward achieving parliamentary democracy. This may account for its not changing the Constitution to fit the new line.

In its treatment of religion, the Ba'th party is in total agreement with non-Ba'th Socialists in the Middle East. The majority of Arab Socialists claim that Islam, the religion of the majority of the Arabs, is a precursor of socialism. Their contention that Islam is Socialist is an attempt to support their claim that their socialism is indigenous to the Arab world.[18]

The Ba'th party has taken a similar stand. Aflaq has accepted Islam as part of Arab heritage and thus, he feels, it does not clash with socialism or nationalism. As a matter of fact, he regards the early Islamic era as the period in which the Arab self was best realized. The life and deeds of the Prophet Muhammad epitomize the Arab self Aflaq is seeking. In the Prophet and his associates Aflaq sees the embodiment of the true and noble Arab spirit. He demands a resurrection (*ba'th*) of that spirit. Aflaq then adds that in the West religion petrified and in the hands of reactionaries became a tool to stifle social progress. This is not the case with Islam. Holding to his view of historical development, he suggests that the Ba'th party, while secular in orientation, embodies a renaissance of the Arab spirit similar to that embodied in Islam.[19]

Ba'th intellectuals, in unison, refer to Islam as a rich part of Arab heritage that cannot and must not be denied.[20] One Ba'th intellectual, Elias Farah, states that Islam is the first "Arab nationalist revolution." He adds that both socialism and Islam have the same end in mind: to provide equal opportunity for all.[21] The Ba'th believes religion to be an essential element for the well-being of man.[22]

Chief among the targets under attack by the Ba'th party is the Communist party's attitude toward religion. The Ba'th has never failed to exploit this issue, which is a constant source of embarrassment to the Communist party in the traditional society of the Arab world.[23] In 1963 the party condemned the charge made by Abdullah al-Sallal, the president of Yemen, that the Ba'th party is irreligious[24] as a "reactionary" method to defame the party. Following Sallal, Nasser attacked the Ba'th as atheistic. With equal vehemence the party defended itself and condemned Nasser as a demagogue who plays on mass sentiment.[25] In a society as sensitive to religious issues as the Arab world, the party could not afford to remain silent in face of these charges. Aflaq hastened to clarify the party's position with regard to religion.[26]

The Ba'th party's view of religion is one of the major reasons for conflict between it and the Communists. Finding itself in traditional Arab society, where the majority of people are Muslim, the party has reconciled itself with religion, accepted it as part of man's personal affairs, and in fact attributed partial responsibility for the Arabs' glorious history to Islam. In the tradition-bound Arab world, even partial rejection of Islam would have been too drastic a step.

No doubt the party's acceptance of religion was prompted by its desire to attract as large a following as possible, while at the same time pointing to the atheism of its rival the Communist party. Added to that is the sincere belief of the majority of Ba'th intellectuals that Islam represents a major Arab contribution to world civilization. The inclusion of the "eternal mission" in Ba'th ideology suggests that the party, while a secular movement, is like Islam prompted by a desire to contribute to world civilization and humanity.

Most Arab Socialist writers using the word "revolution" (*thawrah*) do not necessarily mean bloody revolution. They mean a total change in conditions presently characterized by inertia, sluggishness, and indifference. Yusuf Sayegh, a non-Ba'th Socialist, denies that revolution must mean "blood and fire"; what he sanctions is rather a "revolution in thought and precepts by changing – at the roots – the public way of thinking."[27] Muhammad al-Bahi, an Egyptian Socialist, attempting to prove that Islam is Socialist, denies violence altogether, insisting that "Islam did not depend on violence," [28] while others insist that Arab socialism is an evolutionary socialism that precludes violence.[29]

The Ba'th party calls itself a "struggling revolutionary" party. But the word "revolution" has a special meaning in Aflaq's polemics. Indeed, as Leonard Binder puts it, it "is a romantic non-legalistic conception of revolution."[30] Aflaq's conception of revolution precludes violence. Indeed, he writes in several places that "by revolution [*inqilab*], we understand… the awakening of the Arab spirit."[31] Thus, when Sylvia Haim claims that in Aflaq's writings there is an "insistence on violence,"[32] she is entirely incorrect in her interpretation of both his writings and Ba'th ideology. In the Ba'th Constitution – in the Arabic text – the word "revolution" (*thawrah*) is mentioned only once and the reference is to an *economic*, not a *political*, revolution. The word more often used, *inqilab*, means total transformation. No doubt the difficulty of translating this word contributed to the confusion. But in fact the party on several occasions has condemned violence as a means of achieving political ends.[33] Also, when the party took over the government of Syria in 1963 it did so through a bloodless *coup d'état.*

In one interview Aflaq flatly stated that "violence is not part of our program."[34] Conditions in the Arab world are so degenerate and backward that only a psychological revolution, a change in the Arab personality, can change them. At one point Aflaq defines *inqilab* as the opposition to the present which alone will reconstitute the Arab personality and prepare it to take on the task of modernization and recaptivating the once glorious past.[35]

The transformation demanded by the Ba'th party cannot be achieved through evolution and partial reform. In developed nations partial reform is acceptable because present conditions are not so unbearable. But in Arab society only a complete and rapid transformation, an "*inqilab*, the opposite of the reformist movement,"[36] will do. In another place the Ba'th interprets revolution as "state of mind before anything else" – a state of mind that rejects the putrid conditions of the present and goes beyond the surface of things to the deeper roots of the problem.[37] Article 6 of the party Constitution specifically rejects reform and evolution as a threat to achievement of the party's goals. A true Ba'thist is one who revolts against undesirable elements in himself and in his society. Unless this inner psychological transformation is achieved, no real revolution in the society can be effected. "We want every Arab to understand that he himself is the only way to his own salvation."[38]

The revolution then is not, as Haim says, violent and bloody. Rather it is, as Aflaq states on various occasions, psychological in the sense of opposing current bad conditions in one's own society and the basic instincts in one's self. It is intellectual in that it opposes the traditional ideas of the older leadership and partial reform.[39] It is a moral revolution in that it opposes submissiveness and attempts to build a new Arab whose character rests upon truth, justice, dignity, love, and sacrifice.[40]

The Ba'thist conceives of revolution as the total rejection of the backward conditions of the Arab world. In essence, the party denies that it has any machinery for the overthrow of government by armed force. The revolution called for depends on educating the people and instilling in them those values the party admires. Once each individual is transformed, society as a whole will be transformed. Moreover, partial transformation in each individual is not enough since it will leave him lacking, partial transformation, i.e., reform, in the existing society is not enough either. This *inqilab*, this transformation of the individual and the society, necessitates struggling against colonialism and injustice wherever they appear and giving aid to all liberation movements in the world.[41]

The Ba'th Constitution demands freedom of speech, belief, and association. It does not ask for a one-party state, nor does it demand the right to restrict others from forming political parties. In his writings Aflaq states that "our party" is different from the others because it has a broader perspective on Arab problems and is "national," i.e., not restricted to a single country. He hints, however, that other "local" political parties – especially the Socialist ones, such as the Progressive Socialist party of Lebanon – which demand socialism on the local level, serve only to corrupt and disfigure the meaning of socialism.[42] Nowhere does he demand a one-party state, although his party acquiesced when Nasser abolished political parties after the formation of the U.A.R. Moreover, since the Ba'th's accession to power in Syria in 1963, no other political parties have been allowed to form.

Razzaz concludes that the existence of political parties is a prerequisite to the achievement of "popular democracy." He then goes on to analyze the existing political parties in the Arab world, stating that "most of our political parties in the Arab world are either without a program [meaning a manifest ideology] or have no [real] meaning to their program." In a profound analysis of the growth of political parties in the Arab world, he states that while the struggle for independence and national liberation was being staged, there were some political parties like the Wafd in Egypt and the National Bloc in Syria that commanded the allegiance of a large segment of the populace. With the achievement of independence, however, these parties disintegrated into various groups, led by "personalities" rather than "issues," and were devoid of real social, economic, or political programs. Contemporary political parties, Razzaz concludes, are based on "personalities" not issues. They are "reactionary" in that they arose to fulfill a particular aim; having fulfilled it, they remain in existence. They are "feudalist" and "capitalist" in that they are led by the interests of these groups. Finally, they are "dictatorial" in that they are totally subject to the whims of the leaders rather than to principles and issues.[43]

Razzaz's analysis shows that the Ba'th party is scornful of the "local" political parties in the Arab world. It considers the Muslim Brotherhood reactionary and a tool of American interests.[44] The Ba'th has staged a bitter struggle against the National Syrian Socialist party (PPS) which advocates the Fertile Crescent Scheme for unity. As a result of Ba'th efforts, the party was discredited by 1957. The Ba'th condemns this party as a Fascist organization that serves to disfigure the meaning and content of Arab nationalism.[45] The multitude of political parties are no more than spokesmen for the groups they represent. "They have no real content, and their whole basis is the service of the interests of the groups and leaders behind them.

They only help perpetuate the division of Lebanese society into many *confessions* [religious and ethnic groups]."[46]

In 1949 the Ba'th party refused to attend a political party convention held in Beirut because such parties as the National Syrian Socialist party and others that represent feudalism and capitalism were attending.[47] In 1950 the Ba'th also refused to attend a convention called by the Lebanese Progressive Socialist party, because it did not consider this party or the others invited serious Socialists.[48]

While the Ba'th party since its First National Convention in 1947 has called for cooperation with other Arab "progressive" parties that "fight colonialism and local exploitation,"[49] it seems not yet to have found any such parties to cooperate with except on a temporary basis and only to achieve a particular aim. In fact, the Ba'th has found it propitious at times to cooperate with parties it considered "reactionary." In its attempt to discredit the PPS, the Ba'th cooperated with the *al-Sha'b* (Populist) party in 1954. When by 1957 Ba'th influence was secure, it turned against its former ally the Populist party, "discovering" a plot for which it handed down twelve death sentences.[50] This harshness was calculated to frighten any further conservative opposition. The Ba'th ally in this "terror" drive was the Communist party, but the Ba'th later turned against it too.[51]

Relations of the Ba'th with other political parties in the Arab world are colored by the party's interests. When such cooperation was profitable, the Ba'th did not hesitate to indulge in it whether the party was "progressive" or "reactionary." The degree of cooperation was determined by Ba'th interests. The ideological differences and the clash of interests between the Ba'th and the Communists made cooperation between the two short-lived. Since the European Socialist parties have no branches in the Arab world, as does the Communist party, relations of these with the Ba'th have been restricted to verbal denunciation of them by the Ba'th. The European Socialist parties, in the Ba'th view, have fallen heir to the colonial ambitions of their predecessors the capitalists and have served such ambitions just as well.[52] Any cooperation or rapprochement with them, therefore, is impossible.

With its call for the unity of the entire Arab world from the Atlantic Ocean to the Persian Gulf, the Ba'th party finds itself confronted with Western interests on all sides. With the same intensity of feeling with which it clamors for Arab unity, the party denounces Western interests in this region. Since its First National Convention, and even earlier, one of the chief characteristics of the Ba'th party has been its extreme xenophobia. In the West the party saw the image of a greedy colonialist keeping the Arab land divided in his own interest. Worse, the West had caused the Arabs to lose some territory, as is the case with the Alexandretta District.[53] Later it assisted in the creation and maintenance of the State of Israel. The statement of the First National Convention of the party may be considered classic in its vehement denunciation of the West.[54] On May 7, 1947, Bitar in an editorial in al-Ba'th recommended that the Arabs apply economic pressure on the Western powers by refusing to sell them oil, thus forcing them to alter their position with regard to the Palestine problem. Three days later he recommended in *al-Ba'th* that the Arab countries withdraw from the United Nations, which he claimed had become a "tool" for Zionism and the Western "imperialist" powers.

It was also at the First National Convention that the party recognized the existence of two world power blocs and recommended neutrality.[55] Neutrality in this instance and for the years to come was a blow directed against the Western powers, since the Soviet Union was not at the time embroiled in the affairs of the Arab world. Later, the negative attitude of the party's neutrality was expanded to include the Soviet Union.

After the Soviet vote in the United Nations for the partition of Palestine, Aflaq stated that both the Western and Soviet blocs were hostile to the Arabs.

With the passage of years and the gradual involvement of the Soviet Union in Arab affairs, this negative attitude toward the Soviet bloc changed. After the Suez Canal War in 1956, the term "positive neutrality" came into vogue. Bitar, minister of foreign affairs in Syria in 1957, defined positive neutrality as friendly relations "with all governments regardless of their social, political, or economic regime (orientation)." Then he added that while "we respect" and appreciate the United States' stand during the Suez crisis "we cannot ignore" its vigilant support of Israel. "We consider" the governments of the Soviet bloc "our friend."[56] Khalil states that the party, inspired by its nationalist ideology, advocates a foreign policy that aims at the liberation of all nations from foreign domination and at the promotion of human progress and world peace. He adds that positive neutrality is necessary in order to achieve such a goal since it implies cooperation with both camps.[57]

Since the Soviet Union has no history of colonialism in the Arab world, the conclusion that positive neutrality means friendlier relations with it becomes obvious. Moreover, this positive neutrality explains the party's rejection of "pacts" called for largely by the Western powers. Resting on the principle of neutrality, the party has fought against the Baghdad Pact, the Eisenhower Doctrine, the various mutual defense plans and treaties concluded between Arab and Western powers. The policy of positive neutrality was reaffirmed at the Sixth National Convention in 1963 with a new, and this time explicit, exhortation that it should not be construed to mean "not maintaining friendlier relations with the people of the Socialist World" (Art. 24). Despite these exhortations, relations between the Ba'th party and the international Communist movement have not been too friendly. The Ba'th party has consistently warned the Soviet Union against interfering in the internal affairs of the Arabs and supporting the local Communist parties, which are "anti-Arab nationalism."[58] Since its advent to power in Syria, and while in power in Iraq, the Ba'th has staged a vehement anti-Communist struggle. This has caused Moscow to condemn the Ba'th party as "reactionary."[59]

Along with the Ba'th principle of neutrality is its suspicion of foreign aid from the Western powers. Early in 1947 Bitar stated that "any foreign aid to a weaker nation transforms itself into political influence." Bitar also recommended even the rejection of technical aid since "Foreign experts" turn into "colonial" agents and perpetuate "imperialist" influence. In 1950 the party denounced the Point Four program as an innovation in "American capitalism." The United States wishes to invest its excess capital under the guise of aid. Such is certified by American insistence on certain regulations and "strings attached" to their aid. The "Americans" insist that the recipient country must not nationalize certain concerns and must regulate its monetary and economic policy. This outright interference in the domestic affairs of the recipient country cannot be accepted. The theme that American aid tends to restrict the sovereignty of the recipient country has been a recurrent one.[60]

Enraptured with nationalist ideology, the Ba'th party holds the West responsible for many of the ills of Arab society. The

Ba'th intellectuals decry their treatment by Western powers and never tire of denouncing them. Preoccupied with unity, they blame the West, more than anything else, for their misfortune. Although not a Ba'th writer, Khalaf-Allah typifies the position of the Ba'th party with regard to the Western powers. He states that "Europeans look at the Arabs with materialistic eyes: not as… humans looking at other humans. They consider the Arab Fatherland as a source of profit and an arena of influence. For the sake of partitioning the Arab Fatherland, the Catholic shook hands with the Protestant, the Liberal with the Conservative, the Aristocrat with the Democrat, the Monarchist with the Republican, the Red with the White, the Followers of Jesus with those who killed him."[61] This statement exposes the intense xenophobia of most Arab Socialists, including those of the Ba'th party. Their dislike and mistrust of the West is best exemplified by Hourani's attitude. Asked with whom he feels closer affinity, a British Socialist or a Shaikh from Saudi Arabia, he replied, "The Saudi Arabian Shaikh without any question."[62]

11 Organization and Structure[1]

To perform a "mission," to put a program into action, and to capture power and use it, an organization of some kind is necessary. "Organization exists to facilitate collective activity," in the words of the late V. O. Key.[2] While the functions performed by the Ba'th party are different from those of American political parties, considered by Key, his assessment of the need for organization is nonetheless valid. Since the Ba'th party has always operated in a different milieu from that of the United States, its organization is different from that of American parties.

The Ba'th party is primarily what M. Duverger calls a cell party. Its pyramidal structure begins with the *Halaqah* (Cell) at the bottom and the National Command and the Secretary General at the top. Duverger, however, also states that Communist and certain Fascist parties "alone have the cell as their basis." But the Ba'th party is neither Communist, in that it does not wish to champion the cause of a certain class or to carry out a world-wide revolution, nor Fascist, in that its militia are not party members. Further, the Ba'th differs from both in ideological content and method. The Ba'th party, unlike the Communist and Fascist parties, rules out force and violence.

While the cell is an invention of the Soviet Communist party, the Ba'th party adopted it successfully for its extreme suitability to clandestine activities. In opposition for most of its life, the Ba'th discovered in the manipulable character of the cell a method by which it could survive the repressive measures of governments in most of the Arab world where it had branches.[3]

The cell is at the base of organization in the Arab Ba'th Socialist party.[4] It includes anywhere from three to seven members.[5] This is certainly a much smaller number than the Communist party cells described by Duverger.[6] There are two types of cells that exist side by side in the party: area cells which unite isolated members into one group and work cells based on the type of work performed by members. The cell usually meets once a week in the home of a member. The small size of the group makes such gatherings possible.[7] Coexistent with these two types of cells is a third, *Halqat al-Ansar* (Friend Cells). These latter cells perform two functions: (1) they are the training ground for prospective members, who must spend at least one year in such a cell, and (2) they are designed to attract as many "friends" and sympathizers to the party as possible. This latter function has served the party well, especially in Iraq. No written records are kept of "Friend" cells; the names and duties are memorized by "regulars." This served to protect the lives of the sympathizers from the harsh measures of the monarchist and later the Qasim regime in Iraq. In that country, for instance, the number of regular members never exceeded two thousand while the "Friends" numbered well over thirty thousand in 1963.[9]

The next rung on the party's organizational ladder is what is called *al-Firqah* (the Company). This is composed of from three to seven cells. All the members of the cells composing the Company meet and elect its leadership. The Amin Sir (Keeper of the Secret), or the secretary, as he shall be called henceforward for convenience, is appointed by the leadership of the higher organization, the Division, unless the Company is too far away and communications are difficult, in which case he is elected by the Company's membership. The secretaries of the several cells composing the Company are appointed by its leadership; they are not elected. The area encompassed by a company may include an entire small town, a village, or a section of a city.[11] Two or more companies constitute the next stage in the party's organization, the *Shu'bah* (the Division). The Division has a leadership command elected by a conference of the lower organizations. The Secretary of the Division is appointed by the leadership command of the superior organization. The duties of the command and of the secretary on this level are to receive and execute the decisions and instructions of higher organizations, to submit monthly reports on Division affairs, to scrutinize and examine complaints of lower organizations and of members, and to consider applications for membership and submit them to the higher organization. The Secretary of the Division is the only means of contact with the higher organizations and represents it in party conferences.[12]

Between the Divisional and Regional levels lies the intermediary called *al-Fir'* (Branch), which is composed of at least two Divisions. The area it covers can be a city, a *Qada* (county), or a *Liwa* (department). A conference composed of all the secretaries of the Divisions and a certain number of the command on the Divisional level meets and elects the leadership command of the Branch.[13] The command of the Branch and its secretary general are directly responsible before the Regional Command, the higher organization. The secretary of the Branch is elected by the command of that Branch, a fact which differentiates it from lower organizations. The Branch accepts the new members or rejects them, studies local problems and submits recommendations, is in charge of local party education and propaganda programs, and submits monthly reports to the higher organization. The secretary of the Branch keeps a record of its affairs and represents it in party meetings and conferences.

The Regional level of the party is the most active. A region is an entire country. Jordan, Iraq, Syria, Lebanon, Libya, Kuwait, and every other Arab country, from the Atlantic Ocean to the Persian Gulf, supposedly has its own regional organization. A Regional convention elects the Regional Command, which in turn elects its own secretary.[14] At the convention, the old Regional Command and its secretary may be forced to resign upon a vote of no confidence. The Regional convention also passes on major policy issues affecting the entire Region, considers and approves the budget of the party in that Region, and sends recommendations to the National Command.[15]

The Regional Command assumes the direction of the party politically, culturally, and ideologically. It accepts or expels members, carries on the policy decisions set forth by the highest party organ, the National Command, and may dissolve the leadership of any lower party organ if it deems necessary.[16]

Al-Hizb (the party) "is the national organization which includes all party organizations within and outside the Arab Fatherland."[17] There are Ba'th party organizations outside the Arab world, particularly among students in the United States, Great Britain, and France. The National Convention, which ideally assembles every two years, is the highest decision-making body of the party. The National Convention includes the membership of all the Regional Commands in the Arab world plus a certain number of delegates from lower organizations.[18] This convention elects the National Command and the secretary general of the party. The National Command at the present time must not exceed thirteen. Below is a list of the National Convention's powers and prerogatives:

1. To hear and discuss the recommendations of the National Command and its committees concerning all the problems of the party, and to make appropriate recommendations and decisions.
2. To hear and discuss the programs and policies submitted by the National Command, and to make appropriate recommendations and decisions.
3. To discuss the budget of the National Command, and to make appropriate recommendations and decisions.
4. To elect the National Command.
5. To vote on confidence in the National Command.[19]

The National Command is the highest policymaking and directive organization in the party. All members, leaders, and lower organizations must submit to its authority. It may assume direction of any Region, Division, or any other lower organization when it deems necessary. Such a function, however, has been exercised only once, in Iraq in November, 1963, when the Regional Command was hopelessly divided. It may accept or refuse cooperation with other political parties and governments. It may expel members from the Regional or National Command. It convenes the National Convention and prepares its agenda, and is in charge of all organizational, political, cultural, and financial aspects of the party. The National Command of the party, at present in Damascus, has seven offices dealing with organization, finance, culture and studies, information and propaganda, labor, peasants, and party education. Each office is headed by a member of the National Command.[20] Underlining the importance given party education, in 1963 the party created a "school to educate and graduate" prospective party leaders in Damascus.[21]

Communication between party organizations must be vertical, not horizontal. Contact between cells and companies or even between one region and the next is prohibited. It must go through the higher party organ. Within, the party applies the principle of criticism and self-criticism. Each member can voice his opinions, criticisms, and objections to any issue. But once a decision by the majority is made, the member, cell, or branch must carry it out regardless of personal feelings. Democratic centralism is a principle adhered to by the Ba'th party.

Democracy is achieved by criticism, self-criticism, and the election of higher organs by lower ones. Centralism is achieved by subjection of the minority to the majority and the lower organizations to the higher. A member must carry out the functions and orders assigned to him regardless of his personal opinion. He may voice objection "only after he has done his duty,"[22] and within the proper procedures and channels of the party.

Any citizen in the Arab fatherland or any Arab emigrant overseas may become a member if he accepts the Constitution and principles of the party. He must believe in Arab nationalism, be at least eighteen years of age, and not a member of any other political group. He must take the party oath,[23] be a "true example of the struggling Arab," pay party dues, defend the party, fulfill his duties, and belong to the associations or unions of his trade.[24] The latter requirement is aimed at facilitating the party's infiltration of other associations and groups.

Data as to the exact number of rank-and-file party members are unavailable. Aflaq, other party leaders in Syria, Jordan, and Lebanon, and even regular members refuse to divulge this information. Instead, they say that the party depends on the quality, not quantity, of members. Only the following estimates of membership can be given: Syria – 8,000; Iraq – 2,500; Jordan – 1,000; Lebanon-1,000.[25]

Inquiries about the finances of the party met the same response as those concerning the number of rank-and-file members. The *Internal Rules Manual*, however, states that the party's finances are drawn from monthly dues paid by members, donations, and revenue derived from party publications. The students, a special category, pay a fixed monthly sum plus a ratio of their monthly income determined on a progressive basis. The ratio and exact amount to be paid by the members are not mentioned in the *Manual*. They are decided upon by the Regional Command in each country. The Division may keep 10 per cent of its revenue for its own use: the Branch may keep 25 per cent for its own use. The remainder is to be handed over to the Regional Command. The manner of division of the 85 per cent of the revenue left to the Regional and National organizations is not explained.[26] At the present time, with the party in power in Syria, there is no doubt it receives financial support from the state, although such a statement cannot, at present, be documented.

Ba'th Party Organisation Chart

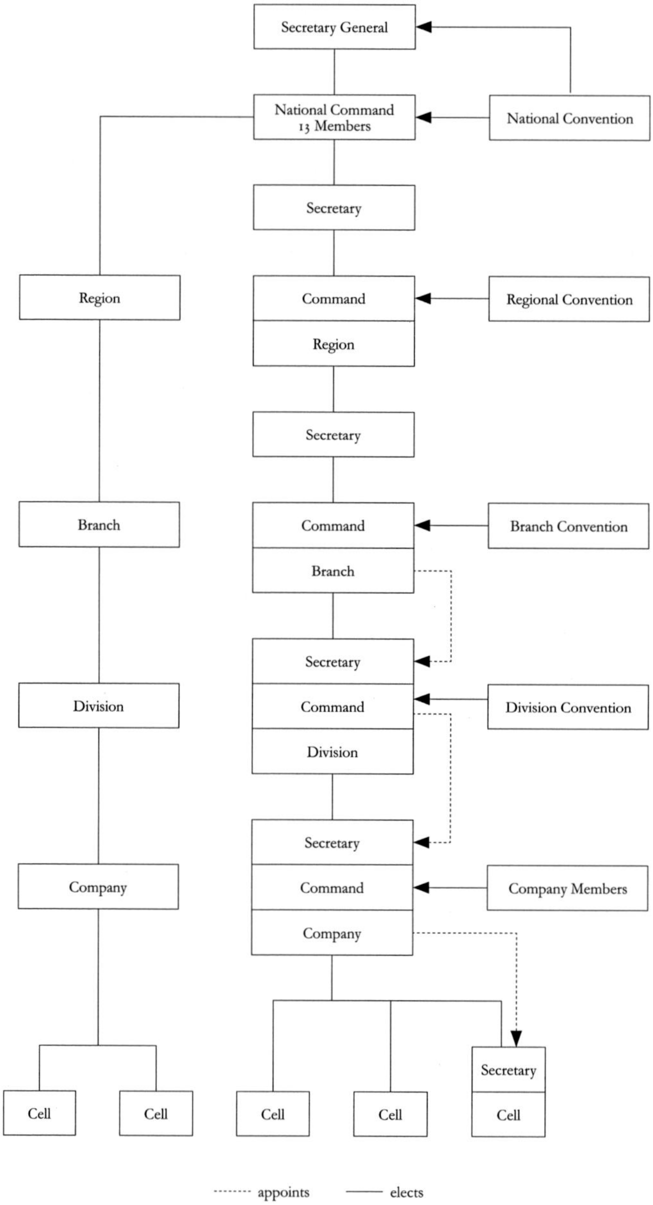

12 Conclusions

The Ba'th party, while primarily a nationalist movement, found in the manipulative character of socialism a means of providing a social content to its nationalism. By the admission of most Ba'th intellectuals and the party's Constitution, the Socialist aspect of the party is ancillary to its nationalism. Regarding itself as the image of the "new" Arab society, and seeing the Ba'thist as the embodiment of the virtues that once made the Arabs great, the party hopes to resurrect the glorious Arab past by transforming the values within each "self" in the Arab world.

The concept of socialism in the party's teaching was incorporated to ameliorate the backward conditions of the Arab world; to help this region industrialize and to provide the people with equal economic opportunity: economic democracy, in the parlance of the party, is practiced for the sake of strengthening the nation economically, militarily, socially, politically, and culturally so that it can stand equal among the great nations of the world and thus achieve the Arabs' "eternal mission" to civilization.

In discussing socialism and liberty, the party is moderate. While it is intensely xenophobic, remnants of Western liberalism can be traced in its ideology. The ideological polemics of the party can be traced to Rousseau rather than to Locke. This is natural considering the French influence in the Levant and the educational background of Aflaq and Bitar.

The actions of the state called for by this party should be performed with an eye to the "national interest." In the name of this vague and undefined principle, liberties may be curtailed and properties may be redistributed, nationalized, or even confiscated. The "general will," the general welfare, clearly is what the party works for, despite the lip service it pays to the individual and liberty. As noted in Chapter 1, the stand of the Ba'th party on the issues of liberty, a strong government, and a single party in practice if not in principle is similar to the stand taken by many leaders and movements elsewhere in the developing world.

The party has been vehemently anti-Communist since its establishment. Specifically it condemns Marxism as too utopian, too difficult to achieve. It deplores the Communist party's "internationalism," its stand against religion, and its dogmatic attitude toward economic determinism and class struggle. Nationalism, as seen by the party, can be used toward humanitarian ends; internally the party calls for a better social system and externally it demands independence, nonalignment, and the championing of liberation movements throughout the world. Taking a pluralistic approach toward society, the party opposes the single-mindedness and materialism of the Communists. While borrowing the internal organization of the Communist party, the Ba'th party has been an ardent foe of communism in the Arab world.

Internally the Ba'th party is organized on the cell basis. Like the Communist party, it adheres to the principle of democratic centralism, and it also insists on collective leadership at the top. Since the party visualizes itself as the vanguard to lead the nation to realization of its goals, its membership is quite restricted: each prospective member is rigorously screened before admission.

Founded in the early 1940s, the Arab Ba'th Socialist party may be considered a reaction to the Communist advance into the Middle East and as a revolt against the backwardness and weakness of the Arabs at mid-twentieth century. While it insists that the socialism it preaches is Arab rather than foreign, its ideology bears traces of Western liberalism. Its insistence on the Arabism of its ideology is a clear manifestation of its nationalism. Its assertion that its socialism is indigenous is similar to the claims of other "modernizing nationalisms" in Asia and Africa. The "unique" spirit of African culture, as Leopold Senghor puts it, cannot be captured by applying a strictly "foreign" ideology. This echoes the Ba'th insistence on the unique spirit of Arab culture. The amalgamation of Western Socialist ideas, Marxism, and certain aspects of the indigenous cultural heritage seems to be a phenomenon shared by the Ba'th with many of the leaders of developing countries.

Insofar as the party holds attitudes similar to those of other parties and groups in the emerging world toward the problems of an underdeveloped country, socialism, and neutrality, it differs greatly from the nonideological groups and parties traditionally found in the Arab world. With amazing tenacity, the party has clung to its ideological aspects as expounded in its Constitution and the writings of its intellectuals. On the altar of unity, the party did not hesitate to sacrifice its separate existence: it was willing to dissolve at Nasser's request in 1958.

Whether being in opposition most of the time or adhering to principles has helped it maintain its identity is difficult to determine. For even while in power, the Ba'th party is still in opposition to those interests in the Arab world that are not sympathetic to its principles. Even within Syria, where the party has been in power since March, 1963, it still faces stiff opposition from the "owner" classes.

In a society like that of Syria, where the extremes of wealth and poverty are so stark, the takeover by the Ba'th party was no mean matter. Thus, the transition of the party from "opposition" to "government" is not so smooth, not so acceptable as, say, the transition of the Labor party in Great Britain from "opposition" to "government."

The party's insistence on the indigenous nature of its socialism and its adherence to its ideology are prompted by both pride and utility – pride in the creativity of the Arabs who need not import their beliefs from abroad and utility in its sincere attempt at instilling a sense of "respectability" in modern Arabs, long accustomed to being ruled by outsiders. To instill in them a sense of respectability might move them toward the action and creativity demanded by the party.

To decide whether the party is sincere, and as honest as it tries to make people believe, is a very difficult task. Indeed, in the context of Arab politics and squabbles, truth is sometimes mixed with myth, facts flavored with propaganda, and seeming truths no more than hearsay. One thing, however, stands out in the Ba'th's favor: So far no politician or party has been able to prove the "corruptibility" of the party – a charge often made, but never proved and rarely believed. Even since the party takeover in Syria, its leaders now Cabinet ministers, high officials, and officers – have not succumbed to the usual temptations of office in which traditional Arab politicians have indulged. No serious charge of corruption has been heard from within or even from outside Syria.

The next question to be posed is whether the party's ideology makes a difference, now that it is in power. The fact is that the Ba'th leaders now in control in Syria seem to be a new breed of Arab politicians – dedicated young men. Whether it is their age that gives them their effervescence and zest, or the ideology of the Ba'th which they espouse, is a question that only time will answer. It appears that the party's ideology is the basis of present government policies in Syria. The party is attempting to put its socialism into practice. While this writer can produce little documentary evidence beyond Ba'th and Syrian government publications to prove this point, the fact remains that anyone can verify these statements for himself. So far, there has been no written record of the party's Socialist activities in Syria. But if the publications of the party and the Syrian government and personal statements from Middle Easterners are to be believed, the Ba'th party is putting its socialism into practice. Banks and large industrial and insurance companies have been nationalized. Land reform is being practiced. Large feudal estates are being broken up, land is being redistributed, and experimental collective farms are being established.

The Ba'th government lays claim to the development of health services and to the building of clinics and schools in the cities and the countryside.[1] The "revolution of rising expectations" has reached Syria as it has other places in the emerging world. For changes have been attempted and made, and Syrian society, governed by the Ba'th party, is becoming more and more attuned to such terminology such as *al-Khitta* (plan), "five-year plan," and "planned society". Such words are becoming familiar in Syria, and they do mean something. Their meaningfulness was evidenced by the Syrian business community's hostility to Ba'th domestic policies in March and April, 1964, at which time strikes and armed revolutions swept through Syria in an attempt to unseat the Ba'th party.

There are difficulties too perhaps too many. Resistance to innovation by "traditional" leadership is a problem. Another problem is the resistance of those elements whose assets and lands have been nationalized. Outside Syria as well as within, there are difficulties of a political nature which are as serious and substantial as those of economic character. The party finds itself having to compete with Nasser. Nasser's image is strong in Syria and he loses little opportunity to foment trouble for the Ba'th regime. The Ba'th idea of Pan-Arabism, a union of all Arab states, places it in direct opposition to those Arab regimes that wish to maintain the status quo. Lebanon, Jordan, and Saudi Arabia are clear examples of regimes bitterly hostile to the Ba'th idea of Arab unity. In these countries, as in the rest of the Arab world, there are vested interests anxious to maintain the status quo. The roots of many of these interests go back to the Ottoman Empire. For many of the Ottoman vilayets' (Districts') boundaries coincided with those "artificial" boundaries created by the Western "imperialists."

Moreover, the Ba'th party's assumption of the role of vanguard to lead the Arabs to unity places it in direct opposition to Nasser, who claims such a role for himself. There is no doubt that competition from Nasser weakens the Ba'th party throughout the Middle East. Nasser, in the eyes of many Arabs, is a successful leader. His success can be observed both on the domestic scene, where reforms are tangible, and on the international scene, where he has emerged as a figure of some importance. Many Arabs are impressed with his role as a leader of the neutral world. The size of Egypt's population alone, the largest in the Arab world, gives Nasser a leading voice in Arab affairs.

The anti-Western attitude of the Ba'th does not endear it to the Western powers. Committed to a policy of maintaining the status quo in the Arab world and held responsible by the Ba'th party for the "division" of the Arab lands in the first place, the Western powers are naturally unsympathetic to the ideology and activity of a party such as the Ba'th. Further, like other nationalist groups in the Arab world, the Ba'th blames the Western powers for the creation and maintenance of the State of Israel. Ba'th hostility to the Western powers deprives Syria of any Western economic or technical aid. Nor would the Ba'th – many Ba'thists say – accept such aid from the Western powers were it forthcoming. One Western diplomat in Beirut noted that Ba'thists will not even meet socially with Western diplomats at embassy parties, to say nothing of negotiating economic or trade agreements. There is no doubt that this hostility to the West "costs" the Ba'th in terms of whatever aid or technical assistance it could get were such hostility not present. On the other hand, Ba'th xenophobia enhances its prestige among the nationalists while at the same time making it impossible for any adversary to accuse the party leaders of being "stooges" or "tools" of Western imperialists.

Nor does Ba'th hostility to the Communist party endear it to the Soviet Union. The Ba'th party attempts to differentiate between the "local" Communist party, which it has fought and continues to fight bitterly, and the Soviet party, with which it tries to maintain friendly relations. This attitude toward the Communists no doubt troubles the Soviet government. At times the Soviet government has taken sides in the disputes and rivalries within the Ba'th party. Early in 1964 the Soviet government hailed Sa'di's splinter group within the Ba'th party as "progressive" while condemning the majority Ba'th, led by Aflaq, as "reactionary." Moreover, the Ba'th's sympathetic attitude toward what it calls the "Yugoslav experiment" has displeased the Soviet Union. Holding a sympathetic attitude towards the "Socialist camp" in general, the Ba'th party found itself "more" sympathetic to the "national" communism of Tito. Since 1949 *al-Ba'th* has given broad coverage to the news and "experiments" of Yugoslavia. And while party polemics and *al-Ba'th* contain little allusion to the Sino-Soviet dispute, the party seems more sympathetic toward the Chinese. After all, the Chinese are Oriental. Also, being less involved in the issues that rock the Middle East, the Chinese are more generous in their declamations championing the Arab cause.

It is indeed amazing that a party like the Ba'th has been able to stay in power as long as it has. What with schisms within its own ranks, Nasser's hostility and active fight against it, the resistance and hostility of the "haves" within Syria, an unfriendly West and a similarly unfriendly East, the party's survival is nothing short of amazing. Nasser's threat to the survival of the Ba'th as the governing party in Syria is serious. At present, and for the foreseeable future, Nasser's hostility will continue. The mere existence of the Ba'th in Syria is a personal affront to him. He will not rest until he sees its downfall, as he did not rest until he saw the downfall of Qasim in Iraq. At the moment the most serious threat to the Ba'th party is the economic difficulties it faces in Syria. Should it be able to solve these – admittedly a difficult task -it might survive Nasser's hostility indefinitely.

Within Syria the only group or power capable of toppling the Ba'th is the army, but the party so far has been able to infiltrate and dominate the officers' group. Discharged anti-Ba'th officers and enlisted men have been given similar, even better-paying positions outside the army. In this way, the party hopes to avoid creating a hard core of discontent and opposition. With the army under control, the Ba'th party has a good chance of surviving.

Throughout the Arab world Damascus has now become acknowledged as a spokesman of Pan-Arabism and socialism.

Just what this will mean in the long run is not clear at the moment. The entire region is in the process of transition. This can be seen in the strong influence and appeal acquired by the Soviet Union and the Socialist camp. In the 1960s the Soviet Union was building the High Aswan Dam in Egypt and giving military aid to Syria, Egypt, Yemen, Iraq, Morocco, and the Sudan. Even Jordan and Tunisia, who have maintained a hostile attitude toward the Communist nations, have already established diplomatic relations with the Soviet Union and received its aid. Between the Ba'th and the Nasserites a lively competition is still going on. The outcome of this competition is of importance to other Arab countries, and perhaps to the world at large. The split in Ba'th ranks in February, 1966, no doubt has weakened the party's position *vis-à-vis* Nasser, but the Ba'th hangs on and is unlikely to be replaced by another group in Syria (except, perhaps, the Communists) in the near future.

European domination over the area is terminated, but the ideas which it generated are still alive – very much alive. The Arab revolution, begun during the First World War, is still in progress, but it has thus far failed to generate a unified ideological basis. And the diversity of the Arab world has defeated efforts at unity. Aflaq and Nasser, both products of this revolution, stand witness to the failure of the Pan-Arab movement. Prophets of change, neither has succeeded in becoming the "Father of his Country" – a unified Arab world. The U.A.R. from 1958 to 1961 was a spontaneous effort torn asunder by centrifugal forces.

The Ba'th party, which like Nasser hoped to lead the revolution, has become only another centrifugal force. Should the Ba'th party soon be ousted from power in Syria, its influence will nevertheless remain. Ideas die hard, and the Ba'th is an ideological movement. Ideological movements are best judged in retrospect, for it is difficult to judge them while the processes they advocate are in progress. If the Ba'th succeeds in holding on to power, as seems likely, Syria will remain a center of anxiety and agitation exporting these to its neighbors. These products are welcome neither among the conservative regimes, which wish to maintain the status quo, nor among the progressive regimes, which see in the Ba'th a militant rival. Propaganda warfare between these various regimes will go on.

Appendix A: Decisions of the Sixth National Convention of the Arab Ba'th Socialist Party, 1963[1]

INTRODUCTION

Following are the general decisions of the Sixth National Convention of the Arab Ba'th Socialist party:

The struggle of the Arab Ba'th Socialist party has been continuous for approximately twenty years. During this period the people, led by the party, have offered many martyrs at the altar of the struggle for Arab national unity, liberty, and socialism. The Arab Ba'th Socialist party was able to outline the course of the Arab struggle with precision and understanding. It was able to crystallize the desires and goals of the Arab peoples in two spheres: the national sphere and the Socialist sphere. Furthermore, the party was able, during the negative aspects of the struggle, to incarnate the Arab peoples' ambitions and their revulsion toward the underdeveloped, exploited, and dismembered Arab present.

During twenty years of struggle the party has been able to incorporate itself truthfully in the struggle of the Arab peoples. It was able to lead successfully such struggles in Syria and Iraq; to deprive aristocracy, reactionaries, and the bourgeoisie of the leadership of Arab nationalism, to convert the nationalist movement into the momentum of the struggle of the millions. This party promises the Arab masses to walk side by side with them

1 Printed in *al-Nahar*, October 29, 1963. Translated by the author.

unhesitatingly and untiringly in their nationalist struggle for Arab unity.

The party has been able to bring into the Arab nationalist movement the spirit of the modern age. It has accomplished this by tying its interests to those of the struggling masses and by linking together the nationalist and Socialist revolutions. Today, the party promises the masses that it will continue to march with fortitude with the struggling masses to achieve the Socialist revolution and to renew the slogans which it has carried and fought for since its inception.

The party contributed toward creation of the first national revolutionary cadre for the Arabs in their modern history when it helped bring about the union of 1958 and sacrificed itself at the altar of that union.

After the destruction of that union, the party was able to reorganize itself, lead the masses, and face courageously the separatist regime that was an enemy of Arab nationalism and unity. This facilitated the downfall of the separatist reactionary regime in Damascus which had been exhausted by the attacks made by the Ba'th. On the morning of March 8, the vanguard of the Arab Ba'th Socialist party were leading forces to bury the black separatist regime.

New circumstances have arisen that will facilitate great victories in the spheres of nationalism and socialism. The Cairo Covenant of April 17 [1964] was the product of the new circumstances brought about by the people's struggle led by the party. The Cairo authorities were not able to understand the new atmosphere of the Arab struggle, thus they refused to cooperate with the party and declared their withdrawal from the Covenant.

Under these new circumstances the Sixth National Convention of the Arab Ba'th Socialist party was convened. On the threshold to positive struggle, the constructive struggle, the Sixth National Convention meets.

It meets full of hope and determination to lead the new battle. It meets with the same faith in the Arab people and with cognizance of the historical responsibility placed upon it.

The Convention commenced its meetings on October 5, 1963, and terminated on October 23, 1963. The Convention discussed the party organization and direction of the authorities in the two Regions and studied some theoretical problems facing the Arab struggle; appropriate decisions were made.

The Convention also discussed the political union of the two Regions – the Syrian and Iraqi – and the application of Socialist measures. It made appropriate decisions.

The Convention discussed Arab international political problems and made appropriate decisions.

What follows are the principal decisions of the Convention. Full explanations of these decisions will be issued later.

ORGANIZATIONAL PROBLEMS OF THE PARTY AND THE PARTY'S RELATION TO THE MASSES AND TO THE AUTHORITIES

1. The Convention studied, in a general way, the organizational problems of the party and reafirmed its principle of collective leadership In party activity; this, to reflect the democracy of the party at the top.

The Convention concluded that the party's experience has confirmed the principle of democratic centralism in which it believes. The establishment of a balance between centralism on the one hand and democracy on the other permits the free and responsible exercise of the party's struggle, and also preserves party unity while on the other hand realizing democracy.

2. In a serious study of the party's situation in Syria and Iraq, the Convention paid particular attention to the forthcoming Socialist revolution. The Convention agreed that the social composition of the party would influence the Socialist revolution. Therefore, the Convention decided that the party's Socialist goals must be a reflection of its social composition since the Socialist revolution would rest on workers and peasants who must be at the base of the revolution and the party at the same time.
3. In these circumstances where the party is in authority in both the Syrian and Iraqi Regions, the Convention warns against the infiltration of the party by opportunists, or the succumbing of some party elements to the temptations of power that will cause them to look down on the non-party masses.

The Convention affirmed that membership in the party could only mean a tremendous responsibility to be borne by the member. Members should confine themselves to carrying out their responsibilities. Their rights are the same as those accorded to any citizen without the addition of any privileges.

The Convention agreed that the nonparty masses have the right to criticize and oversee party members. The Convention considers this supervision by the nonparty masses a natural right of the people that guarantees that process of rapport between the people and the party and between the party and the authorities.

This popular supervision was considered a means to check against the temptations of power and a means to check against the rise of bourgeois tendencies within the party.

The Convention emphasized that careful attention be paid to the behavior of prospective party members, that requirements for membership be made more stringent, and that the period of party training be lengthened to make certain of the prospective member's characteristics and readiness to struggle.

4. Regarding the relation between the party and the state, the Convention decided upon the necessity of complete separation between the state and the party. It cautioned against the possibility of party involvement in the routine of day-to-day government. The Convention considers the party as leader and director of the basic political problems of the state.

The Convention recognized the necessity of having a larger proportion of party leadership devoted to the direction of party activity.

DECISIONS CONCERNING SOME THEORETICAL PROBLEMS DEALING WITH THE PARTY IDEOLOGY AND THE ARAB NATIONAL STRUGGLE

5. The Convention discussed a number of problems of the Arab struggle. It discussed some of the theoretical problems dealing with Arab unity, socialism, popular democracy, and the party's stand *vis-à-vis* international Socialist thought. The Convention recognized the two basic characteristics of the party's ideology, pragmatism and revolutionism, within the national framework.

The Convention then criticized some of the outdated opinions and thoughts left behind as the party ideology advanced. Such criticism allows the ideological evolution of the party to meet future needs while maintaining continuity with the party's heritage, in a manner that guarantees the ideological and organizational unity of the party and provides for revolutionary and scientific solutions to the problems of the Arab national struggle.

PROBLEMS OF THE SOCIALIST PROGRAM IN THE TWO REGIONS OF SYRIA AND IRAQ

6. The Convention discussed the problems of conversion to a Socialist regime in the Regions of Syria and Iraq and decided

to proceed with it on a democratic basis and with popular participation. Following a scientific discussion of the sociopolitical and class composition in the two Regions of Syria and Iraq, the Convention reiterated that the party should be based in the masses in preparation for the establishment of a revolutionary and democratic experiment in the two Regions that will influence the course of events in the entire Arab fatherland and provide the objective circumstances for interaction with other movements in the Arab fatherland.

7. On the basis of a scientific analysis of economic and political conditions in the two Regions, the Convention concluded that the bourgeoisie is unable to carry out any positive task in the economic sphere. Furthermore, the opportunism of the bourgeoisie qualifies it for the role of ally to the new colonialism. The workers, peasants, revolutionary civil and military intelligentsia, and the petit bourgeoisie were considered the proper forces for achievement of the Socialist revolution in its initial stage.

8. In an attempt to visualize the extent of Socialist evolution in the two Regions, and guided by Socialist experiments elsewhere in the world, the Convention asserted the necessity of democratic workers' participation in administration in the two Regions during the stage of state capitalism.

The Convention cautioned against bureaucratic tendencies and stressed the necessity for a continual curbing and eventual liquidation of such tendencies.

9. The Convention paid particular attention to the growth of governmental agencies and the relation of these to the party and the masses.

The Convention approved a detailed policy of a revolutionary and democratic development of these agencies in a manner that would permit them to participate fully in the process of conversion to socialism. The Convention asserted that the principal task would be proper evolution rather than mutation. Evolution should be the basis, mutation the exception. Such a plan is necessitated by humane considerations and by a faith in the citizens' consciousness.

As for the land problem, the Convention concluded with revolutionary and Socialist decisions. The Convention agreed on the necessity of take-off from a revolutionary basis, and considered the agricultural revolution as a necessary step toward a quick economic development in the industrial sector. Thus the goal of establishing collective farms, administered by the peasants themselves, in those lands covered by agricultural reform, was considered the proper Socialist take-off point for the oncoming change in social relationships. Such a revolutionary goal, coupled with peasant participation in the agricultural sphere, is a necessary element in the success of the Socialist revolution.

10. The Convention also asserted the importance of Socialist planning in the regional and Arab spheres. Planning was considered the practical method by which all the national material, human, and natural resources could be scientifically and practically utilized. The Convention also emphasized industrialization and industrial development. Investments should be centered in those more important spheres that guarantee real national economic development, rather than in those ostentatious accomplishments that do not increase real production.

11. The Convention laid out a Socialist policy in the field of social services. It drew attention to the apparent paradox between ostentatious and unnecessary spending in government and the low standard of living of the masses. Austerity should be practiced by the well-to-do and the government agencies as well.

The Convention considered the problems of education and the establishment of compulsory education. It stressed the need to eradicate illiteracy and to give the education of youth a scientific and national coloring that would go hand in hand with human knowledge. The education plan should correspond with the requirements of development and should stress higher specialization. It should look to an expansion of the scientific fields in the universities and to raising their standards.

The Convention agreed on the necessity of expanding services in the rural areas and the poor and distant districts. Free and socialized medicine was considered the most basic aspect of Socialist thought. The Convention put forth the policy to execute this program beginning with expansion of medical school facilities and expansion of present government medical services until the eventual liquidation of private medicine.

12. The Convention studied the National Guard program. Despite some of the shortcomings and mistakes of this program it was considered a safeguard of the revolution. The Guard should be expanded and developed to become capable of fulfilling revolutionary tasks and educating the masses. Any mistakes committed by members of the National Guard should be dealt with firmly.

The Convention affirmed the right of popular organizations for workers, students, professionals, and women that are within the national Socialist line. It affirmed the associations' relative autonomy with regard to the state as long as the latter is in the process of achieving its Socialist program. The existence of such associations was considered a necessity dictated by the interests of groups and classes. The Convention affirmed the right of the working class to have political parties.

13. The Convention paid particular attention to ideological education in the Armed Forces and affirmed the right of its members to practice their full political rights. The Convention

considered the organic incorporation of the revolutionary civilian and military vanguard as the only way to create an ideological interaction between the two groups. This would mean a practical unity of action and thought and would incorporate the popular and armed forces in a combined Socialist effort. Ideological education for the armed forces would create a new and revolutionary understanding between the officers and the men.

The Convention affirmed the necessity of compulsory military service in an underdeveloped country where such service could become a school for peasant soldiers, thus sharing in the eradication of illiteracy in the rural areas.

CONTEMPORARY PROBLEMS OF THE ARAB STRUGGLE

14. Following Cairo's withdrawal from the Tripartite Unity Agreement, the party finds itself compelled to establish unity between Syria and Iraq. Thus the Convention agreed on the principle of establishing a federal union between the Syrian and Iraqi Regions. The Convention regarded the new union as a step toward complete Arab unity and one capable of fusing the revolutionary energies in the two Regions. The new state was considered as a stage in the struggle for complete unity, and open for others to join.

The Convention affirmed that the biggest unionist stride is that which brings Egypt to the new nation on the basis of democracy, regional equality, and collective leadership.

15. The Convention considered the reactionary aggression by the Maghrib on the Algerian revolution. The essence of the problem was not a mere border dispute; rather, the Convention considered the aggression only as another aspect of the struggle between progressivism and reaction in the African part of the

Arab fatherland. The Convention insisted that the support of the Algerian revolution, with all its national, Socialist, revolutionary, and Arab characteristics, is a guarantee of the success of the unionist Socialist revolution in the entire Arab fatherland.

Therefore, the party stands unhesitatingly with the Algerian revolution against the Maghrib reactionary aggression supported by the new and old colonialism. It calls on the governments of Syria and Iraq to offer the Algerian revolution any assistance it may require.

16. The first aspect of the resistance of Arab reaction is portrayed in its aggression on the Algerian revolution. The second aspect is its conspicuous and frank subservience to colonialism – a subservience that compels it to betray the Arab national cause daily. Thus the repressive measures utilized by the reactionary Maghrib authorities against *Al-Ittihad al-Watani Li al-Quwah al-Sha'biyyah* [The National Union of Popular Forces] are an aspect of subservience to imperialism and a defense of the imperialist spheres of influence in the Maghrib. The Convention decided to condemn the repressive measures taken against *Al-Itthad al-Watani Li al-Quwah al Sha'biyyah* and declare its support of the latter against the forces of reaction and imperialism.

17. The Convention carefully considered the problem of diversion or pumping of the waters of the River Jordan and considered such a scheme a supreme military danger to the Arab fatherland. Thus the party calls on all the Arab peoples and their governments to resist this danger by force. The governments of Syria and Iraq in particular must resist this danger. It also calls on the United Arab government to resist this scheme even by the use of force and to cooperate in this endeavor with Syria and Iraq.

18. The Convention considered the Yemenite revolution and saw in it another aspect of the struggle between the Arab reactionary

forces and the Arab peoples. The Convention saw in the Yemenite revolution a revolutionary take-off point to save the Arab south and the Arabian peninsula from the reactionaries and imperialist stooges. The Convention calls on all the progressive Arab forces to rally around the Yemenite revolution and support it against the reactionaries. In particular, the Convention calls on the revolutionary authorities in Syria and Iraq to aid and support the Yemenite revolution. Such support should be viewed as a duty imposed by Arab destiny and an element in the defeat of reaction.

19. The Convention discussed the positive and negative aspects of Abdel Nasser's regime and reiterated the importance of the presence of the United Arab Republic, quantitatively and qualitatively, in any union.

The positive aspects of Abdel Nasser's regime prompt the party to accept a union with it. The negative aspects, however, compel the party to accept Abdel Nasser's regime only as a partner but not as the basis of the union. The party considers this a condition that permits the process of correction and interaction of the revolutionary Arab movements. The Convention affirmed that Abdel Nasser's autocratic regime had imposed on the party an unnecessary struggle with it.

The Convention agreed on the necessity of halting this struggle and finding mutual points of understanding among the libertarian Arab movements.

20. The Convention studied carefully the development of the contemporary Arab problem in Palestine and concluded the necessity of recruiting the Palestinian Arabs as the first tool in the liberation of Palestine.

The Convention recommends the establishment of a Palestine Liberation Front and calls on all Arab governments, and on Syria and Iraq in particular, to offer all available resources to the establishment of this Front. All the necessary tools and revolutionary leadership should be provided. The Front must be kept out of disputes among Arab states.

21. From its deep faith in the unity of the entire Arab world, the Convention stresses the necessity of establishing a Progressive Arab Front to include the entire Arab fatherland.

22. The Convention reafirmed the basic revolutionary policy that has been pursued by the party since its establishment and that endeavors to support all national liberation movements against imperialism. The Convention exposed the recent methods of cooperation between the bourgeoisie and neoimperialism in defining the party's stand *vis-à-vis* imperialism by explaining its role as a Socialist party belonging to a persecuted and colonized people. Therefore, the Convention cautioned against the belief that the construction of a Socialist society that places the people's interest first cannot be completed without entailing a struggle against imperialism, and against every aspect of the exploitation of man.

23. The Convention affirmed the policy of nonalignment with international power blocs, and neutrality in the daily disputes of the blocs.

24. But nonalignment should not be construed as a bar against closer and friendlier relations with the peoples of the Socialist camp.

25. The Convention affirmed the necessity of strengthening the ties with the nations of the Third World, to which we belong and which pursues the policy of positive neutrality. Closer ties will mean strengthening the Front against imperialism.

26. The Convention decided to fight all types of racial discrimination in the world and to consider such a phenomenon as another characteristic of colonial capitalism. The Convention

views South Africa as a new kind of Israel in Africa. The party stands against racial discrimination in this nation and extends its helping hand to all peoples struggling against the new and old imperialism.

Appendix B: Constitution of the Arab Ba'th Socialist Party[2]

FUNDAMENTAL PRINCIPLES

First Principle: Unity and Freedom of the Arab Nation

The Arabs form one nation. This nation has the natural right to live in a single state and to be free to direct its own destiny.

The Party of the Arab Ba'th therefore believes that:

1) The Arab fatherland constitutes an indivisible political and economic unity. No Arab country can live apart from the others.

2) The Arab nation constitutes a cultural unity. Any differences existing among its sons are accidental and unimportant. They will all disappear with the awakening of the Arab consciousness.

3) The Arab fatherland belongs to the Arabs. They alone have the right to administer its affairs, to dispose of its wealth, and to direct its destinies.

Second Principle: Personality of the Arab Nation

The Arab nation is characterized by virtues which are the result of its successive rebirths. These virtues are characterized by vitality and creativeness and by an ability for transformation and renewal. Its renewal is always linked to growth in personal freedom, and harmony between its evolution and the national interest.

---

2 Translated by Sylvia Ham, *Arab Nationalism: An Anthology* (Berkeley: University of California Press, 1962), pp. 233-41.

The Party of the Arab Ba'th therefore believes that:

1) Freedom of speech, freedom of assembly, freedom of belief, as well as artistic freedom, are sacred. No authority can diminish them.

2) The value of the citizens is measured once all opportunities have been given them – by the action they take to further the progress and prosperity of the Arab nation, without regard to any other criterion.

Third Principle: The Mission of the Arab Nation

The Arab nation has an eternal mission. This mission reveals itself in ever new and related forms through the different stages of history. It aims at the renewal of human values, at the quickening of human progress, at increasing harmony and mutual help among the nations.

The Party of the Arab Ba'th therefore believes that:

1) Colonialism and all that goes with it is a criminal enterprise. The Arabs must fight it with all possible means, just as they must take it on themselves to help, according to their physical and moral abilities, all peoples fighting for their freedom.

2) Humanity constitutes a whole, the interests of which are solidarity and the values and civilization of which are common to all. The Arabs are enriched by world civilization and enrich it in their turn. They stretch a fraternal hand to other nations and collaborate with them for the establishment of just institutions which will ensure for all the peoples prosperity and peace, as well as moral and spiritual advance.

GENERAL PRINCIPLES

Article 1. The Party of the Arab Ba'th is a universal Arab party. It has branches in all the Arab countries. It does not concern itself with regional politics except in relation to the higher interests of the Arab cause.

Article 2. The headquarters of the party is for the time being located in Damascus. It can be transferred to any other Arab city if the national interest should require it.

Article 3. The Party of the Arab Ba'th is a national party. It believes that nationalism is a living and eternal reality. It believes that the feeling of national awakening which intimately unites the individual to his nation is a sacred feeling. This feeling has within itself a potential of creative power; it binds itself to sacrifice, it seeks the exercise of responsibilities, and it directs the individual personality in a concrete and active manner.

The national idea to which the party appeals is the will of the Arab people to free themselves and to unite. It demands that the opportunity be given to it to realize in history its Arab personality, and to collaborate with all the nations in all the fields which will ensure the march of humanity toward welfare and progress.

Article 4. The Party of the Arab Ba'th is a Socialist party. It believes that socialism is a necessity which emanates from the depth of Arab nationalism itself. Socialism constitutes, in fact, the ideal social order which will allow the Arab people to realize its possibilities and to enable its genius to flourish, and which will ensure for the nation constant progress in its material and moral output. It makes possible a trustful brotherhood among its members.

Article 5. The Party of the Arab Ba'th is a popular party. It believes that sovereignty is the property of the people, who alone are the source of all authority. It believes that the value of the state is the outcome of the will of the masses from which it issues and that this value is sacred only to the extent that the masses have exercised their choice freely. That is why, in the accomplishment of its mission, the party relies on the people with whom it seeks to establish intricate contact, the spiritual, moral, material, and physical level of whom it is trying to raise, in order that the people may become conscious of its personality and that it may become able to exercise its right in private and public life.

Article 6. The Party of the Arab Ba'th is revolutionary. It believes that its main objectives for the realization of the renaissance of Arab nationalism or for the establishment of socialism cannot be achieved except by means of revolution and struggle. To rely on slow evolution and to be satisfied with a partial and superficial reform is to threaten these aims and to conduce to their failure and their loss.

This is why the party decides in favor of:

1) The struggle against foreign colonialism, in order to liberate the Arab fatherland completely and finally.

2) The struggle to gather all the Arabs in a single independent state.

3) The overthrow of the present faulty structure – an overthrow which will include all the sectors of intellectual, economic, social, and political life.

Article 7. The Arab fatherland is that part of the globe inhabited by the Arab nation which stretches from the Taurus Mountain, the Pocht-i-Kouh Mountains, the Gulf of Basra, the Arab Ocean, the Ethiopian Mountains, the Sahara, the Atlantic Ocean, and the Mediterranean.

Article 8. The official language of the state, as well as that of all the citizens, is Arabic. It alone is recognized in correspondence and in teaching.

Article 9. The emblem of the Arab state is that of the Arab revolution begun in 1916 to liberate and unify the Arab nation.

Article 10. An Arab is he whose language is Arabic, who has lived on Arab soil, or who, after having been assimilated to Arab life, has faith in his belonging to the Arab nation.

Article 11. To be excluded from the Arab fatherland: whoever has fought for or has belonged to a factious anti-Arab association, whoever has lent himself inside the Arab fatherland to colonial ends.
Article 12. The Arab woman enjoys all the rights of citizenship. The party struggles to raise up woman's level in order to make her fit to exercise these rights.
Article 13. The party strives to give all the citizens the same opportunities in the field of schooling and livelihood in order that, in the various aspects of human activity, everyone should be equally able to show his real abilities and to develop them to the maximum.

THE WAY: INTERNAL POLICY OF THE PARTY

Article 14. The regime of the Arab state will be a constitutional parliamentary regime. Executive power is responsible before the legislative, which is directly elected by the people.
Article 15. The national tie is the only tie that may exist in the Arab state. It ensures harmony among all the citizens by melting them in the crucible of a single nation and counteracts all religious, communal, tribal, racial, or regional factions.
Article 16. The administrative system of the Arab state is a system of decentralization.
Article 17. The party strives to make popular feeling universal and to make the power of the people a living reality in the life of the individual. It undertakes to give the state a constitution guaranteeing to all Arab citizens absolute equality before the law, the right to express their opinions in absolute freedom, and a true choice of their representatives, thus ensuring for them a free life within the framework of the law.
Article 18. A single code of laws is to be established freely for the whole of the Arab nation. This code will be in conformity

with the spirit of the times and will take into account the past experiences of the Arab nation.

Article 19. The judicial power will be independent. It will be free from inference by other powers and enjoy total immunity.

Article 20. The rights of citizenship are granted in their totality to every citizen living on Arab soil who is devoted to the Arab fatherland and who has no connection with any factious association.

Article 21. Military service is compulsory in the Arab fatherland.

FOREIGN POLICY OF THE PARTY

Article 22. The foreign policy of the Arab state will be guided by the interests of Arab nationalism and of the eternal mission of the Arabs which seeks to establish in cooperation with other nations a free, harmonious, and secure world, continuously advancing in progress.

Article 23. The Arabs will struggle with all their power to destroy the foundations of colonialism and of foreign occupation and to suppress all foreign political or economic influence in their country.

Article 24. Since the Arab people is the sole source of power, all treaties, pacts, and documents concluded by governments which detract from the total sovereignty of the Arabs will be abrogated.

Article 25. Arab foreign policy seeks to give a true picture of the will of the Arabs to live in freedom, and of their sincere desire to see all other nations enjoy the same liberty.

ECONOMIC POLICY OF THE PARTY

Article 26. The Party of the Arab Ba'th is a Socialist party. It believes that the economic wealth of the fatherland belongs to the nation.

Article 27. The present distribution of wealth in the Arab fatherland is unjust. Therefore a review and a just redistribution will become necessary.

Article 28. The equality of all the citizens is founded on human values. This is why the party forbids the exploitation of the work of others.

Article 29. Public utilities, extensive natural resources, big industry, and the means of transport are the property of the nation. The state will manage them directly and will abolish private companies and foreign concessions.

Article 30. Ownership of agricultural land will be so limited as to be in proportion to the means of the proprietor to exploit all his lands without exploitation of the efforts of others. This will be under the control of the state and in conformity with its over-all economic plan.

Article 31. Small industrial ownership will be so limited as to be related to the standard of living of the citizens of the state as a whole.

Article 32. Workers will participate in the management of their factory. In addition to their wages fixed by the state-they will receive a proportion of the profits, also fixed by the state.

Article 33. Ownership of immovable property is allowed to all the citizens so long as they do not exploit it to the harm of others, and so long as the state ensures for all citizens a minimum of immovable property.

Article 34. Property and inheritance are two natural rights. They are protected within the limits of the national interest.

Article 35. Usurious loans are prohibited between citizens. One state bank is to be founded to issue currency, which the national output will back. This bank will finance the vital agricultural and industrial plans of the nation.

Article 36. The state will control directly internal and external trade in order to abolish the exploitation of the consumer by the producer. The state will protect them both, as it will protect the national output against the competition of foreign foods and will ensure equilibrium between exports and imports.

Article 37. General planning, inspired by the most modern economic ideas, will be organized so that the Arab fatherland will be industrialized, national production developed, new outlets opened for it, and the industrial economy of each region directed according to its potential and to the raw material it contains.

SOCIAL POLICY OF THE PARTY

Article 38. Family, Procreation, Marriage.

§1) The family is the basic cell of the nation. It is for the state to protect, to develop, and to help it.

§2) Procreation is a trust given in the first place to the family, and then to the state. Both must ensure its increase, and look to the health and education of the descendants.

§3) Marriage is a national duty. The state must encourage it, facilitate it, and control it.

Article 39. Public Health. The state will build, at its expense, institutions of preventive medicine, dispensaries, and hospitals which will meet the needs of all citizens, for whom the state ensures free medical treatment.

Article 40. Labor.

§1) Labor is an obligation for all those who are capable of it. It is for the state to ensure that work is available to every citizen, whether intellectual or manual.

§2) The employer must ensure at the least a decent standard of living for his employee.

§3) The state sees to the maintenance of all persons incapable of work.

§4) Just laws will be promulgated to limit the workman's daily hours of work, to give him the right to paid weekly and annual holidays, to protect his rights, to ensure social security for him in old age, and to indemnify him for any cessation of work, whether partial or total.

§5) Free workmen's and peasants' unions will be established and encouraged, so that they may constitute an instrument efficient in the defense of their rights, in raising their standard of living, in developing their abilities, in increasing the opportunities offered to them, in creating among them a spirit of solidarity, and in representing them in joint works councils.

§6) Joint works councils will be created in which the state and the unions of workmen and peasants will be represented. These councils will have power to decide the issues arising among the unions, the works managers, and the representatives of the state.

Article 41. Culture and Society.

§1) The party seeks to develop a general national culture for the whole Arab fatherland which shall be Arab, liberal, progressive, extensive, profound, and humanist; it attempts to disseminate it in all sections of the population.

§2) The state is responsible for the protection of the liberty of speech, of publication, of assembly, of protest, and of the press, within the limits of the higher Arab national interest. It is for the state to facilitate all the means and the modalities which tend to realize this liberty.

§3) Intellectual work is one of the most sacred kinds. It is the state's concern to protect and encourage intellectuals and scientists.

§4) Within the limits of the Arab national idea, every freedom will be given for the foundation of clubs, associations, parties, youth groupings, and tourist organizations, as well as for obtaining profit from the cinema, radio, television, and all the other facilities of modern civilization in order to spread generally the national culture, and to contribute to the entertainment of the people.

Article 42. Separation of the classes and differentiation among them are abolished. The separation of the classes is the consequence of a faulty social order. Therefore, the party carries on its struggle among the laboring and oppressed classes of society so that such separation and differentiation will come to an end and the citizens will recover the whole of their human dignity and will be enabled to live in the shadow of a just social order in which nothing will distinguish one citizen from another except intellectual capacity and manual skill.

Article 43. Nomadism. Nomadism is a primitive social state. It decreases the national output and makes an important part of the nation a paralyzed member and an obstacle to its development and progress. The party struggles for the sedentarization of nomads by the grant of lands to them, for the abolition of tribal customs, and for the application to the nomads of the laws of the state.

POLICY OF THE PARTY IN EDUCATION AND TEACHING

The educational policy of the party aims at the creation of a new Arab generation which believes in the unity of the nation, and in the eternity of its mission. This policy, based on scientific reasoning, will be freed from the shackles of superstitions and reactionary traditions, it will be imbued with the spirit of optimism, of struggle, and of solidarity among all citizens in the carrying out of a total Arab revolution, and be the cause of human progress.

Therefore the party decides as follows:
Article 44. A national Arab stamp will mark all the aspects of intellectual, economic, political, architectural, and artistic life. The party establishes once again the links of the Arab nation with its glorious history and urges it toward a future even more glorious and more exemplary.
Article 45. Teaching is one of the exclusive functions of the state. Therefore, all foreign and private educational institutions are abolished.
Article 46. Education at all stages shall be free for all citizens. Primary and secondary education shall be compulsory.
Article 47. Professional schools with the most modern equipment shall be established, where education shall be free.
Article 48. Teaching careers and all that relates to education are set aside for Arab citizens. An exception to this rule is made in the instance of higher education.

AMENDMENT OF THE CONSTITUTION

Single Article. The fundamental and general principles of the Constitution cannot be amended. Other articles may, however, be amended, provided that two-thirds of the General Council of the party agree thereto, on a motion put by the Executive Council, or by a quarter of the members of the General Council, or by ten members of the Party Organization.

Appendix C: Syrian Provisional Constitution, 1964[3]

CHAPTER 1

Article 1.

§1) The Syrian Region is a Sovereign Socialist Democratic Popular Republic and it is a part of the Arab fatherland.

§2) The Arab people of Syria are part of the Arab nation, they believe in unity and work toward its achievement.

Article 2. Sovereignty in the Region belongs to the people.

Article 3. Islamic jurisprudence is a principal source of the law-Islam is the religion of the state.

Article 4. Arabic is the official language.

Article 5. The capital of the Republic is Damascus.

Article 6. The flag of the Republic is as follows: its length twice its width – it is of three equal and parallel colors, at the top is red, then white, then black. The white part contains three green five-pointed stars in a straight line and equidistant from each other. The emblem of the Republic and its anthem shall be designated by law.

CHAPTER 2. BASIC PRINCIPLES

Article 7. By law, citizens are equal in their rights and duties.

Article 8. The state guarantees citizens their liberty, safety, and equality of opportunity.

---

3 Printed in *al-Nahar*, April 4, 1964. Translated by the author.

Article 9. Individual liberty is guaranteed – a man is innocent until proven guilty by law. It is illegal to investigate anyone or detain him except in accordance with the law. Right of defense is guaranteed by law.
Article 10. Crime and punishment are defined by law.
Article 11. The law is effective only from the date of its passage, and it shall not be retroactive; the only exception to this according to the law is in matters of a noncriminal nature.
Article 12. It is illegal to enter houses or to search them except under the conditions and procedures defined by law.
Article 13. Public liberties are guaranteed and the law shall regulate the manner of their practice.
Article 14.

§1) It is illegal to exile citizens from the fatherland.

§2) Every citizen has the right to reside and to travel in Syria, unless forbidden by a legal judgment or in accordance with general health and safety regulations.

Article 15. Political refugees shall not be extradited because of their political views or their defense of liberty.
Article 16. Freedom of belief is guaranteed, and the state respects all religions and guarantees the liberty of their practice provided they do not contradict the public laws.
Article 17.

§1) Education is a right of every citizen.

§2) The state is interested in the growth of a generation strong in body, mind, and character, with faith in its spiritual heritage and pride in its Arab virtues.

Article 18.

§1) Work is a right of every citizen and is a duty dictated by honor. The state should provide work to citizens and guarantee it by building a Socialist national economy which will raise their standard of living.

§2) The state will protect labor and guarantee workers just compensation for their labor; it will limit working hours and also guarantee social security and regulate the rights of leisure and holiday.

§3) Labor organizations are guaranteed their independence, their responsibility in building the national economy on Socialist principles is clarified. This shall be stated by law.

Article 19.

§1) The state will provide for every citizen and his family in emergency cases, illness, disability, orphanage, or old age.

§2) The state will protect the health of the citizen and will facilitate for him the means of hospitalization and medicine.

Article 20.

§1) The family is the basic unit of society and is under the state's protection.

§2) The state shall protect and encourage marriage and shall remove material and social impediments to it.

Article 21.

§1) To defend the fatherland is a sacred duty of all citizens.

§2) Military service is compulsory and shall be regulated by a special law.

Article 22. Citizens shall exercise their rights and enjoy their liberties guaranteed by law, provided they do not infringe on the safety of the fatherland, national unity, the bases of the Republic, and the popular Socialist aims of the revolution.

Article 23. The state shall place all the products of the fatherland as well as its energies in the service of the people according to a plan prohibiting exploitation and aiming at increasing the national income and its just distribution according to the abilities of the contributors.

Article 24.

§1) Natural resources are the property of the people.

§2) The Socialist society is based on collective ownership of the means of production.

Article 25. Ownership of the means of production shall be as follows:

1. State ownership represented by the public sector that shoulders the great burden of the economic plan including public utilities, major means of transportation, and those means of production dealing with the basic needs of the people.
2. Collective ownership, meaning ownership by all the producers.
3. Private ownership is a partner in the growth provided it does not inhibit the growth of the public sector or the building of the Socialist economy.

Article 26. Private property is protected, the law shall regulate its social function. Private property shall be expropriated only in the public interest, and a just compensation according to the law shall be paid.

Article 27. The law shall define the maximum limits of property.

Article 28. The state encourages cooperation and shall attempt to bolster and protect all cooperative establishments.

Article 29. The state may nationalize, by law, any firm or establishment which is connected with the public interest and shall pay an adequate compensation for it.

Article 30. The right of inheritance is protected according to the law.

CHAPTER 3. THE AUTHORITIES

Article 31. The National Revolutionary Council is in charge of the legislative powers and shall supervise the activities of the executive authorities.

Article 32. The National Revolutionary Council is charged with the following duties:

1. To elect the president, vice president, and members of the Executive Council.
2. To amend the Provisional Constitution and to draft the permanent Constitution.
3. To conduct a public plebiscite.
4. To decree the number of universities; define their duties; consolidate, abolish, or change their titles.
5. To establish the general policy outlines of the state and to approve the provisional [economic] plan.
6. To draw up the budget, levy taxes, lower them, or abolish all or part of them.
7. To decide on matters of war and peace.
8. To vote confidence or withdraw it from the Cabinet or any of its members.

Article 33. The National Revolutionary Council shall be composed of its present membership and representatives of the people; their numbers and the manner of representation shall be defined by law.

Article 34. The National Revolutionary Council, in its first meeting, shall elect its president and the members of his staff.

Article 35.

§1) The Council shall hold three sessions annually. It shall definitely meet at the beginning of October and decide, according to its internal rules, the times for its two subsequent sessions.

§2) The president of the National Revolutionary Council may call special sessions at the request of the Council, or if one-quarter of the membership demands a special session in writing.

Article 36. Members of the National Revolutionary Council shall enjoy immunities during its sessions, and they cannot be prosecuted criminally, nor can a judgment against them be executed except by permission of the National Council. They cannot be detained except if caught in a public criminal act of which the Council is notified immediately.

Article 37. Prior to assuming their duties, each member of the National Council shall publicly take the following oath: "I do swear by God that I shall be faithful to the Constitution and shall defend it, the independence of the fatherland, and the public interest. I shall respect the laws of the land, honorably execute my duties, and work for the aims of the revolution: unity, liberty, and socialism."

Article 38. A law shall define the compensation and expenses of the members of the Council.

Article 39. No member of the National Council may exploit his position in any manner.

Article 40. The National Council may, by assent of an absolute majority of its members, grant general amnesty on crimes committed before that amnesty.

Article 41. The National Council, at any time, may form committees or deputize one or more of its members to investigate any matter, and it is the duty of all ministers and government employees to submit any documents, certificates, or plans that may be requested of them.

Article 42. The sittings of the Council are not legal unless attended by an absolute majority of its members.

Article 43. Members of the Executive Council and all members of the National Council have the right to suggest laws.

Article 44.

§1) The National Council may vote passage of a law issued by the Executive Council within fifteen days (of its issuance by the Executive Council).

§2) If the Council, by an absolute majority, designates the law for prompt action, it must be acted upon within the designated period, and should it not be issued by the Executive Council within the said time limit, the president of the National Council may decree it immediately.

Article 45. Any member may address questions and interpolations to the Cabinet, which must reply at the time designated proper by the internal rules.

Article 46. In its internal rules, the National Council shall define the proper methods of discussion, questions, interpolations, voting, the duties of the various offices, committees, and all other activities of the Council.

CHAPTER 4. THE EXECUTIVE COUNCIL

Article 47. The executive powers shall be vested in the Executive Council and the Cabinet within the limits laid down by the Constitution.

Article 48.

§1) The Executive Council shall be composed of a president, vice president, and five members elected by the National Revolutionary Council from its membership.

§2) The Executive Council is responsible to the National Revolutionary Council for all phases of its activities.

Article 49. Prior to assuming their duties, the president of the Executive Council and its members shall take the following oath: "I do swear by God that I shall be faithful to the Constitution and shall defend it, the independence of the fatherland, and the public interest. I shall respect the laws of the land, honorably execute my duties, and work for the aims of the revolution: unity, liberty, and socialism."

Article 50. The Executive Council may appoint or remove Cabinet members; it has the right to issue a private amnesty, grant medals, and appoint or remove the chiefs of political missions.

Article 51. The Executive Council may, if the need arises, and in the absence of the National Council, issue any decision which is within the original jurisdiction of the National Council provided that it is placed before the consideration of the Council immediately upon its reconvention and that the Council does not reject it by a two-thirds majority of its membership. If the Council rejects it, then it shall be disregarded as of the date of its rejection.

Article 52. The Executive Council with the concurrence of the Cabinet shall conclude treaties and agreements and shall notify the National Revolutionary Council of their conclusion. These shall, after their conclusion, ratification, and publication, according to the law, have the force of law. Peace treaties, alliances, and all other treaties dealing with the sovereignty of the state and those granting privileges or concessions to foreign companies are not effective unless ratified by the National Revolutionary Council.

Article 53.

§1) The Executive Council may declare by decree a state of emergency and may call for partial mobilization provided that the action be placed before the National Council at its first session following such action.

§2) The Executive Council may call for total mobilization in case of aggression against the country or any other Arab country provided that the National Council be called for a special session to approve the action.

Article 54.

§1) The Executive Council draws up the internal and external policies of the State and supervises the activities of the Cabinet.

§2) The Executive Council has the right to annul the decisions of the Cabinet or those of any of its ministers, if these be contrary to the Constitution or the laws or detrimental to the public interest.

Article 55. The Executive Council may appoint or dismiss civil or military officials within the boundaries of the law.

Article 56. The president of the Executive Council shall accept the credentials of foreign embassies and shall represent the state in international conferences.

Article 57. The president of the Executive Council shall sign all laws, and all declarations, statutes, or regulations issued by the Executive Council and referred to him. The president of the Executive Council shall function as the head of state in conformity with this Provisional Constitution.

Article 58. No member of the Executive Council may hold the position of minister or deputy minister.

Article 59. The Cabinet shall be composed of the prime minister and ministers; it shall be possible to appoint one or more deputy prime ministers, ministers without portfolio, and deputy ministers, and all shall be subject to the special regulations dealing with ministers.

Article 60. The prime minister shall be a member of the National Revolutionary Council.

Article 61. The Cabinet shall be collectively responsible to the National Council, each minister individually responsible for his own ministry in executing the public policy.

Article 62. The Cabinet shall be responsible for executing affairs of state and unifying and coordinating business between the ministers and the various public agencies. It shall also be responsible for drawing up and executing the development plan, and for drawing up the programs and plans for its realization according to the public good. It shall also be responsible for maintaining domestic peace, the safety of the state, protection of the rights of citizens, drawing up of the budget, executing it, and conducting affairs of state in the field of international relations.

Article 63. The Cabinet, presided over by the prime minister or his deputy, shall meet to consider the following matters:

1. Draft legislation.
2. Regulatory laws.
3. Drafting of public and special budgets.
4. Internal and external policy.
5. Any matters suggested – with the consent of the president or the prime minister – by any of the ministers or the prime minister.
6. Other matters defined by law.

Article 64.

§1) The prime minister shall conduct the Cabinet meetings when presiding.

§2) He shall coordinate the activities of various ministries.

§3) The prime minister alone may call for a vote of confidence in his Cabinet by the National Council.

§4) The prime minister may delegate some of his functions to any Cabinet member.

Article 65. Upon resignation, or withdrawal of confidence from the Cabinet, the ministers shall continue their duties until the new Cabinet has been formed.

CHAPTER 5. JUDICIAL AUTHORITY

Article 66. Judges shall be independent with no power over them but the laws; no authority may interfere with the affairs of justice.

Article 67. All judgments shall be issued in the name of the Syrian Arab people.

Article 68. The law shall define the judicial branch and its jurisdiction.

Article 69. Judges shall not be subject to removal except in accordance with the law.
Article 70. The law shall define the qualifications for appointment and transfer of judges or for disciplinary action against them.
Article 71. Public prosecution is a judicial authority which shall lie within the jurisdiction of the minister of justice; its functions and duties, and its relations with the judges, shall be defined by law.
Article 72. The law shall define the role and duties of the special courts and shall define the qualifications for who shall preside over them.

CHAPTER 6. FINANCIAL AFFAIRS

Article 73. The government shall prepare the budget. The National Revolutionary Council alone has the right to approve it.
Article 74. The law shall define the manner of preparation of the budget, independent budgets, addenda and special budgets, and the manner of presenting it to the National Council and the manner of approval.
Article 75. The date for the beginning of the fiscal year shall be designated by law.
Article 76. If the National Council is unable to approve the budget prior to the beginning of the fiscal year for which it has been planned, then the Cabinet may open monthly credits on the basis of one-twelfth of the previous year's budget. Revenues shall be collected according to the laws in effect at the end of the last fiscal year.
Article 77. Final accounts for the fiscal year shall be considered by the National Revolutionary Council. Termination of accounts shall be done by law.
Article 78. Introduction of taxes, or their modification, cannot be done except by law.

Article 79. Final and Provisional Regulations.

§1) Present legislation shall remain in effect temporarily until amended in accordance with this Constitution.

Article 80. This Provisional Constitution shall remain in effect until the people agree on a permanent Constitution.

Notes

AUTHOR'S INTRODUCTION

1. The attempted *coup* was averted on the morning of Dec. 18, 1965 and a number of leftist officers were arrested. See *New York Times*, December 30, 1965.
2. *New York Times*, December 30, 1965, and January 3, 1966.
3. Attempts at closer ties with Nasser were begun earlier by President Hafiz. See *New York Times*, October 16, 1965.
4. *New York Times*, February 26, March 10, and March 28, 1966.
5. As late as January 1966 the secretary general of the party denied the existence of such a split between the civilians and the military. See *al-Ahrar*, January 1, 1966.
6. *Al-Ahrar*, March 1, 1966; and *New York Times*, March 13, 1966.
7. *Al-Ahrar*, March 1, 1966.
8. *New York Times*, March 13, 1966.
9. *Ibid.*, March 22, 1966.
10. *Ibid.*, April 14, 1966. Bakdash left Syria in February, 1958, for East Europe in a protest against the union concluded then between Syria and Egypt. The Communist party in Syria was not happy with the union especially under Nasser.
11. *Ibid.*, April 14 and April 24, 1966.

PREFACE TO THE SECOND EDITION

1. Kamel Abu Jaber, *Memories: An Oasis in Time*, London: Hesperus Press, (2023), p.129. For an academic history of the

JNM, see Betty Anderson, *Nationalist Voices in Jordan: the Street and the State*, Austin: University of Texas Press, (2005)

2. This rendition of the meeting with Madadha was related to me by Kamel Abu Jaber during what would prove our last encounter, in of all places, an ice cream parlor in Khilda, the outlying suburb of western Amman that he had retired to with his wife Loretta in his last years.

3. The early chapters of Abu Jaber's *Memories* discuss his family origins and the creation of the Yadudah estate. They also preserve a press cutting detailing his father, Saleh Frayh Abu Jaber's, love of Bedouin lore and attachment to the land. His cousin Rauf Abu Jaber offers an academic account of the origins of the family farm in Yadudah in his *Pioneers over the Jordan: the Frontier Settlement in Transjordan* 1851–1914, London: I.B. Taurus (1989).

4. Hanna Batatu, *The Old Social Classes and the Revolutionary Movements of Iraq*, Princeton: Princeton University Press (1978).

5. The term given by Malcolm Kerr to the struggle between Nasser and the conservative Arab regimes. See Kerr, *The Arab Cold War: Gamal 'Abd al-Nasser and his Rivals*, Oxford: Oxford University Press, (1971).

6. Abu Jaber, *Memories*, p. 129.

7. Kamel Abu Jaber, *The Arab Ba'th Socialist Party*, Syracuse, NY: Syracuse University Press (1966), p.15. Looking back in later years, Abu Jaber would recall that he was 'most impressed by the mild-mannered, soft-spoken and kindly founder of the party, Michel Aflaq, whose intellectual wanderings with me through several lengthy interviews in both his office and his home enriched my research and left me with a sense of sadness about Arab affairs.' See Abu Jaber, *Memories,* p. 130.

8. For al-Tall's attempt in June 1971 to bring these Ba'thists, along with other former members of the JNM into a 'working plan'

focused on armed conflict with Israel see his 'Khittat 'Amal,' in Wasfi al-Tall, *Kitabat fi al Qadaya al-'Arabiyyat*, Amman: Dar al-Liwa' (1976), pp. 103-104.

9. See in particular Patrick Seale, *Asad of Syria: the Struggle for the Middle East*, London: I.B. Taurus (1988); Hanna Batatu, *Syria's Peasantry the Descendants of its Lesser Rural Notables and their Politics*, Princeton: Princeton University Press (1997); Nikolaus Van Dam, *The Struggle for Power in Syria: Politics and Society under Asad and the Ba'th Party*, London: I.B. Taurus (2011).

10. I have taken this term from Michel Seurat, *Syrie: L'Etat de Barbary*, Paris: Presses Universitaires de France, (2015).

11. For a brilliant analysis of the utility of a cult of personality to the power of Hafez al-Asad, see Lisa Wedeen, *Ambiguities of Domination: Politics, Rhetoric and Symbols in Contemporary Syria*, Chicago: University of Chicago Press (1999).

12. Abu Jaber, *Arab Ba'th Party*, p. 95.

13. The term is taken from the title of a notorious book penned by Kanaan Makiyya (under the pseudonym Samir al-Khalil) on Saddam's Iraq, see *Republic of Fear: the Politics of Modern Iraq*, Berkley: University of California Press (1989). It is worth noting that more recent work using the Ba'th party archives captured after the US invasion of Iraq uncover a different view of Saddam's rule. While most certainly violent, it also drew on the social support ensured by the vast distribution of state patronage through the Ba'th Party, a pattern of politics much closer to the egalitarian vision of the old Ba'thists than the gory spectacles of violence that Makiyya puts center stage. See Lisa Blaydes, *State of Repression: Iraq under Saddam Hussein*, Princeton: Princeton University Press (2018); Joseph Sassoon, Saddam Hussein's Ba'th Party: Inside an Authoritarian Regime, Cambridge: Cambridge University Press, (2012).

1. BEGINNINGS OF ARAB SOCIALISM

1. "Al-Ghina Wa al-Faqr" (Wealth and Poverty), al-Muqtataf, XIII, No. 9 (June, 1889), 580-81.

2. "Al-Ijtima'iyyah Wa al-Ishtirakiyyah" (Socialism and Communism), *al-Hilal*, XVI, No. 5 (February, 1908), 281-82. The word *Ishtirakiyyah* then was used to denote communism.

3. Clovis Maqsud, *Nahwa Ishtirakiyyah Arabiyyah* (Toward an Arab Socialism) (2d ed.; Beirut: Dar Munaimneh, 1958), p. 57.

4. Shibli Shumayyil, *Majmu'at al-Doctor Shibli Shumayyil* (Collection of Doctor Shibli Shumayyil) (Cairo: Matba'at al-Ma'aref, 1908), pp. 154, 183. For further discussion of Shumayyil's ideas, see Allush Naji, *al-Thawri al-Arabi al-Muasir* (The Contemporary Arab Revolutionary) (Beirut: Dar al-Tali'ah, 1960), pp. 97-99.

5. "Al-Ishtirakiyyah al-Sahihah" (The True Socialism), *al-Muqtataf*, XLII, No. 1 (January, 1913), 9. While this magazine was anti-Socialist in policy, it allowed Shumayyil to defend his ideas in it.

6. "Tarikh al-Ishtirakiyyah Fi Ingliterrah" (History of Socialism in England), *al-Hilal*, XVIII (March, 1910), 335-38.

7. *Al-Ishtirakiyyah* (Socialism) (Cairo: al-Matba'ah al-Ahliyyah, 1913), pp. 2, 22. Musa used the term "machine" to denote technological progress.

8. *Ibid.*, pp. 14, 17-20.

9. The Wafd party established by Saad Zagloul in 1920 campaigned for Egyptian independence from Britain and was the largest party in Egypt until the 1952 Nasser revolution.

10. Salamah Musa, *Tarbiyyat Salamah Musa* (Salamah Musa's Growth) (Cairo: Muassasat al-Khanji, 1958), p. 166.

11. Maqsud, *Nahwa*, p. 57; see also the newspaper *al-Sahafah*, April 8, 1959.

12. Nicola Haddad, *al-Ishtiraktyyah*, pp. 34, 36-44, 50, 55, 60, 77.

13. *Ibid.*, pp. 66, 77-80. Haddad clearly refers to George's idea of a high progressive tax.
14. *Ibid.* pp. 58-61. For further discussion of Haddad's ideas see N. Haddad, "Al-Ishtirakyyah, Ma Tatabaluhu wa Ma La Tatublubuhu (Socialism, What It Asks for and What It Does Not), *al-Hilal*, XXVI (July, 1918), 783-88; Maqsud, *Nahwa*, p. 57; and Naji, *al-Thawri*, pp. 199-204.
15. Maqsud, *Nahwa*, p. 57; and *al-Sahafah*, April 8, 1959.
16. Ali al-Khalil, "The Socialist Parties in Syria and Lebanon" (un-published Ph.D. dissertation, The American University, Washington, D.C., 1962), p. 67. Also in *al-Sahafah*, April 8, 1959; and Maqsud, *Nahwa*, p. 57.
17. Nabih Faris, "The Arabs in Search of a Political Ideology," *al Abhath*, XV, No. 1 (March, 1962), 35. Mr. Faris states that this was the first Socialist party in the Middle East, which is certainly wrong, as indicated above. Actually the party was banned in 1924 by the government of Sa'd Zaghloul and Salamah Musa was arrested, but it continued precariously until 1930, when it completely disintegrated. See Salamah Musa, *al-Adab wa al-Hayat* (Life and Literature) (Cairo: Dar al-Nashr al-Masriyyah, 1956), p.
18. Khalil, "The Socialist Parties," p. 70.
19. Majid Khadduri, *Independent Iraq* (London: Oxford University Press, 1960), pp. 69, 70.
20. *Ibid.*, pp. 70, 71.
21. Such a point is aptly expounded by G. Majdalany in Walter Z. Laqueur (ed.), *The Middle East in Transition* (New York: Praeger, 1958), p. 341. See also Sidney Lens, "A Report on Asian Socialism," *Dissent* (Winter, 1955), p. 56; and Khalil, "Socialist Parties", p. 66.
22. See Mortoe Berger, *The Arab World Today* (New York: Doubleday, 1962), p. 362.
23. *Al-Sahafah*, April 7, 1959.

24. *The Politics of Social Change in the Middle East and North Africa* (Princeton: Princeton University Press, 1963), p. 235.
25. Lens, "A Report," p. 56.
26. In *Middle East in Transition*, p. 337.
27. T. al-Maqdisi and G. Lusian, *al-Ahzab al-Siyasiyyah fi Lubnan* (Political Parties in Lebanon) (Beirut: Maktabat Haykal al-Gharib, 1959), p. 16.
28. Clovis Maqsud, "al-Ahzab al-Ishtirakiyyah Fi al-Iraq (Socialist Parties in Iraq), 1946-1956," *al-Thaqafah al-Arabiyyah*, IV, No. 1 (February, 1961), 8.
29. Gamal Abdel Nasser, *The Philosophy of the Revolution* (Buffalo: Economica Books, 1959), pp. 53, 71.
30. "Forum Interviews Michel Aflaq," *Middle East Forum* (February, 1958), p. 9.
31. Interview, Dr. Ali Jabir, Beirut, February 11, 1964. Dr. Jabir is a cofounder of the party and a close friend of Aflaq.
32. Both Halpern, *Politics of Social Change*, p. 240, and Walter Z. Lagueur, "Syria on the Move," *The World Today*, XIII, No. 1 (January, 1957), 18, state that Aflaq was a Communist until 1943. In my interview with Aflaq on January 16, 1964, Afaq stated, "I was never a Communist for one moment in my life."
33. Interview, Michel Aflaq, Damascus, February 16, 1964.
34. Interview, Dr Ali Jabir, Beirut, February 11, 1964
35. "Statement of the Students of Michel Aflaq," Damascus, October, 1942. (A leaflet which was distributed in the streets.)
36. "Statement," Damascus, June 15, 1943. (One sheet signed by Aflaq and Bitar and distributed in the streets.)
37. *Al-Ba'th*, November 18, 1949.
38. Interview, Michel Aflaq, Damascus, January 16, 1964.
39. Razzaz was one of the founders of the party.

40. Michel Aflaq, *Fi Sabil al-Ba'th al-Arabi* (Toward Arab Resurrection) (Beirut: Dar al-Tali'ah, 1959), p. 11. See also Leonard Binder, "Radical Reform Nationalism in Syria and Egypt, I," *The Muslim World*, XLIX, No. 2 (April, 1959), 102.
41. Interview, Dr. Ali Jabir, Beirut, February 11, 1964.
42. Bitar's criticisms of Sa'di may be found in *al-Nahar*, January 8, 1964. The Syrian Region of the party in Damascus expelled him on January 24, 1964; see *al-Nahar*, January 24, 1964.
43. *Al-Siyasah al-Arabiyyah Bayn al-Mabda Wa al-Tatbiq* (Arab Politics Between Principle and Practice) (Beirut: Dar al-Tali'ah, 1960), p. 9.
44. See the *New York Times*, March 28, 1966.
45. *Civilization on Trial* (New York: Oxford University Press, 1948), p. 23.
46. "Democracy in the Middle East, Its State of Prospect," *Middle Eastern Affairs*, VI, No. 4 (April, 1955), 103.
47. *The Ideologies of the Developing Nations* (New York: Praeger, 1963), p. 40.
48. *New York Times*, March 19, 1966.
49. Quoted in *al-Ahrar*, February 9, 1966.
50. Quoted in *ibid.*, February 6, 1966.
51. *Ibid.*, February 9, 1966.

2. THE ADVENT OF THE ARAB BA'TH SOCIALIST PARTY

1. Interview, Dr. Ali Jabir, Beirut, February 11, 1981.
2. In a speech by Aflaq quoted in *al-Ba'th*, January 30, 1947.
3. Al-Ba'th al-Arabi, "Statement," June 15, 1943. (Leaflet.)
4. Al-Ba'th al-Arabi, "Statement," Damascus, November 14, 1943. (Leaflet.)
5. Al-Ba'th al-Arabi, "To the Arab Nation," Damascus, June 9, 1945 (Leaflet.)

6. Al-Ba'th al-Arabi, "For the National Struggle," Damascus, May 20, 1945. (Leaflet).
7. Al-Ba'th al-Arabi, "Comments on the Speech of His Excellency the President," Damascus, March 8, 1945. (Leaflet.)
8. "The Socialist Parties," pp. 117-18.
9. *Al-Ba'th*, February 26, 1947.
10. Al-Ba'th al-Arabi, "Our Opinion on the Covenant of the Arab League," Damascus, April 12, 1945. (Leaflet.)
11. *Al-Ba'th*, November 1, November 17, and November 23, 1946.
12. *Al-Ba'th*, November 29, 1946; al-Ba'th al-Arabi, "Millions of Arabs Demand Unity, Liberty and Socialism," Damascus, November 29, 1954. (Leaflet.)
13. *Al-Ba'th*, February 2, 1947.
14. *Al-Ba'th*, December 13, 1946, and February 17, 1947.
15. Khalil, "The Socialist Parties," p. 119; see also *al-Ba'th*, April 16, 1947.
16. *Al-Ba'th*, March 20, 1947.
17. Since the party holds that the Arab world is one entity, it refers to these international conventions as National Conventions. The same is true of its international command, which it refers to as the National Command.
18. *Al-Ba'th*, April 6, 1947.
19. This comprehensive statement appeared in *al-Ba'th*, April 13, 1947. Further clarification appeared April 16, 1947.
20. Incidentally, the party refers to the Persian Gulf as the Arab Gulf.
21. *Al-Ba'th*, April 16, 1947.
22. *Al-Ba'th*, May 7, 1949.
23. *Al-Ba'th*, May 10, 1947.
24. *Al-Ba'th*, April 4 and May 8, 1948.
25. *Al-Ba'th*, February 16, 1948.

26. *Syria and Lebanon* (London: Oxford University Press, 1946), p. 100.
27. *The Meaning of the Disaster*, trans. R. B. Winder (Beirut: Khayat's College Book Cooperative, 1956), pp. 2, 6, 17, 38.
28. Maqsud, *Nahwa*, p. 76.
29. Clovis Maqsud, *Azamat al-Yasar al-Arabi* (Crisis of the Arab Left) (Beirut: Dar al-Ilm Li al-Malayin, 1960), p. 5.
30. *Ma'alim al-Hayat al-Arabiyah al-Jadidah* (Contours of the New Arab Life) (4th ed.; Beirut: Dar al-Ilm Li al-Malayin, 1960), pp. 10-11.
31. Arab Ba'th party, "A Note to Husni al-Zaim," Damascus, May 24, 1949, pp. 1-4. Also found in *Nidal al-Ba'th* (Ba'th Struggle) (Beirut: Dar al-Tallah, 1963), I, 292-97.
32. Khalil, "The Socialist Parties," p. 121.
33. *Al-Ba'th*, November 18, 1949. Aflaq resigned November 15 when the election results became known.
34. This party was created by Anton Sa'adeh in 1947. He was executed by Riad al-Solh's government in Lebanon in 1950. This party condones the use of violence and uses Fascist organization and tactics. See Arnold Hottinger, *The Arabs* (London: Thames & Hudson, 1963), pp. 230-31.
35. *Al-Ba'th*, November 28, 1949.
36. Hottinger, *The Arabs*, p. 255; Khalil, "The Socialist Parties," pp. 120-24.
37. *Nidal al-Ba'th*, II, 180.
38. Khalil, "The Socialist Parties," p. 123.
39. See for instance their leaflet, "Shishakli Kindles Civil and Minorities Strife," September 25, 1952. Several other such leaflets are collected in *Nidal al-Ba'th*, II, 178-210.
40. Khalil, "The Socialist Parties," p. 122.
41. "Tension Between Syria and Lebanon," *Mideast Mirror*, IV, No. 35 (January 10, 1953), 1.

3. DRIFT TO THE LEFT, 1954-58

1. *Middle East in Transition*, p. 327.

2. Constitution of the Arab Socialist Party (Damascus: Matba'at al-Ilm, n.d.).

3. For a discussion of the differences between these two bases, see Maurice Duverger, *Political Parties*, trans. Barbara North and Robert North (New York: Wiley, 1954), p. 23-36.

4. Walter Z. Laqueur, "Syria on the Move," *The World Today*, XIII, No. 1 (January, 1957), 19.

5. Interview, Michel Aflaq, Damascus, January 16, 1964; see also Khalil, "Socialism and Socialist Movements in the Arab World." (unpublished Master's thesis, American University of Beirut, 1958), p. 69.

6. *Al-Ba'th*, May 6, 1954, see also Nidal al-Ba'th, II, 243.

7. Laqueur, "Syria on the Move," The World Today, p. 20; see also *Nidal al-Ba'th*, IV, 15.

8. *Nidal al-Ba'th*, II, 255, 257.

9. *Al-Ba'th*, September 26, 1954; see also Khalil, "The Socialist Parties," p. 112.

10. *Middle East in Transition*, p. 328.

11. Sidney N. Fisher, ed., *The Military in the Middle East* (Columbus: Ohio State University Press, 1963), p. 62.

12. "Social Reform: Factor X," *Atlantic Monthly*, CXCVIII, No, 4 (Octo-ber, 1956), 137.

13. Ann Dearden, *Jordan* (London: Robert Hale, Ltd., 1958), p. 104; see also *al-Ba'th*, February 11, 1955.

14. Dearden, *Jordan*, p. 83.

15. *A Soldier with the Arabs* (London: Hodder and Stoughton, 1957), p. 431.

16. For a full discussion of the politics of Jordan and particularly of the Ba'th, see *ibid.*, pp. 431-39; and Dearden, *Jordan*, pp. 101-25.

17. See *al-Ba'th*, January 22, February 26, and March 6, 1955.
18. *Nidal al-Ba'th*, III, 1O10; see also Khalil, "The Socialist Parties," p. 126; and Sidney N. Fisher, ed., The Military, p. 63.
19. Fisher, *The Military*, p. 63.
20. Glubb, *A Soldier*, p. 431.
21. Hottinger, *The Arabs*, p. 255. Serraj was never a Ba'thist.
22. Hottinger, *The Arabs*, p. 276; Glubb, A Soldier, p. 431; and Fisher, The Military, p. 62.
23. *Nidal al-Ba'th*, III, 43-53; see also Khalil, "The Socialist Parties," p. 127.
24. *Nidal al-Ba'th*, III, 9-10, 22.
25. *Ibid.*, 9-13; see also Salah al-Bitar, *Al-Siyasah al-Arabiyyah Bayn al-Mabda Wa al-Tatbiq* (Arab Policy in Principle and Practice) (Beirut: Dar al-Tali'ah, 1960), p. 84.
26. Bitar, *Al-Siyasah*, p. 177; see also Hottinger, *The Arabs*, pp 270-71.
27. Bitar, *Al-Siyasah*, 141.
28. Charles Issawi, "Negotiation from Strength," International Affairs, XXXV, No. 1 (January, 1955), 1, 3.
29. *Nidal al-Ba'th*, III, 62-63, 73; see also al-Ba'th, May 4, 1956.
30. R. N. Nolte and W. R. Polk, "Toward a Policy for the Middle East," *Foreign Affairs*, XXXV, No. 4 (July, 1958), 647.
31. Walter Z. Laqueur, "The National Bourgeoisie," *International Affairs*, XXXV, No. 3 (July, 1959), 327-28.
32. Charles Issawi, "Middle East Dilemmas: An Outline of Problems," *Journal of International Affairs*, XIII, No. 2 (1959), 107.
33. G. E. Wheeler, "Russia and the Middle East," *International Affairs*, XXXV, No. 3 (July, 1959), 300.
34. Khalil, "The Socialist Parties," p. 126.
35. *Al-Ba'th*, April 20, 1956.
36. *Al-Ba'th*, May 20 and June 1, 1956.

37. See *Mideast Mirror*, VIII, No. 42 (October 21, 1956), 12; Khalil, "The Socialist Parties," p. 129; and *al-Ba'th*, June 22, 1956.
38. *Al-Ba'th*, July 6, 1956.
39. See *ibid.*, August 17 and September 7, 1956.
40. Printed in *ibid.*, January 18, 1957.
41. *Ibid.*, January 25, 1957.
42. *Ibid.*, March 29, 1957.
43. *Ibid.*, May 17, 1957. Actually it was King Hussein's personal courage that toppled the Nabulsi-Abu-Nuwar (Socialist-Ba'thist) coalition that was planning a *coup d'état* against him. See Glubb, *A Soldier*, p. 436.
44. Israel attacked the Syrian village of al-Tawafiq and a few days later Adan Menderis attacked Syria as Communist. *Al-Ba'th*, August 9, September 13, and September 25, 1957. On October 4, 1957, the Ba'th paper welcomed Khrushchev's threat that Turkey would be attacked if it attacked Syria. See also Nevill Barbour, "Impressions of the United Arab Republic," *International Affairs*, XXXVI, No. 1 (January, 1960), 21.
45. On Soviet influence see Claire Sterling, "Syria, Communism, Nasserism and a Man Named Serraj," *The Reporter*, XVI, No. 13 (June 27, 1957), 17.
46. Hourani was elected to this office on October 18, 1957. See *al-Ba'th*, same date.
47. Fisher, *The Military*, p. 66. See also Hottinger, *The Arabs*, p. 276; and New York Times, February 2, 1958. The party was very much concerned about growing Communist influence in the military and popular spheres. Though it did not admit it at the time, this was one of the reasons that compelled it to press for unity with Egypt. Sa'dun Hamadi, an Iraqi Ba'th intellectual and a former minister of agricultural reform in Iraq, admitted later that this was one of the reasons (perhaps the main one)

that prompted the party's drive for unity. See Sa'dun Hamadi, *Nahnu Wa al-Shuyu'iyyah Fi al-Azamah al-Hadirah* (We and the Communists in the Present Crisis) (Beirut: Dar al-Tali'ah, n.d.), pp. 48-49. See also Arab Ba'th Socialist party (Lebanon), "Our View of Arab Unity" (pamphlet), September 16, 1962, pp. 45, 54, and "The Meaning of the UAR," *The World Today*, XIV, No. 3 (March, 1958), 94.

48. For a discussion of events in this period, see Hottinger, *The Arabs*, pp. 276-77; C. E. Cremeans, *The Arabs of the World* (New York: Praeger, 1963), pp. 159-82, See also "Rift in the Left Lute." *The Economist*, CLXXXV,, No. 5960 (January 25, 1958), 299; and "Pan Arab Challenge to Ankara," *The Economist*, CLXXXVI, No. 5071 (February 1, 1958), 379 80.

49. In an internal party directive published in *Nidal al-Ba'th*, III, 162.

50. Fisher, *The Military*, p. 66, states that the Ba'th aligned itself with the right to avert Communist ascendancy. This was true when the Ba'th cooperated with President S. al-Quwately, certainly a rightist in the eyes of the Ba'th. See also Hottinger, *The Arabs*, p. 277; and "The Atlantic Report: Syria," *Atlantic Monthly*, CCIX, No. 1 (January, 1962), 19.

51. *Al-Ba'th*, February 8, 1958.

4. BA'TH AND THE U.A.R.

1. *Al-Sahafah*, January 2, 1959; see also Simon Jargy, "Le Déclin d'un Parti," *L'Orient*, No. 11 (1959), p. 28, on Ba'th faith in Nasser.

2. Interview, Damascus, January 16, 1964; see also Jargy, "Le Déclin," p. 29.

3. *New York Times*, February 2, 1958.

4. Emile Bustani, "Can Arab Unity Survive?" *New Statesmen*, LXIII, No. 1608 (January 5, 1962), 5.

5. *New York Times*, March 24, 1958.

6. *Ibid.*, July 10, 1958.
7. *Ibid.*, September 28, 1958.
8. Khalil, "The Socialist Parties," p. 141.
9. *New York Times*, September 28, 1958.
10. *Al-Sahafah*, March 18, April 5, and April 8, 1959.
11. *Ibid.*, September 2, 1959; interview, Michel Aflaq, January 16, 1904; and Jargy, "Le Déclin,' p. 34.
12. Based on interview, Michel Aflaq, January 18, 1964, and other Ba'th members.
13. George Kirk, *Contemporary Arab Politics* (New York: Praeger, 1961), p. 103; see also Khalil, "The Socialist Parties," p. 140; and "Political Quarrels in Syria," *Mideast Mirror*, II, No. 35 (April 30, 1959), 2.
14. *Al-Sahafah*, July 12, 1959.
15. *New York Times*, October 22 and December 30, 1959, and January 1 and January 5, 1960; see also *Christian Science Monitor*, October 22, 1959.
16. *Al-Sahafah*, December 21, 1959, and January 3, 1960. Such declarations were to change after the break-up of the U.A.R. in 1961.
17. There is no written history or even an allusion to the Ba'th party in Iraq at this early stage of its development. The account presented here was given by Iraqi students at the American University of Beirut and other Iraqis I met in Lebanon. Fearing reprisals from the Iraqi government, they insist upon being kept anonymous. The interviews upon which most of the account is based – it has been verified by accounts from others who were for or against the party – were conducted in Beirut, March 16 and 18, 1964, and in Damascus, March 25, 1964.
18. *Al-Ba'th*, January 22, 1955. The party led many antigovernment demonstrations which led to the arrest of a large number of its members.

19. Many Iraqi Ba'thist exiles claim that the Ba'th party was one of the major elements assisting Qasim in his *coup d'état* which toppled the monarchy. (Based on an interview in Damascus, March 25, 1964.)
20. Interview, Michel Aflaq, Damascus, January 16, 1964.
21. Hottinger, *The Arabs*, p. 279.
22. *Al-Sahafah*, January 22, 1959.
23. I could not find the text of the statements made by Rikabi against the Ba'th party. I did, however, find a list of them in a statement by the Ba'th in Lebanon, August, 1961, itemizing Rikabi's accusations and defending themselves against them.
24. Interview, Michel Aflaq, Damascus, January 16, 1964.
25. Based on interview with Iraqi students, Damascus, March 22, 1964.
26. *Al-Sahafah*, January 15, 1960. Certain members of the Ba'th party admit that the Regional party in Iraq had been preparing for Qasim's assassination since April, 1959. One member – presently an Iraqi exile in Syria – informed me he was among those arrested on October 10, 1959, the day of the unsuccessful attempt on Qasim's life. He was sentenced to death but not executed. He spent two years and four months in prison and was released when the Qasim regime was overthrown. This member claims the National party command in Syria certainly knew of the plot to assassinate Qasim. Interview, Anonymous, Damascus, March 25, 1964.
27. Fuad al-Rikabi, *al-Qawmiyyah, Harakatuhah Wa Muhtawahah* (Nationalism: Movement and Content) (Cairo: Dar al-Kitab al-Arabi, 1963), p.118.
28. Interview with Mr. Sa'dun Hamadi, former minister of agricultural reform in Iraq and a prominent Ba'th leader, Beirut, March 11, 1964.
29. *Al-Ishtiraki*, Baghdad, January, 1963.
30. Interview, Anonymous, Damascus, March 25, 1964.

5. THE BREAK-UP OF THE U.A.R.

1. H. Seton-Watson, *Neither War Nor Peace* (New York: Praeger, 1960), p. 219. For further discussion of the "hydraulic societies," see Karl Wittfogel, "Chinese Society: A Historic Survey," *Journal of Asian Studies* (May, 1957), p. 354. Jebran Majdalany, a leader of the Ba'th party in Lebanon, makes the claim that Egyptians are traditionally accustomed to "submissiveness" whereas Syrians are not. According to him, this was one of Nasser's difficulties in Syria. (Interview, Beirut, August 29, 1963.)

2. Malcolm Kerr, "The Emergence of Socialist Ideology in Egypt," *Middle East Journal*, XVI, No. 2 (Spring, 1962), 127-14.

3. *Nidal al-Ba'th*, IV, 247, 248.

4. Cremeans, *The Arabs*, pp. 170, 171; interview, Michel Aflaq, Damascus, January 16, 1964. See also "The Atlantic Report: Syria," *The Atlantic Monthly*, CCIX, No. 1 (January, 1962), 19. As early as March, 1960, the party complained that in a one-man-rule government no one has any real authority except the individual on top. The one-man type of government depends on a "dictator" aided by "experts" – experts who are consulted only when the dictator wishes. See *Nidal al-Ba'th*, IV, 139 40.

5. Interview, Anonymous, a former Ba'th member and a Hourani partisan, Beirut, November 28, 1963. For further information on the topic see Khalil al-Kallas, *Aradnaha Wihda Wa Araduha Mazra'a* (We Wanted a Union, But They Wanted a Plantation) (Damascus: Matba'at al-Jamhuriyyah, 1962). Kallas was minister of national economy in the U.A.R. and one of the Ba'th ministers who resigned in 1959. See also A. Abdul Karim, *Adwa' Ala Tajribat al-Wihdah* (Lights on the Unity Experience) (Damascus: Maktabat Atlas, 1962), 30, 213.

6. After the break-up of the union, the Ba'thists made public a torrent of complaints and criticisms of the police methods. Such a stand was taken by the leaders in their writings and speeches

and in *al-Ba'th*. For an example of this, see *al-Ba'th*, September 8, 1962; see also *Nidal al-Ba'th*, IV, 133, 138, and 141.

7. Interview, F. Shbaqlu, Beirut, November 23, 1963.

8. Cremeans, *The Arabs*, p. 172. According to *Nidal al-Ba'th*, IV, 200, the "National Union" was supposed to have come into existence immediately after the formation of the U.A.R. But in fact it came into existence in the early part of 1959. It was a state party which was to include everyone in the society. Egyptian Socialists justified this arrangement on grounds that their brand of socialism denied "class struggle." The National Union should not be viewed as a political party, they claimed; rather, as a movement all the people could join. Afif Bahnasi, *Al-Madkhal ila al-Ishtirakiyyah al-Arabiyyah* (Entrance to Arab Socialism) (Damascus: Maktabat Hussein al-Nuri, 1958), p. 151. See also Abdul Aziz Izzet, "Kaif Nuhagiq al-Demoqratyyah wa al-Adalah al-Ijtimaiyyah" (How to Achieve Democracy, Socialism, and Social Justice), *Al Majallah al-Masriyyah Li al-Ulum al-Siyasiyyah*, No. 10 (January, 1962), pp. 35-36; and Muhammad al-Bahi, *Falsafat al-Ishtirakiyyah* (Philosophy of Socialism) (Cairo: Kutub Qawmiyyah, n.d.), p. 29.

9. Khalil, "The Socialist Parties," 138-40; *Nidal al-Ba'th*, IV, 200-04.

10. Interview, J. Majdalany, Beirut, August 29, 1963; *Nidal al-Ba'th*, IV, 145. On the other hand, Egyptian Socialists extol their own pragmatism. On this point see Muhammad Hatim, *Hawl al-Nazariyyah al-Ishtirakiyyah* (Concerning the Socialist Theory) (Cairo: Kutub Qawmiyyah, 1959), p. 24; Ahmad Abu al-Majd, "*al-Mithaq al-Watani: Ahdafuhu, Madmunuhu*" (The National Union, Aims and Content), *Al-Majallah al-Masriyyah Li al-Ulum al-Siyasiyyah*, No. 12 (March, 1962), p. 90.

11. Khalil, "The Socialist Parties," pp. 141, 142.

12. Interview, J. Majdalany, Beirut, August 29, 1963; see also A. 'Abdul Daim, *Al-Ishtirakiyyah wa al-Demoqratiyyah* (Socialism

and Democracy) (Beirut: Dar al-Adab, 1961), pp. 14-15; and "Socialism and State Capitalism," *Al-Sahafah*, August 1, 1960.

13. Yasin al-Hafiz et al., *Fi al-Fikr al-Siyasi* (Concerning Political Thought) (Damascus: Dar Dimishq, 1963), I, 44. See also Naji Allush, *Fi Sabil al-Harakah al-Arabiyyah al-Thawriyyah al-Shamilah* (Toward a Comprehensive Arab Revolutionary Movement) (Beirut: Dar al-Taliah, 1963), p. 11.

14. *Fi al-Fikr*, 51.

15. Allush, *Fi Sabil*, I, 13-15.

16. A. K. Zuhur, *Fi al-Fikr al-Siyasi*, II, 200. See also Arab Ba'th Socialist party, "About the Unity Trial," Damascus, February, 1962, p. 13 (Pamphlet); and another Ba'th publication entitled, "No Unity without Democracy, Damascus, June, 1962, p. 5 (Leaflet).

17. "Pan Arab Challenge to Ankara," *The Economist*, I, CLXXVI, No. 5971 (February 1, 1959), 379.

18. Khalil, "The Socialist Parties," 145; see also *New York Times*, September 30, 1961; and *Christian Science Monitor*, October 23, 1961.

19. The Arab Ba'th Socialist party, "A Statement," October 5, 1961.

20. See Allush, *Al-Thawrah*, p. 128.

21. For further information on their views see A. al-Rimawi, *Al-Mantiq al-Thawri Li al-Harakah al-Arabiyyah al-Hadithah* (Revolutionary Logic of the Modern Arab Movement) (Cairo: Dar al-Ma'rifah, 1961); and F. al-Rikabi, *Al-Qawmiyyah, Harakatuhah wa Muhtawahah* (Nationalism, Movement, and Content) (Alexandria: Dar al-Kitab al-Arabi, 1963).

22. "Political Quarrels in Syria," *Mideast Mirror*, II, No. 35 (August 30, 1959), 3; see also A. Abdul Karim, *Adwa Ala*, p. 216.

23. *Al-Sahafah*, July 11, 1959. The Ba'thist candidates were clearly unhappy and withdrew from the elections. See Allush, *al-Thawrah*, p. 140.

24. Allush, *al-Thawrah*, p. 140.
25. *Al-Sahafah*, December 31, 1959; and Allush, *al-Thawrah*, pp. 140-41.
26. Allush, *al-Thawrah*, p. 143.
27. Mahmud Abdul-Rahim, *Qiyadat Hizb al-Ba'th al-Murtadah* (Retreat-ing Ba'th Party Leadership) (Cairo: al-Dar al-Qawmiyyah Li al-Tiba'ah Wa al-Nashr, 1963), p. 33. In fact, Bitar, who signed this document, later acknowledged this act to be a regrettable error on his part; see also Allush, *al-Thawrah*, pp. 371-72.
28. "Hourani Calls for Views on Arab Union," *Mideast Mirror*, XIV, No. 18 (May 5, 1962), 8.
29. "Hourani Replies to Abdel Nasser," *Mideast Mirror*, XIV, No. 22 (June 2, 1962), 5.
30. "Hourani Again Attacks Nasser," *Mideast Mirror*, XIV, No. 23 (June 9, 1962), 7.
31. Arab Ba'th Socialist party, *Nazratunah ila al-Wihdah al-Arabiyyah* (Our View on Arab Unity) (no publisher, September, 1962), p. 81. This pamphlet reflects the views of the so-called Hourani group in Lebanon. In fact, they agreed with Hourani on most of his views regarding Nasser. They disagreed on the personality of Hourani himself whom they regarded as an opportunist and "traditional" political leader.
32. Interview, Anonymous, Beirut, November 23, 1963.
33. Arab Ba'th Socialist party, *Nazratunah ila al-Wihdah al-Arabiyyah*, September, 1962.
34. Arab Ba'th Socialist party, "Concerning the Unity Trial," Damascus, February, 1962. This statement was also published in *al-Ba'th*, July 28 and August 11, 1962.
35. The word "region" was used to signify each country belonging to the union in 1958. Northern Region referred to Syria, while Southern Region referred to Egypt.

36. Arab Ba'th Socialist party, "A Statement to the People," Beirut, May, 1962. (Pamphlet.) This statement was also published in Allush, *al-Thawrah*, pp. 357-64. See also *New York Times*, April 11, 1963.
37. "Ba'thists Call for Union," *Mideast Mirror*, XIV, No. 22 (June 2, 1962).
38. "Syrian Call for Federal Union with Egypt," *Mideast Mirror*, XIV, No. 23 (June 9, 1962).
39. Abdul Rahim, *Qiyadat*, pp. 47, 55. See also the party's publication in Lebanon, "Closure of the Ba'th Newspaper Is a Direct Attack on Liberty," Beirut, October 13, 1962. The newspaper was closed on October 8, 1962, and was not reissued until after the March 8, 1963, Ba'th party *coup d'état* which toppled the Syrian "secessionist" government. See also "Syrian Government Reshuffled," *Mideast Mirror*, XV, No. 8 (February 23, 1963).
40. *Al-Ba'th*, October 6, 1962.
41. Sati' al-Husari, *al-Iqlimiyyah, Judhurhah wa Budhurhah* (Provincialism, Roots and Seeds) (Beirut: Dar al-Ilm Li al-Malayin, 1963).
42. *Al-Ahram*, Cairo, October 4, 1961. This and other Egyptian newspapers carried on a vehement attack against the Ba'th party.
43. Muhamad Hasanein Haykal, *Ma Alladhi Jara Fi Suriyyah* (What Happened in Syria) (Cairo: Kutub Qawmiyyah, 1962).
44. See, for instance, Nihad al-Ghadiri, *al-Kitab al-Aswad* (The Black Book) (Damascus: Matabi' al-Alf Ba, 1962), a vicious attack on the Ba'th party.

6. THE BA'TH PARTY IN IRAQ, 1963

1. This Court, popularly known in the Middle East as the Mahdawi Court, was notorious for its mishandling of justice. It was organized after the Qasim regime took over in 1958 and was abolished by the Ba'th in 1963.

2. *Al-Ishtiraki* (The Socialist), IX, January, 1963. This was an underground Ba'thist newspaper in Iraq.
3. Interview, Anonymous, Damascus, March 25, 1964. This man was one of the plotters in the attempted assassination of Qasim on October 7, 1959. He was arrested and sentenced to death; the sentence, however, was not carried out and he spent only two years and four months in prison after which he was released by the Ba'th regime. He has been a political exile in Syria since Aref's purge of the Ba'th in November, 1963.
4. Interview with T. Aziz, Damascus, March 25, 1964. This man was the chief editor of the Ba'th newspaper *al-Jamahir* (The Masses) in Baghdad until the Aref purge. Presently he is a political exile in Damascus. See also *al-Hayat*, February 16, 1963.
5. "Syrian Ministers Stick to Resignations," Mideast Mirror, XV, No. 7 (February 16, 1963). For details, see *al-Hayat*, March 14, 1963.
6. Arab Ba'th Socialist party, Lebanon, "In Memory of the Union between Syria and Egypt," February 22, 1963. (Leaflet.)
7. Arab Ba'th Socialist party, Lebanon, "The Arab Ba'th Socialist Revolution in Iraq is the Property of the Arab People Everywhere," February 14, 1963. (Leaflet.)
8. "Iraq and Suggested Union with Syria," *Mideast Mirror*, XV, No. 8 (February 23, 1963); see als*o al-Hayat*, February 15, 1963.
9. *Al-Hayat*, March 10 and March 15, 1963.
10. *Ibid.*, February 23, 1963.
11. *Al-Ba'th*, March 15 and March 20, 1963.
12. *Ibid.*, April 7 and April 9, 1963.
13. *Al-Hayat*, March 19, 1963.
14. *Ibid.*, March 24, 1963.
15. *Al-Ba'th*, April 25, 1963.
16. *New York Times*, May 3, 1963.
17. *Ibid.*, April 7, 1963.

18. *Al-Ba'th*, May 9, 1963.
19. *New York Times*, May 12, 1963. The government of Jundi in Syria resigned after Cairo charged that he was only a front man for the Ba'th party. The resignation of the government in Iraq was also preceded by the resignation of the five pro-Nasser ministers. See also *New York Times*, May 13, 1963.
20. *Al-Ba'th*, May 15, 1963.
21. Quoted in *ibid.*, May 19, 1963.
22. *New York Times*, May 21, 1963.
23. *Al-Ba'th*, May 28, 1963.
24. *Ibid.*, July 1, 1963.
25. *Ibid*, July 20, July 22, and July 25, 1963; *al-Hayat*, July 19, July 23, and July 25, 1963.

7. SYRIA, THE BA'TH PARTY, AND THE LOSS OF IRAQ
1. *Al-Ba'th*, July 23, 1963.
2. *Al-Hayat*, July 25, 1963; *al-Ba'th*, July 26, 1963.
3. *Al-Ba'th*, July 26, 1963.
4. *Al-Hayat*, August 7, 1963.
5. *Al-Ba'th*, August 1, 1963.
6. Arab Ba'th Socialist party (Jordan), "Statement," August, 1963. (Leaflet.)
7. *Al-Nahar*, August 22, August 23, and August 24, 1963.
8. *Ibid.*, July 23, 1963.
9. *Ibid.*, July 30, 1963.
10. *Mahadir Muhadathat al-Wihdah* (Minutes of the Unity Talks) (Cairo: Muasassat al-Ahram, 1963). For a defense of the Ba'th view on these talks, see Riad Taha, *Mahadir Muhadathat al-Wihdah* (Minutes of the Unity Talks) (Beirut: Dar al-Kifah, 1963).
11. *Al-Ba'th*, June 23 and July 11, 1963.
12. *Al-Hayat*, July 27, 1963.

13. *Al-Ba'th*, October 23, 1963; *al-Nahar*, November 1, 1963.
14. *Al-Ba'th*, September 16, 1963. This newspaper account was verified in an interview with N. Farzali, president of the ASO in 1963 and a Ba'th party member, Beirut, January 19, 1964.
15. A discussion of the practical reasons for Nasser's "withdrawal" from the proposed union can be found in *al-Nahar*, August 26, 1963; and *Lisan al-Hal*, August 27, 1963.
16. *Al-Nahar*, September 24, September 26, September 27, and September 28, 1963.
17. See Appendix A for complete text of the Convention decisions.
18. *Al-Nahar*, November 2, 1963.
19. In *Lisan al-Hal*, November 5, 1963. This paper published a photo of a map, attributed to the convention, of the stages by which the annexation was to be put into effect.
20. *Al-Nahar*, November 7 and November 8, 1963; a*l-Ba'th*, October 25 and November 7, 1963.
21. Al-Nahar, November 14, 1963; *Newsweek* (November 25, 1963), p. 20; *Lisan al-Hal*, November 14, 1963.
22. *Al-Nahar*, November 2, 1963.
23. *Ibid.*, November 14, November 15, and November 17, 1963; Time (November 20, 1963), p. 28.
24. *Al-Nahar*, November 18, 1963; see also *al-Yaum*, November 19, 1963.
25. Al-Nahar, November 19, 1963; al-Ba'th, November 19, 1963.
26. Interview, Beirut, December 6, 1963. Mr. Rahal was chairman of the department of political science at the American University of Beirut and a prominent member of the Syrian National Socialist party.
27. Interview, Beirut, March 6, 1964.
28. Interview with Mr. A. J. K., a Ba'thist Saudi student at the Syrian University in Damascus, June 7, 1964.

29. Interview, Damascus, March 26, 1964. Mr. Shagrah is presently a political exile in Damascus. Two of his brothers, both Ba'thists, were killed in the Shawwaf uprising (1959) against the Qasim regime. He was in jail in Iraq from 1959 to 1963, at which time he was released by the Ba'th goverment.
30. *Al-Nahar*, November 10, 1963; see also *al-Ahad*, November 24, 1963.
31. See *Newsweek* (November 25, 1963), p. 40.
32. *Al-Nahar*, November 20, 1963.
33. *Ibid.*, November 19 and November 29, 1963.
34. *Al-Ahad*, November 24, 1963.
35. See Appendix A, Article 3.
36. See *ibid.*, Article 12.
37. *Al-Nahar*, December 4, 1963; see also *Lisan al-Hal*, December 7, 1963.
38. The text of the agreement was published in *al-Nahar*, May 27, 1963.
39. *Al-Nahar*, January 8, 1964.
40. Interview, A. S., Beirut, February 6, 1964. The exact date of Bitar's expulsion has never been published. A. S., a Ba'thist student at the American University of Beirut, does not wish his name revealed.
41. *Al-Anwar*, February 28, 1964; *al-Hayat*, February 7, 1964; *al-Nahar*, February 7, 1964.
42. *Al-Nahar*, February 27, 1964. Also interview with Mr. Fawwaz Tarabulsi, Beirut, March 6, 1964. Tarabulsi also led a group of twenty party members to split from the party in February, 1964. His reasons for splitting were the same as those forwarded by the Sa'di group. However, his group is independent of the Sa'di group. They consider Sa'di a demagogue.
43. *Al-Nahar*, February 28, March 3, and March 4, 1964; *al-Ba'th* March 2, 1964.
44. Quoted in *al-Nahar*, March 6, 1964.

45. See the Damascus Chamber of Commerce Statement to the Minister of Economy in Syria, in *ibid.*, February 12, 1964.
46. *Ibid.*, September 25, 1963.
47. *Al-Ba'th*, March 19 and March 20, 1964; see text of the agreement in *ibid.*, March 27, 1964.
48. *Al-Nahar*, February 25, 1964.
49. *Al-Ba'th*, February 20, February 24, and February 25, 1964; and *al-Nahar*, February 21, February 25, and February 26, 1964.
50. *Al-Nahar*, March 7, 1964.
51. *Al-Hayat*, April 9, April 21, April 22, and April 24, 1964.
52. *Al-Nahar*, April 24, 1964.
53. *Al-Hayat*, June 13, 1964.
54. *Ibid.*, February 16, 1963.
55. This Parliament was dissolved on March 28, 1962.
56. Details of this period and of the *coup d'état* may be found in *al-Hayat*, March 14, 1963.
57. See details in *al-Nahar*, July 28, 1963.
58. *Al-Hayat*, July 19, 1963.
59. For an excellent commentary on Hafiz cooperation with the party, see *al-Nahar*, July 31, 1963.
60. For a good discussion see *al-Nahar*, July 3, 1964.
61. For further information on the military-civilian roles in Syria, see *al-Hayat*, February 9, 1964.
62. Interview, Damascus, June 6, 1964.
63. On this point see *al-Nahar*, February 25, 1964.
64. *Al-Nahar*, March 3, 1964.

8. BA'TH IDEOLOGY

1. Asoka Mehta, *Studies in Asian Socialism* (Bombay: Bharatiya Vidya Bhavan, 1959), p. 89.
2. In Laqueur, *The Middle East in Transition*, p. 23.

3. The attack by some Ba'thists on this lack of theory will be discussed later.
4. "Ahdafunah al-Ishtirakiyyah 'ala Du' al-Mu'tamar al-Watani Li al-Quwa al-Sha'biyyah" (Our Socialist Goals in the Light of the National Convention of Popular Forces), *al-Majallah al-Masriyyah Li al-Ulum al-Siyasiyyah* (Egyptian Political Science Journal), No. 12 (March, 1962), p. 16.
5. *Hawl al-Nazariyyah al-Ishtirakiyyah* (Concerning the Socialist Theory) (Cairo: Kutub Qawmiyyah, 1959), p. 24. On this point one cannot help but agree with Mr. Hatim: In Britain "nationalization was stressed as a practical remedy rather than as a political end." Carl Brand, "The British Labor Party and Nationalization," *The South Atlantic Quarterly*, XIII, No. 2 (Spring, 1959), 155. Also, Herbert Morrison observed that "one of the reasons for socializing the basic industries is that it would not be safe to rely on persuasion that they [private industries] conform to national policy." In V. V. Ramandham, *Problems of Public Enterprise* (Chicago: Quadrangle, 1959), p. 35.
6. "Al-Mithaq al-Watani: Ahdafuhu, Madmunuhu" (The National Charter: Goals and Content), *al-Majallah al-Masriyyah Li al-'Ulum al-Styasiyyah*, No.12 (March, 1962), p. 90.
7. *Fi Sabil al-Ba'th* (Toward Resurrection) (Beirut: Dar al-Taliah, 1959), pp. 9-11, 34, 35.
8. *Fi Sabil* (2d ed.; Beirut: Dar al-Tali'ah, 1963), pp. 7, 42.
9. *Ibid.*, p. 43. Further analysis of this point can be found in Leonard Binder, *The Ideological Revolution in the Middle East* (New York: Wiley, 1964), pp. 160-63. Also by the same author, "Radical Reform Nationalism in Syria and Egypt, I & II," *The Muslim World*, XIX, Nos. 2, 3 (April and July, 1959).
10. "Makanat al-Ta'mim fi Bina al-Mujtama' al-Arabi al-Ishtiraki," (The Role of Nationalization in Building the Arab Socialist Society), *al-Thaqafah al-Arabiyyah*, IV, No. 1 (February, 1961), 20.

11. A. K. Zuhur *et al.*, *Fi al-Fikr al-Siyasi* (Damascus: Dar Dimishq, 1963), 1, 142, 145, 154, 157.
12. Charles Issawi, "Middle East Dilemmas," p.108
13. Malcolm H. Kerr, "Tho Emergence of Socialist Ideology in Egypt" *The Middle East Journal*, XVI, No. 2 (Spring, 1962), 127.
14. *Politics of Social Change*, p. 239.
15. This contradicts Morroe Berger's contention that Arab Socialists are willing to "adopt any plan that will help them industrialize and raise the standard of living," The Arab World Today, p. 381.
16. Sidney Lens, "A Report," p. 57.
17. *Al-Falsafah al-Ishtirakiyyah , wa al-Demoqratiyyah al-Ta'awuniyyah* (Socialist Philosophy and Democratic Cooperation) (Cairo: Dar al-Qawmiyyah, 1962), pp. 98.
18. *A Soldier*, p. 431.
19. Lens, "A Report," p. 56. The writer suggests this to be true of socialism in Asia in general.
20. In Laqueur, *The Middle East*, p. 340.
21. *Ma'rakat al-Masir al-Wahid* (Battle for the Same End) (Beirut: Dar al-Adab, 1959), pp. 30, 33.
22. *Al-Siyasah al-Arabiyyah Bain al-Mabda wa al-Tatbiq* (Arab Politics between Principle and Practice) (Beirut: Dar al-Taliah, 1960), pp. 43, 44, 137.
23. Gebran Majdalany, in Laqueur, *The Middle East*, p. 341.
24. *Al-Siyasah*, p. 139.
25. *Mawduat ila Mutamar Ishtiraki Arabi* (Subjects for an Arab Socialist Conference) (Damascus: Dar Dimishq, 1963), p. 54.
26. *Dirasat Fi al-Qawmiyyah* (Studies in Nationalism) (Beirut: Dar al-Taliah, 1960), p. 30.
27. *Ibid.*, p. 29.
28. *Al-Siyasah*, p. 33.

29. *Mawdu'at*, pp. 44, 46.
30. Sa'dun Hamadi, *Nahnu wa al-Shuyu'iyyah Fi al-Azamah a -Hadirah* (We and the Communists in the Present Crisis) (Beirut: Dar al-Taliah, n.d.), p. 14.
31. *Politics of Social Change*, p. 237. See also *al-Ba'th*, March 7, 1947, where an editorial by Bitar demanded an end to all operations of foreign companies in Syria so that independence could be complete.
32. *Al-Ba'th*, January 20, 1951. In 1952 the Ba'th called on the Lebanese government to nationalize all foreign companies. See also *al-Ba'th*, January 19, 1952.
33. *The Arab World*, p. 328. See also Nejla Izzedin, *al-Alam al-Arabi* (The Arab World), trans. M. A. Ibrahim, M. Dweyik, M. Y. Nejm, and B. E. al. Dajjani (Beirut: Dar Ihya al-Kutub al-Arabiyyah, 1953), p. 437.
34. *Azamat al-Yasar al-Arabi* (Crisis of the Arab Left) (Beirut: Dar al-Ilm Li al-Malayin, 1960), p. 5. See also Adib Nassur, *Qabla Fawat al-Awan* (Before It Is Too Late) (Beirut: Dar al-Ilm Li al-Malayin, 1955), p. 42.
35. *Al-Ba'th*, January 23, 1948.
36. *Nahnu Wa*, p. 10.
37. *Al-Ba'th*, January 23, 1958.
38. Bitar, *al-Siyasah*, p. 137; Hamadi, *Nahnu*, p. 14; Zuhur et al., *Fi al-Fikr*, I, 125; see also *al-Sahafah*, December 7, 1958.
39. *Al-Ba'th*, January 23, 1948.
40. Aflaq, *Ma'rakat*, p. 10.
41. In Hafiz et al., *Fi al-Fikr*, II, 127.
42. A. Abdul-Daim, *Al-Ishtirakiyyah Wa al-Demoqratiyyah* (Socialism and Democracy) (Beirut: Dar al-Adab, 1961), pp. 17-21,
43. Aflaq, *Fi Sabil*, pp. 193, 195, 210.
44. *Ibid.*, p. 208.

45. Munif al-Razzaz, *Limadha al-Ishtirakiyyah al-An* (Why Socialism Now?) (Pamphlet) (1957), pp. 15, 16.
46. Ali Al-Khalil, "Arab Socialism: A Force for Freedom and Unity," *The Student*, VII (October, 1959), 18.
47. *Ma'rakat*, p. 29; see also *Fi Sabil*, p. 221.
48. *Al-Sahafah*, July 18, 1959; see also Appendix B, Article 42.
49. Khalil, *The Student*, p. 18; see also Aflaq, *Fi-Sabil*, p. 208.
50. *Al-Sahafah*, October 11, 1959.
51. Aflaq, *Fi Sabil*, p. 208. Ba'th treatment of these issues will follow later.
52. Khalil, "The Socialist Parties in Syria and Lebanon" (Ph.D. dissertation, American University, Washington, 1962), pp. 98-99; *al-Sahafah*, April 11, 1959.
53. See Glubb, *A Soldier*, 431; Hottinger, *The Arabs*, 276.
54. Interview, A. T. al-Azzuz, Damascus, March 25, 1964.
55. Sami Ayub, *Al-Hizb al-Shuyu'i Fi Suriyyah Wa Lubnan* (The Communist Party in Syria and Lebanon) (Beirut: Dar al-Huriyyah, 1959), pp. 175, 177, 178. The PPS is a militant nationalist party that advocates the Fertile Crescent Scheme of unity of Greater Syria alone. It adopts certain Fascist techniques.
56. "The Meaning of the UAR," *The World Today*, XIV, No. 3 (March, 1958), 94.
57. Aflaq, *Fi Sabil*, p. 211.
58. A. Mehta, *Socialism and the Peasantry* (Bombay: Praja Socialist Pub-lication, 1953).
59. Clovis Maqsud, *Nahwa Ishtirakiyyah Arabiyyah* (Toward an Arab Socialism) (2d ed.; Beirut: Dar Muneimneh, 1958), p. 53.
60. R. N. Nolte and W. R. Polke, "Toward a Policy for the Middle East," *Foreign Affairs*, XXXV, No. 4 (July, 1958), 650; see also Guy Wint and Peter Calvocoressi, *Middle East Crisis* (Aylesbury: Penguin Books, 1957), p. 19.

61. *Ma'rakat*, pp. 133, 155.
62. Aflaq, *Fi Sabil*, p. 202.
63. M. Naccache, "The Outside Lane," *Middle East Forum*, XXXVI, No. 1 (January, 1960), 7.
64. Interview, Michel Aflaq, Damascus, January 16, 1964.
65. *The Student*, p. 19.
66. Aflaq, *Fi Sabil*, p. 201.
67. *Azamat al-Yasar al-Arabi* (Beirut: Dar al-Ilm Li al-Malayin, 1960), pp. 95, 97. No Arab Socialist party, including the Ba'th, agreed to attend the First Asia Socialist Conference, held in Rangoon, Burma, 1912. Their refusal was due to the presence of the Mapai Socialist party from Israel. See Saul Rose, *Socialism in Southern Asia* (London: Oxford University Press, 1959), p. 9. Arab Socialist parties refused to attend the second convention held in Bombay, India, 1956, for the same reason, *ibid.*, 249. See also David J. Saposs, "The Split Between Asian and Western Socialism," *Foreign Affairs*, XXXII, No. 4 (July, 1954), 588-94.
68. Lens, "A Report," 56.
69. Maqsud, *Azamat*, 21.

9. BA'TH SOCIALISM

1. "The Socialist Parties," pp. 86, 87.
2. *Dirasat Fi al-Ishtirakiyyah* (Studies in Socialism), (Beirut: Dar al-Taliah, 1960), p. 19. This article was printed in al-Ba'th, July 29, 1950.
3. *Al-Ba'th*, October 7, 1950.
4. *Al-Sahafah*, January 29, 1959; Wint and Calvocoressi, *Middle East Crisis*, p. 19.
5. *Limatha*, p. 14. Also see Abu Maizer, "Makanat al-Tamim," p. 19.
6. Abdul-Daim, *Al-Ishtirakiyyah Wa*, pp. 27-28.
7. *Fi al-Fikr al-Siyasi*, II, p. 122.

8. In Haim, *Arab Nationalism*, p. 205.
9. *The Ideological*, p. 184.
10. On this point see L. Binder, "Radical Reform Nationalism in Syria and Egypt, II," *The Muslim World*, XLIX, No. 3 (July, 1959), 217.
11. *Fi Sabil*, p. 45. This article is translated and can be found in Haim, *Arab Nationalism*, p. 242.
12. *Fi Sabil*, p. 45.
13. Aflaq in Haim, *Arab Nationalism*, p. 248. See also Khalil, "The Socialist Parties," p. 103.
14. *Al-Sahafah*, October 11, 1959.
15. In *Nidal al-Ba'th*, I, 60.
16. *Fi Sabil*, p. 185; see also *al-Sahafah*, June 6, 1960.
17. *Al-Siyasah*, p. 11.
18. *Fi Sabil*, pp. 185-86.
19. Khalil, "The Socialist Parties," p. 107.
20. *Al-Ba'th*, January 8, May 2, May 3, May 5, and May 26, 1950.
21. *Al-Ba'th*, April 9, 1954; *Nidal al-Ba'th*, II, p. 227.
22. *The Meaning*, pp. 43 44.
23. "Al-Arab Fi al-Nisf al-Thani Min al-Qarn al-Ishrin," (The Arabs in the Second Half of the Twentieth Century), *Al-Abhath*, IV, No. 2 (June, 1951), 140-41.
24. For example see Faiz Sayegh, *Al-Ba'th al-Qawmi* (National Renaissance) (Beirut: Maktabat al-Wajib, 1946), p. 141.
25. See Edward Shills, "The Concentration and Dispersion of Charisma," *World Politics*, XL, No. 1 (October, 1958), 1-19, for interesting insight into the problem of the political elite and the way they attempt to legitimize them-selves.
26. Bitar, *al-Siyasah*, pp. 11-12.
27. Khalil, "The Socialist Parties," p. 91.
28. Razzaz, *Ma'alim*, p. 46.
29. *Al-Ishtirakiyyah*, pp. 21-22, 23, 25.

30. See Abdul Daim, *Al-Ishtirakiyyah*, p. 28.
31. *Ibid.*
32. *Fi Sabil*, pp. 116-17.
33. Halpern, *Politics of Social Change*, p. 236; *The Economist* (September 24, 1960), p. 1197.
34. *Al-Sahafah*, August 1, 1960.
35. *Ibid.*
36. *Al-Ishtirakiyyah*, pp. 21, 76.
37. "*Forum Interviews* Michel Aflaq," *Middle East Forum* (February, 1958), p. 10.
38. For example see *al-Ba'th*, March 7, March 12, April 13, 1947, and January 20, 1950.
39. *Al-Ba'th*, April 13 and November 16, 1947.
40. "The Socialist Parties," p. 92. See also Appendix B, Article 32.
41. See Francis Coker, *Recent Political Thought* (New York: Appleton Century, 1934), p. 195.
42. Razzaz, *Ma'alim*, pp. 199-200. The party views cooperative societies as another means by which socialism may be effected. See *al-Ba'th*, January 20, 1951; and Appendix A.
43. Abu Maizer, *Makanat*, p. 19; and Abdul Daim, *al-Ishtirakiyyah*, p. 44.
44. *Ma'alim*, p. 200.
45. *Mawdu'at*, p. 46.
46. Collective farms have been added to the party ideology since the Sixth National Convention in 1963. See Appendix A.
47. Eva Garzouzi, "Land Reform in Syria", *Middle East Journal*, XVII, No. 1 (Winter-Spring, 1963), 83. This article gives the details of land reform in Syria.
48. *Mawdu'at*, p. 49.
49. Razzaz, *Ma'alim*, p. 204.
50. *Al-Ba'th*, January 24, 1950, August 11, 1951, and August 6, 1963.

51. *Ma'alim*, p. 195.
52. "The Socialist Parties," p. 93.
53. *Makanat*, p. 19.
54. *Fi al-Fikr al-Siyasi*, I, 164.
55. *Makanat*, p. 19.
56. *Al-Nahar*, February 7, 1964.
57. *Fi Sabil*, p. 209; see also Razzaz, *Ma'alim*, pp. 129-30.
58. *Al-Ishtirakiyyah*, p. 49.
59. William Ebenstein, *Today's Isms* (New York: Prentice-Hall, 1954), p. 180.
60. G. B. Shaw (ed.), *Fabian Essays in Socialism* (New York: Humboldt Publishing Company, 1891), p. 141.

10. BA'TH ORIENTATION
1. On this point see Leonard Binder, "Radical Reform Nationalism in Syria and Egypt, II," *The Muslim World*, XLIX, No. 3 (July, 1959), 229; and by the same author, "The Constitution of the Arab Resurrection Socialist Party of Syria," *The Middle East Journal*, XIII, No. 2 (Spring, 1959), 195.
2. *Ma'rakat*, p. 27; Fi Sabil, p. 50.
3. *Fi Sabil*, pp. 161, 296.
4. Aflaq, *Fi Sabil*, p. 161. Also quoted erroneously in Haim, p. 71. Haim translates the latter part as "our swords against them."
5. "The Socialist Parties," p. 83.
6. In his introduction to *Fi Sabil*, pp. 8-9.
7. Abdul Daim, *Al-Ishtirakiyyah*, p. 51.
8. Interview, Damascus, March 26, 1964. Mr. Aysami was ousted from his post in the party after the February 1966 *coup* led by leftist Ba'thists.
9. Interview, Beirut, November 14, 1963.
10. *Al-Hayat*, March 13, 1963.

11. *Al-Ba'th*, March 5 and April 13, 1947.
12. *Ma'alim*, p. 36.
13. Abdul Daim, *Al-Ishtirakiyyah*, p. 28.
14. *Al-Ba'th*, December 15 and December 29, 1951; see also *Fi al-Fikr al-Siyasi*, II, 135.
15. Murkos, *Mawdu'at*, p. 67; see also John S. Badeau, "The Revolt Against Democracy," *International Affairs*, XIII, No. 2 (1959), 149-56.
16. *Al-Ishtirakiyyah*, p. 29.
17. Murkos, *Mawdu'at*, pp. 67-70.
18. The idea that Islam is Socialist may be found in the writings of non-Ba'th Socialists such as Bahi, *Falsafat*, pp. 16-20; Shaikh Mahmud Abu al-Uyun, "Al-Ishtirakiyyah Fi al-Islam" (Socialism in Islam), *Al-Hilal*, LIX, No. 11 (November, 1951), 18-22; Ahmad Ferraj, *Al-Islam Din al-Ishtirakiyyah* (Islam the Religion of Socialism) (Cairo: Kutub Qawmiyyah, n.d.); Anwar al-Khatib, *Al-Naz'ah al-Ishtirakiyyah Fi al-Islam* (Socialist Tendency in Islam) (Beirut: Dar al-Ilm Li al-Malayin, 1956); R. A. A. al-Sharbasi, *Mabadi al-Ishtirakiyyah Fi al-Islam* (Socialist Principles in Islam) (Cairo: Kutub Thaqafiyyah, n.d.); M. al-Siba'i, *Ishtirakiat al-Islam* (The Socialism of Islam) (Cairo: al-Dar al-Qawmiyyah, 1960), and Khalid M. Khalid, *Min Huna Nabda* (From Here We Start) (Cairo: Dar al-Nil, 1950); also Mauli Afhab al-Din Ahmad, *Islam and Western Socialism* (Surrey: The Working Muslim Mission, n.d.). This writer states that "Islam does admit that for complete social peace, the social system must be based on economic justice," p. 13. Nasser, *The Philosophy of the Revolution*, p. 60, sees in religion a useful tool; and in a speech on July 22, 1961, he stated that the Caliph Omar was the first to nationalize and distribute land among the peasants; Kerr, "The Emergence," p. 140. Another defense of Islam as a just economic order may be found in "The

Challenge of Communism and Islam," *The Muslim Sunrise*, XXV, No. 4 (Fourth Quarter, 1953), 3-5.

19. *Fi Sabil*, pp. 29, 43, 52, 57, 205. For further treatment of Aflaq's view on Islam see Haim, ed., *Arab Nationalism*, pp. 62-64; and Binder, "Radical… I," *The Muslim World*, pp. 106-07.

20. Murkos, *Mawdu'at*, p. 3.

21. *Dirasat Fi al-Qawmiyyah*, pp. 40, 45.

22. Khalil, "The Socialist Parties," p. 99.

23. For example see Aflaq, *Fi Sabil*, p. 203, where he states that communism is a danger to spiritualism. It is antireligion. See also *al-Sahafah*, April 11, April 12, and August 2, 1959.

24. *Al-Nahar*, July 24, 1963.

25. *Al-Ba'th*, July 30, 1963.

26. See *al-Nahar*, July 31 and August 1, 1963.

27. "Nahwa Sighah 'Arabiyyah Li al-Ishtirakiyyah" (Toward an Arab Form of Socialism), *al-Abhath*, XIV, No. 4 (December, 1961), 532.

28. *Falsafat al-Ishtirakiyyah* (Philosophy of Socialism) (Cairo: Kutub Qawmiyyah, n.d.), p. 34.

29. See the writings of these two non-Ba'th Socialists: Abdul Qadir Hatim, *Hawl al-Nazariyyah al-Ishtirakiyyah* (Concerning Socialist Theory) (Cairo: Kutub Qawmiyyah, 1959), p. 39; and Maqsud, *Azamat*, p. 76, who also uses the word "revolution" to signify total change rather than actual violence.

30. "Radical Reform Nationalism in Syria and Egypt, II," *The Muslim World*, XLIX, No. 3 (July, 1959), 218.

31. *Fi Sabil*, p. 175.

32. *Arab Nationalism*, p. 70.

33. The party's condemnation of violence and of political assassination in particular has been reaffirmed on several occasions. Jebran Majdalany stated that the party is definitely

against the use of violence. This attitude, he added, stems from its faith in the people to effect change without employing violent tactics such as those used by the Communists. Interview, Beirut, August 29, 1963. See also *al-Ba'th*, December 28, 1949; *al-Sahafah*, January 15 and September 5, 1960.

34. *Middle East Forum* (February, 1958), p. 10.

35. *Fi Sabil*, p. 176. There is, however, a minority of Ba'th intellectuals who believe that violence and force are necessary to achieve their goals. These, ho-ever, do not represent the party line. Representative of these is Dr. Jamal al-Atasi, in *Fi al-Fikr al-Siyasi*, II, 129.

36. *Fi Sabil*, pp. 153, 167.

37. *Al-Sahafah*, June 6, 1960.

38. *Al-Ba'th*, September 10, 1950, and August 11, 1951.

39. *Ibid.*, February 28, 1950, and April 9, 1954.

41. See Appendix B, Principle III and Articles 3 and 6.

42. *Ma'rakat*, p. 19.

43. *Ma'alim*, pp. 74, 75, 78-81.

44. *Al-Ba'th*, April 20, 1957.

45. The propaganda attacks of the Ba'th party on the PPS commenced in late 1950. See *al-Ba'th*, December 9, 1950, through January 27, 1951. See also Khalil, "The Socialist Parties," p. 126; and Fisher (ed.), *The Military*, p. 63.

46. *Al-Ba'th*, August 1, 1960.

47. *Ibid.*, January 19, 1949.

48. Maqsud, *Nahwa*, p. 74.

49. *Al-Ba'th*, April 13, 1947, and January 20, 1951.

50. Fisher, *The Military*, pp. 62, 65.

51. For a discussion of Ba'th Communist cooperation and later discord see above, pp. 38-45 *passim*.

52. *Al-Ba'th*, March 10, 1951, *al-Sahafah*, November 22, 1958.

53. *Al-Ba'th*, February 2, 1947.

54. For text see *al-Ba'th*, April 13, 1947.
55. *Ibid.*
56. *Ibid.*, March 29, 1957.
57. "The Socialist Parties," p. 101; see also "Two Worlds," *Mideast Mirror*, IX, No. 35 (September 1, 1957), 13.
58. *Al-Sahafah*, October 1, 1959; *al-Ba'th*, June 19, 1963.
59. *Al-Hayat*, July 25, 1963.
60. *Al-Ba'th*, March 20, March 26, and April 5, 1947, and November 25, 1950.
61. *Al-Falsafat al-Ishtirakiyyah al-Demoqratiyyah al-Ta'awuniyyah* (The Socialist, Democratic Cooperative Philosophy) (Cairo: al-Dar al-Oawmiyyah, 1962), p. 13.
62. *Middle East Forum* (March, 1957), p. 33.

11. ORGANIZATION AND STRUCTURE

1. See organization chart on p. 162.
2. *Politics, Parties and Pressure Groups* (New York: Crowell, 1958), p. 345.
3. Barbara Roth and Robert Roth (trans.), *Political Parties* (New York: Wiley, 1954), p. 27, 31, 39.
4. The basis of this description of Ba'th organization in *Al-Nizam al-Dakhili* (The Internal Rules Manual) (1963), hereafter cited as Internal Rules.
5. *Ibid.*, p. 11.
6. Roth and Roth, *Political Parties*, p. 28.
7. *Internal Rules*, p. 7.
8. Interview, A. T. al-Azzuz, Damascus, March 25, 1964.
9. Interview, Anonymous, Beirut, March 6, 1964. These numbers are only estimates even by regular party members. My questions as to the exact number of members in each country drew silence from all the party leaders I interviewed.

10. *Internal Rules*, pp. 11-13.
11. Interview, Anonymous, Amman, July 12, 1963.
12. *Internal Rules*, pp. 14-16.
13. *Ibid.*, p. 17. Not mentioned is how often this conference is held and the exact number of delegates.
14. The frequency of these conventions is not mentioned.
15. *Ibid.*, pp. 18, 19, 20, 22.
16. *Ibid.*, p. 21.
17. *Ibid.*, p. 22.
18. For the exact numbers and ratios see *Internal Rules*, pp. 23-24.
19. *Ibid.*, p. 24.
20. *Ibid.*, pp. 25-30.
21. Interview with a Tunisian student at the University of Damascus, June 3, 1963. This student works at the Culture and Studies Office at the National Command Headquarters, Damascus; also National Command directive No. 8/1/m, May 22, 1964, Damascus.
22. *Internal Rules*, pp. 4-5.
23. Quoted above, p. 117.
24. *Internal Rules*, pp. 6-11.
25. Interview, Anonymous, Beirut, March 6, 1964.
26. *Internal Rules Manual*, pp. 43-45.

12. CONCLUSIONS

1. Little documentary evidence beyond Syrian Ba'th government publications can be produced. On land reform in Syria before and since Ba'th advent see Eva Garzouzi, "Land Reform in Syria," Middle East Journal, XVII, No. 1 (Winter-Spring, 1963), 83-90. On Ba'th government achievements in education see *al-Ba'th*, January 27 and January 30, 1964. On housing see *al-Ba'th*, February 9, 1964. On agricultural reform see *al-Ba'th*,

February 27, March 3, March 6, March 12, March 13, March 16, and March 17, 1964. On workers participation in the management of nationalized industries, profit-sharing, and labor reform, see *al-Ba'th*, January 29, February 9, March 2, March 12, and March 16, 1964. On health reforms see *al-Ba'th*, April 5, 1964. While these notations are by no means exhaustive, it is hoped they will give an idea of Ba'th claims as to its accomplishments.

Bibliographic Essay

This essay may be useful to the reader as an indication of publications used in the preparation of this book and as a starting point for further research on the topic of Arab socialism. It does not cover the whole body of materials used; nor is it a comprehensive discussion of sources on every aspect of the Arab world. It has been restricted largely to those books dealing primarily with Arab socialism and a few of the more important background studies.

Despite the fact that the list of published books on the Arab world is impressive, few deal even remotely with the topic of this book. Passages and impressions appear here and there, yet no extensive study of this major Arab Socialist movement has appeared yet. The following books on comparative politics were valuable: G. A. Almond and J. S. Coleman, *The Politics of the Developing Areas* (Princeton: Princeton University Press, 1960); L. Binder, *The Ideological Revolution in the Middle East* (New York: Wiley, 1964); V. M. Dean, *The Nature of the Non-Western World* (New York: New American Library, 1959); S. Haim, ed., *Arab Nationalism: An Anthology* (Berkeley: University of California Press, 1962); M. Halpern, *Politics of Social Change in the Middle East and North Africa* (Princeton: Princeton University Press, 1964); M. Kaplan, ed., *The Revolution in World Politics* (New York: Wiley, 1962); W. Z. Laqueur's studies, *Communism and Nationalism in the Middle East* (New York: Praeger, 1956) and *The Middle East in Transition* (New York: Praeger, 1958); D. Lerner, *The Passing of Traditional Society* (Glencoe, Illinois: Free Press, 1958); H. B. Sharabi, *Governments and Politics of the Middle East in the Twentieth Century* (Princeton: Van Nostrand, 1962); and P. E. Sigmund, ed., *The Ideologies of the Developing Nations* (New York: Praeger, 1963). All of the above books contributed substantially to the author's understanding of the political and social climate of the Arab world. Binder's book, the most recent, offers fresh and good insight into the ideological climate of the Arab world. Haim's and Halpern's books are indispensable to the study of the contemporary nationalist revolution. Haim's book traces the nationalist revolution to its beginnings, while Halpern's is an excellent study of the major ideologies in the Middle East. Extremely helpful were Laqueur's book, *The Middle East in Transition*, and Sigmund's book. The latter is a fresh comparative study that relates the ideologies in the developing nations to each other.

The quantity of sources tracing and discussing Western socialism is so impressive that I shall make no attempt to include any here. English-language studies on Asian socialism are few. The most helpful were: Adhab al-Din Ahmad, *Islam and Western Socialism* (Surrey: The Working Muslim Mission, n.d.); A. Datta, *Socialism, Democracy and Industrialization* (London: Allen & Unwin, 1962); and A. Mehta's three good books, *Democratic Socialism* (Hyder Abad: Chefana Prakashan, Ltd., 1951); *Socialism and Peasantry* (Bombay: Praja Socialist Publication, 1953); and *Studies in Asian Socialism* (Bombay: Bharatiya Vidya Bhavam, 1959). A good book on Asian socialism in English is Saul Rose, *Socialism in Southern Asia* (London: Oxford University Press, 1959).

There are so many studies of the history of the Middle East that no attempt was made to include them here. Of those dealing with contemporary politics in the Arab World, Morroe Berger's

The Arab World Today (New York: Doubleday, 1962) was most helpful and stimulating. E. Childers, *Common Sense about the Arabs* (London: Gollancz, 1960), is stimulating but often elementary. C. E. Cremeans, *The Arabs of the World* (New York: Praeger, 1963), is a good background study. A. Hottinger's *The Arabs* (London: Thames & Hudson, 1963) is an excellent study of contemporary politics in the Middle East written by a man who has a deep understanding of Arab politics. C. Kirk's *Contemporary Arab Politics* (New York: Praeger, 1961) could have been a better book were it not for the author's thinly camouflaged anti-Arab sentiment. G. Lenczowski, *The Middle East in World Affairs* (3rd ed.; Ithaca: Cornell University Press, 1962), is an exhaustive scholarly study of Arab politics nation by nation. H. Z. Nusseibeh's *The Ideas of Arab Nationalism* (Ithaca: Cornell University Press, 1956) is a scholarly exposé of the topic, while C. Zurayk's book, *The Meaning of the Disaster*, translated by R. B. Winder (Beirut, Khayat's College Cooperative, 1956), is indispensable for an understanding of the frustrations of modern Arab nationalists.

For the researcher who reads Arabic and who is interested in early Arab Socialist ideas, the following works by Salamah Musa are a must: *al-Ishtirakiyyah* (Socialism) (Cairo: al-Matba'ah al-Masriyyah al-Aliyyah, 1913); and *Tarbiyat Salamah Musa* (Salamah Musa's Growth) (Cairo: Muassasat al-Khanji, 1958). The former book, really a small pamphlet, was the first Arab book on socialism, while the latter traces the growth of an Egyptian-Arab nationalist with Socialist tendencies. The latter was translated and published in 1961 (Leiden: E. J. Brill) with an excellent introduction by L. O. Schuman. Nicola Haddad's book, *al-Ishtirakiyyah* (Socialism) (Cairo: Dar al-Hilal, 1920), and Shibli Shumayyil's work, *Majmu'at al-Doctor Shibli Shummayil* (Collected works of Doctor Shibli Shumayyil) (Cairo: Matba'at al-Ma'arif,

1908), should be read by all those interested in the origins of Arab socialism. Clovis Maqsud's works, *Ma'na al-Hiyad al-Ijabi* (Meaning of Positive Neutrality) (Beirut: Dar al-Ilm Li al-Malayin, 1960); *Nahwa Ishtirakiyyah Arabiyyah* (Toward an Arab Socialism) (2nd ed.; Beirut: Dar Muneimneh, 1958); *Sira' al-Sha'b al-Arabi Ma' al-Shuyu'iyyah al-Alamiyyah* (The Arab People's Struggle with International Communism) (Cairo: Dar al-Qahirah, 1959); and *Azamat al-Yasar al-Arabi* (Crisis of the Arab Left) (Beirut: Dar al-Ilm Li al-Malayin, 1960) are some of the more sophisticated studies on Arab politics. Naji Allush's voluminous works are sophisticated too but at times too dull and repetitive. The most important of Allush's works are: *al-Thawri al-Arabi al-Mu'asir* (The Contemporary Arab Revolutionary) (Beirut: Dar al-Tali'ah, 1960); *Fi Sabil al-Harakah al-Arabiyyah al-Thawriyyah al-Shamilah* (Toward the Complete Arab Revolutionary Movement) (Beirut: Dar al-Tali'ah, 1963); and *al-Thawrah Wa al-Jamahir* (Revolution and the Masses) (Beirut: Dar al-Tali'ah, 1963). *Judhur al-Ishtirakiyyah* (Roots of Socialism) (Beirut: Dar al-Taliah, 1964), edited by the present author, is a collection of the works of S. Musa and N. Haddad. The introduction to this work discusses early Arab Socialist thought and movements.

For purposes of comparison and for a better understanding of the general trend of thought in Arab socialism, mainly the Nasserite Socialist movement, the following works are necessary: S. Abu al-Majd, *al-Bina al-Ishtiraki* (The Socialist Edifice) (Cairo: al-Dar al-Qawmiyyah, 1961); S. Afrah, *al-Ta'awuniyyah Fi Mutamainah al-Ishtiraki* (Cooperation in our Socialist Society) (Cairo: Kutub Qawmiyyah, n.d.); A. Baha al-Din, *al-Thawrah al-Ishtirakiyyah* (The Socialist Revolution) (Cairo: al-Maktabah al-Thaqafiyyah, 1962); M. al-Bahi, *Falsafat al-Ishtirakiyyah* (Philosophy of Socialism) (Cairo: Kutub Qawmiyyah, n.d.);

A. Hatim, *Hawl al-Nazariyyah al-Ishtirakiyyah* (Concerning the Social Theory) (Cairo: Kutub Qawmiyyah, 1959); A. I. Khalaf-Allah, *al-Falsafah al-Ishtirakiyyah al-Demoqratiyyah al-Ta'awuniyyah* (The Socialist Democratic Cooperative Philosophy) (Cairo: al-Dar al-Qawmiyyah, 1961). This latter work is an interestingly intense anti-Western tirade. The works of two former Ba'th leaders, Fuad al-Rikabi and Abdullah al-Rimawi, should be read with an eye to understanding the mentality and method of those Ba'thists who are impatient with the Ba'th party and whose sympathies and loyalties tend to be pro-Nasserite. Enlightening are Rikabi's *Ala Tariq al-Thawrah* (On the Road to Revolution) (Cairo: al-Dar al-Qawmiyyah, 1962); al-Qawmiyyah, Harakatuhah Wa Muhta-wahah (Nationalism, Content and Activities) (Cairo: Dar al-Kitab al-Arabi, 1963); and Rimawi's, *al-Mantiq al-Thawri Li al-Harakah al-Qawmiyyah al-Arabiyyah* (The Revolutionary Logic to the Arab Nationalist Movement) (Cairo: Dar al-Ma'rifah, 1961); and *al-Qawmiyyah Wa al-Wihdah Fi al-Harakah al-Qawmiyyah al-Arabiyyah al-Hadithah* (Unity and Nationalism in the Modern Arab National Movement) (Cairo: Dar al-Ma'rifah, 1961).

The literature by Ba'th Socialist intellectuals is not as extensive as one would expect from a party which regards itself as a vanguard to lead the masses. Below is a partial list of works by Ba'th intellectuals. Abdullah Abdul Daim, *al-Ishtirakiyyah Wa al-Demoqratiyyah* (Socialism and Democracy) (Beirut: Dar al-Adab, 1961) is a sophisticated, well-written work. This author is concerned primarily with youth and education. The following works by Aflaq are central to any study of the Ba'th party: *Fi Sabil al-Ba'th* (Toward Resurrection) (Beirut: Dar al-Taliah, 1959); and *Ma'rakat al-Masir al-Wahid* (Battle of the Same End) (Beirut: Dar al-Adab, 1959). Aflaq also coauthored *Dirasat Fi al Qawmiyyah* (Studies in Nationalism) (Beirut: Dar al-Tali'ah, 1960); and

Dirasat Fi al-Ishtirakiyyah (Studies in Socialism) (Beirut: Dar al-Tali'ah, 1960). Aflaq's writings are frequently contradictory, vague. As they are wrapped in mystical terminology and romanticism, it is frequently difficult to discover what Aflaq is aiming at. Aflaq's, Razzaz', and Bitar's works are acknowledged by all as the fountainhead of Ba'th doctrine. Bitar's *al-Siyasah al-Arabiyyah Bayn al-Mabda Wa al-Tatbiq* (Arab Politics between Principle and Practice) (Beirut: Dar al-Tali'ah,1960) is a clear and concise discussion of his ideas and beliefs. Munif al-Razzaz' *Ma'alim al-Hayat al-Arabiyyah al-Jadidah* (Characteristics of the New Arab Life) (Beirut: Dar al-Ilm Li al-Malayin, 1960) is an impressively clear and interesting work that merits extensive attention.

Fi al-Fikr al-Siyasi (On Political Thought) (2 vols.; Damascus: Dar Dimishq, 1963), a collection of writings by a number of young Ba'th intellectuals, is the most recent serious work by the party. While it does not represent the central theme of Ba'th doctrine, it is interesting since it represents the leftist tendencies within the party. Sa'dun Hamadi, onetime minister of agrarian reform in Iraq and a top Ba'th leader, has written two impressive works that warrant attention: *Nahnu Wa al-Shuyu'iyyah Fi al-Azamah al-Hadirah* (We and the Communists in the Present Crisis) (Beirut: Dar al-Tali'ah, n.d.); and *Nahwa Islah Zira'i Ishtiraki* (Toward Agricultural Reform) (Beirut: Dar al-Tali'ah, 1964). A final and most important work on the Ba'th has been published since 1963 in several volumes by the Tali'ah publishing house in Beirut. *Nidal al-Ba'th* (The Ba'th Struggle), 7 vols., is a collection of Ba'th statements, pamphlets, speeches by Ba'th leaders and certain party communications dating back to the establishment of the party. While it is quite dull and repetitious in places, it does offer the researcher access to sources which otherwise would be difficult to obtain. Its greatest weakness is that it does not include many "secret" party communications.

An essential primary source of information about the Ba'th party in particular and the Arab world in general is a number of English-language periodicals devoted primarily to Middle Eastern studies. Among these are: *The Middle East Journal* (Washington); *The Muslim World* (Hartford); *Middle Eastern Affairs* (New York); *Middle East Forum* (Beirut). The following issues of other journals were useful too: *International Affairs* (London, January, 1954, January, 1955, January, 1958, January, 1959, and January, 1960); *World Politics* (New Haven, October, 1956, April, 1962, October, 1962, January, 1963, and July, 1964); *The World Today* (London, January, 1957, March, 1958, July, 1960, and November, 1961). In addition, a number of other English periodicals which frequently print articles dealing with the contemporary problems of the Middle East were used and, again, these cannot be included. The author has also relied heavily on a number of Arabic magazines, including *al-Hilal* (Cairo, February, 1908, March, 1910, March, 1916, June and July, 1918, and January, 1923); *al-Muqtataf* (Cairo, June, 1889, March, 1890, August and September, 1894, and January, 1913); *al-Abhath* (Beirut, March, 1949, June, 1951, December, 1959, December, 1961, and March, 1962); *al-Majallah al-Masriyyah Li al-Ulum al-Siyasiyyah* (Cairo, January, 1962, March, 1962, April, 1962, and July, 1962); *al-Thaqafah al-Arabiyyah* (Beirut, April, 1959, and February, 1961); and *al-Tali'ah* (Damascus, March and June, 1936).

The nature of this book demanded heavy reliance on interviews and newspapers. The most prominent leaders of the Ba'th party and certain non-Ba'thists were interviewed and citations are given in the text. Of English-language newspapers, the New York Times was an important source. Of Arabic newspapers, I relied heavily on the Ba'th party newspaper *al-Ba'th*. I know of only one collection of this newspaper in existence. Even this collection, owned by Dr. Bashir al-Dauk, owner of al-Tali'ah publishing house in Beirut, is not complete. I also used *al-Sahafah*, another Ba'th party newspaper, which was published only for the duration of the union between Syria and Egypt (1958-61). A complete collection of *al-Sahafah* may be found in the library at the American University of Beirut in Lebanon. For the most recent events I also relied on another Ba'th party newspaper, *al-Ahrar*, which has been published in Beirut since 1964.

For independent points of view on current events – sometimes hostile to the Ba'th party – I relied on *al-Hayat* (Beirut), a collection of which may be found at the Princeton University Library. *Al-Nahar* (Beirut) is an excellent independent paper which I used extensively. In addition, I relied on the following Arabic newspapers: *al-Anwar* (Beirut), *al-Hurriyyah* (Beirut), and *al-Muharrir* (Beirut). These last three newspapers are extremely anti-Ba'th and pro-Nasser.

Party publications, leaflets, and pamphlets cannot be found in the United States and are indeed difficult to find even in Syria. The American University of Beirut has been collecting some of these for a number of years now, and a modest quantity of them may be found there. I relied heavily on personal collections in the Middle East.

Index

Index

About the Author

H.E. Dr. Kamel S. Abu Jaber (1932–2020): BA (Pol. Sc.), PhD (Pol. Sc.) Syracuse University; postdoctoral programme Oriental studies, Princeton University.

Lecturer, Syracuse University (USA) 1965; Asst. Prof., University of Tennessee (USA) 1965–67; Associate Prof., Smith College (USA) 1967–69; Associate Prof., University of Jordan, Amman 1969–71, Prof. 1971–72, 1979–80, Dean, Faculty of Economics & Commerce 1972–79, President, Council of Consultation, Tech Services & Studies Center 1982–84, Director, Strategic Studies Center 1984–85, Prof. Political Sc 1985–89; Minister of National Economy 1973, of Foreign Affairs 1991–93; Director, Queen Alia Social Welfare Fund 1980–82; Visiting Prof., Emory University Carter Center, Atlanta (USA) 1989; Senator, Jordan Upper House of Parliament 1993–97; President: Jordan Institute of Diplomacy 1997, Higher Media Council; Visiting Prof., Hong Kong Baptist University 2008–2009; Visiting Prof. St. Anthony's College, Oxford University UK; Visiting Prof. Calgary University in Alberta, Canada; Director, Royal Institute for Interfaith Studies 2010–2013.

SELECT PUBLICATIONS

The Arab Ba'th Socialist Party: History, Ideology and Organisation (1966), *The United States of America and Israel* (1971), *The Israel Political System* (1973), *The Jordanians and the People of Jordan* (1980),

Economic Potentialities of Jordan (1984), *Political Parties and Elections in Israel* (1985), *The Palestinians: People of the Olive Tree* (1993); notable encyclopaedia articles include *Jordan* (1974) in Britannica, *The Bedouins (*1984) World Book Encyclopaedia; and over 30 papers and articles published in national and international journals and conference proceedings.

The Arab Ba'th Socialist Party (1966), *The Jordanians* (1980), *The Palestinians: People of the Olive Tree* (1993) and *Sheepland* (2005) were recently republished by Hesperus Press.

MEMBERSHIPS & AWARDS

Jordan Order of the Star – First Class (Kawkab Order) 1976; Honorary Doctorate, University of Buenos Aires (Argentina) 1980; Silver Medallion, Queen Alia Jordan Social Welfare Fund 1981; Commander, Swedish Royal Order of the Polar Star 1989; Order of the Sacred Tomb (1st Class), Orthodox Patriarchate of Jerusalem and the Holy Land 1992; Bernardo O'Higgins award, Chile, 1994; European Academy of Arts and Sciences, 1996; Distinguished Professor Award University of Jordan 2022; Awarded the Centennial Cross for his service to his country in 2022 posthumously. Honorary member of the Confucius society; Honorary member of the Onondaga Indian tribe of Upstate New York; Member board of trustees and secretary general, Royal society for the conservation of Nature 1977; Counsellor for West Asia of the International Union for Conservation of Nature 1991; Member board of trustees and secretary general, Jordan World Affairs Council 1978; Honorary Member, Jordanian Arab University Women's Alumni 1984; Member board of trustees Petra University Jordan 2013–May 29, 2020.